Adolescents At Risk

ADOLESCENTS AT RISK

A Guide to Fiction
and Nonfiction for Young Adults,
Parents, and Professionals

JOAN F. KAYWELL

GREENWOOD PRESS
Westport, Connecticut • London

Library of Congress Cataloging-in-Publication Data

Kaywell, Joan F.
    Adolescents at risk : a guide to fiction and nonfiction for young
adults, parents, and professionals / Joan F. Kaywell.
        p.   cm.
    Includes bibliographical references and index.
    ISBN 0-313-29039-3 (alk. paper)
    1. Teenagers—United States—Books and reading.   2. Young adult
fiction—Bibliography.   3. Young adult literature—Bibliography.
I. Title.
Z1037.K28   1993
[PS643]
028.1'62—dc20   93-20834

British Library Cataloguing in Publication Data is available.

Library of Congress Catalog Card Number: 93-20834
ISBN: 0-313-29039-3

First published in 1993

Greenwood Press, 88 Post Road West, Westport, CT 06881
An imprint of Greenwood Publishing Group, Inc.

Printed in the United States of America

The paper used in this book complies with the
Permanent Paper Standard issued by the National
Information Standards Organization (Z39.48-1984).

10 9 8 7 6 5 4 3 2

To

Christopher S. Maida and Stephen M. Kaywell,

the special boys in my life

Contents

Preface

Adolescents At Risk: A Guide to Fiction and Nonfiction for Young Adults, Parents, and Professionals grew out of my increasing concern about the problems confronting today's youth. There are so many problems affecting adolescents these days that a separate term *at-risk* has emerged in the literature. All teenagers are *at-risk*, some more so than others. This reference book provides helpful information so that young adults, parents, and professionals such as teachers, media specialists, guidance counselors, social workers, psychologists, psychiatrists, clergy, and anyone else who wants to help young adults may have access to information that will help them do so.

This text is built on the premise that literacy is the key to growth and understanding of oneself and others. The problem that exists, however, is that a lot of teenagers' problems are exacerbated by illiteracy. At present, anyone can go to a library and conduct an ERIC search to find information about any given problem. The results include abundant lists and annotations of books, most of which do not deal specifically with kids and most of which are written on advanced reading levels. This text is a collection of current or classic resource materials available specifically for young adults. I have provided annotations of these books in 14 at-risk categories, ranging from alienation and identity issues to stress and suicide. The annotations are written so that adolescents and adults may read and understand them easily. The books that I have included are written at the junior high or middle school reading levels. It is my firm belief that it is through reading that we develop our abilities to understand our problems and the problems of others.

Parents experiencing a divorce may want to examine the chapter "Divorced and Single Parents" in order to recommend a book for their children to read. If parents read along with their children, it might be easier to discuss a character's situation and relate it to reality rather than asking their children to describe feelings they don't know how to articulate. A psychiatrist with a strong addictions background might find the chapter on "Alcohol and Drugs" particularly useful for bibliotherapy or group therapy sessions. By teaming with a psychologist, a school's guidance counselor might be instrumental in creating an innovative intervention strategy for substance abuse prevention for adolescents in school. An English teacher, using any one of the chapters, might assign a different novel per student in order to study multiple perspectives. Afterwards, students may conduct research in the library to find facts relevant to a specific problem and write literary criticisms about whether or not the author adhered to reality in developing characters.

It is my hope that new approaches for helping adolescents at risk will emerge as a result of the availability of this text as a resource.

Acknowledgments

My first thanks must go to Lynne Laveley from the University of South Florida's Institute for At-Risk who hired me for two consecutive summers to compile young adult literature for at-risk adolescents. From that summer of 1991, I had a focus to direct my efforts in helping teenagers. Next, I'd like to thank Ted Hipple and Don Gallo for suggesting that I submit this manuscript to the Greenwood Publishing Group. I am grateful to Barbara Rader, the Senior Editor for School and Library Reference, who thought this manuscript deserved a chance and offered her invaluable expertise in its development. Also, I'd like to thank Ann LeStrange and Liz Leiba for their lay-out and production assistance.

A special thanks is extended to Heidi Quintana who willingly gave up part of her summer vacation to help me with the library research. Thanks to Paul Nehrig and Lisa Holland who helped proofread the manuscript one last time. Another special thanks is offered to Susan Maida who graciously helped me with the printing and formatting of this book. Thanks Heidi, Paul, Lisa, and Susan!

Thanks to my family and friends, and various faculty, staff, and students at the University of South Florida for supporting me and giving me the time and encouragement necessary to complete this task, especially Ben Johnson and Howard Johnston. And finally, I'd like to thank the people at the American Academy of Child and Adolescent Psychiatry and all of the countless folks who donate time serving the various hotlines and providing information for those people who are at risk.

Organization

This book is divided into 14 chapters, each dealing with a specific problem area. Although the first chapter "Growing Up: Alienation and Identity" is the most benign chapter, it sets up all of the following chapters. For example, the next two chapters, "Youth with Disabilities" and "Homosexuality" are larger problems often stemming from alienation and identity problems.

Chapters Four, Five, and Six deal with family issues resulting in problems for adolescents: "Divorced and Single Parents," "Adopted and Foster Families," and "Abuse." Chapters Seven and Eight, "Eating Disorders" and "Alcohol and Drugs," deal with adolescents who want to be in control but are out of control. Chapters Nine, Ten, and Eleven are particularly interconnected problems: "Poverty," "Dropouts and Delinquency," and "Teenage Pregnancy." The last three chapters, "AIDS," "Death and Dying," and "Stress and Suicide" represent the most serious problems confronting today's teenagers.

Each chapter follows the same format: an introductory paragraph followed by startling information about the topic; information on what to do and where to go for help including addresses and 800 numbers for additional information; annotated young adult novels arranged alphabetically according to the author's or editor's last name; annotated nonfiction books written specifically for teenagers; and a listing of journal articles, journal themes, and other books that are easily accessible and readable.

All chapters stand alone, and each is cross-referenced to other chapters that may overlap. For example, a young adult book dealing with stress and suicide may also be about abuse. The complete annotation may be found in the chapter "Stress and Suicide" but may be only listed in the chapter titled "Abuse" with a reference to "See Stress and Suicide." Awards given to novels are listed whenever possible and are found at the end of the annotations.

CHAPTER 1

Growing Up:
Alienation and Identity

All adolescents go through a stage of struggling with their identity and wondering how they fit in with their family, their peers, and the rest of the world. Sometimes while coming to terms with their identities, adolescents feel alienated or disconnected from the world. These feelings are exacerbated when families are fragmented and people are moving. During a time of extreme emotional and physical changes, young people are searching to belong which is found by socializing with others. Standing out from the crowd brings unwanted attention, and alienation deters one's emotional growth. Teenagers experiencing extreme feelings of alienation are more prone to suicide, alcohol and drug abuse, pregnancy, and violence. Perhaps this short piece by an unknown author best describes what teenagers are "growing" through:

> Put the personality of a child in the body of a man or a woman. Furnish a need to be loved and a fierce desire to be independent. Allow a need to be self-directing but leave out any idea of what direction to take. Add an enormous amount of love but also the fear that it may not be accepted or returned. Give physical and sexual powers without any knowledge or experience of how to use them in a society whose values and achievements are essentially incomprehensible and certainly unattainable and whose concerns are seemingly misplaced and insecure. Then you have just begun to understand the problems of adolescence.

STARTLING INFORMATION ABOUT ALIENATION AND IDENTITY

- More and more young people are being raised in families where the adults have less and less time for them. (Eitzen, 1992)

- Alienation is responsible for many problems confronting adolescents. (Calabrese, 1989)

- Alienated students involve themselves in unsafe activities with their peers, either as victims or aggressors. (Tucker-Ladd, 1990)

- Boys tend to rebel and disobey; whereas, girls express their difficulty by depressed moods. (Petersen, 1987)

- Mobility affects over 8 million adolescents each year. (U.S. Census Bureau, 1983)

- Older adolescents have more difficulty adjusting to family moves because of the increasing importance of peer groups. (American Academy of Child & Adolescent Psychiatry, *Facts for Families*, 1992)

- The primary and most pervasive changes occurring during adolescence are puberty and school change. (Petersen, 1987)

WARNING SIGNS OF ALIENATION AND IDENTITY PROBLEMS

- Poor achievement, low self confidence caused by repeated sense of failure, unhappiness, depression.

- Passive withdrawal, hopelessness, apathy.

- Changes in appetite, sleep disturbances, other dramatic changes in behavior.

- Irritability, violent forms of behavior such as vandalism and destruction of property.

WHAT TO DO AND WHERE TO GO FOR HELP

- Remember that success brings success.

- If someone you know feels alienated, engage him or her in activities that are social and inclusive.

- If a daughter or son is a senior in high school when a move is planned, consider the possibility of letting her or him stay with a trusted family until after graduation.

- Get professional help: Call crisis intervention centers, mental health clinics, hospitals, a family physician, a clergy, a guidance counselor, or a teacher. For more information, write to the American Academy of Child & Adolescent Psychiatry, 3615 Wisconsin Avenue, NW, Washington, D.C., 20016-3007.

Annotated Young Adult Novels Dealing with Alienation and Identity

1.01. Blume, Judy. (1970). *Are you there, God? It's me Margaret.* New York: Dell. 149 pp. (ISBN: 0-440-40419-3)

Margaret Simon, an 11-year-old going on 12, moves with her family from New York City to the suburbs of New Jersey. She has to adjust to a new school, new friends, and new surroundings. Margaret also has to deal with her fears of wearing a bra, getting her period, and deciding on a religion. Because Margaret's father is Jewish and her mother is Catholic, they are allowing Margaret to choose her own way. Margaret's search leads to confusion, some lack of identity, and a need for belonging. (Great Stone Face Award)

1.02. Blume, Judy. (1974). *Blubber.* New York: Dell. 153 pp. (ISBN: 0-440-90707-1)

This novel vividly illustrates the cruelty of peer pressure as seen through the eyes of one of the aggressors, Jill Brenner, a well-to-do suburban 5th grader. The innocent victim of the abuse is Linda Fischer, nicknamed "Blubber" because of her weight and her oral report on whales. Lifting up her skirt, eating chocolate-covered ants, and kissing Wendy's sneakers are just a few things Jill and her friends make Blubber do. Because teachers and parents are clueless as to what's going on, Jill continues to harass Blubber until one day the tables are turned and Jill finds herself the one who's being alienated and abused by her so-called friends. Jill's whole world temporarily collapses until she confronts her own self-identity and finally gets a mind of her own. She learns the Golden Rule, "Do unto others as you would have them do unto you," the hard way. (a New York Times Outstanding Book of the Year)

1.03. Blume, Judy. (1986). *Then again, maybe I won't.* New York: Dell. 164 pp. (ISBN: 0-440-48659-9)

Because Tony's father has invented an incredible, new electric charge, this means a lot of money for the Miglione family. Tony realizes, however, that life is not always fun and full of laughter. The money means moving away from his old neighborhood, trying to make new friends, and worst of all, seeing his mother try to be somebody she's not. Tony eventually learns from the people around him that life isn't really so bad, but it is most important for a person to stick to his morals and pride.

1.04.   Calvert, Patricia. (1986). *Yesterday's daughter*. 138 pp.

          See Adopted and Foster Families

1.05.   Cleary, Beverly. (1991). *Fifteen*. New York: Avon Books. 192 pp. (ISBN: 0-380-70920-1)

          This is the story of a teenage girl who learns to like and accept herself for who she is as a result of her first real relationship with a boy.

1.06.   Cole, Brock. (1992). *The goats*. New York: Farrar, Straus, & Giroux. 184 pp. (ISBN: 0-374-42576-0)

          Two 13-year-old teenagers of the opposite sex are the victims of what is intended to be a harmless prank. Labelled as "goats," Laura and Howie are stripped and marooned overnight on a small island. The two are devastated, escape off of the island, and decide to leave the camp and disappear for good. They meet many people during their journey, some who are willing to help while others will not. Eventually, they discover their own inner strengths and decide that they cannot run forever. (a New York Times Book Review Notable Book, an ALA Best Book for Young Adults, & a *School Library Journal* Best Book of the Year)

1.07.   Colman, Hila. (1985). *Claudia, where are you?* 168 pp.

          See Dropouts and Delinquency

1.08.   Cooney, Caroline B. (1990). *The face on the milk carton*. New York: Bantam Books. 184 pp. (ISBN: 0-553-28958-6)

          Janie Johnson is a typical sophomore whose only concern is not being too ordinary. She gets her wish and her life is turned upside down when she sees herself as a three-year-old on a milk carton. Janie is in complete denial since her parents are so loving and couldn't possible have done such a thing. Or could they?

1.09.   Corcoran, Barbara. (1986). *I am the universe*. New York: Atheneum. 136 pp. (ISBN: 0-689-31208-3)

          While in the 8th grade, Katharine Esterly, better known as Kit, receives an English assignment that really gets her thinking. She has to write a composition on the topic, "Who I Am." She knows she hates math and her braces, but there are a lot of other things as well: She's concerned about her little brother's problems at school, her big brother's girlfriends, her mother's frequent headaches, and a short story contest. It seems as though her entire life revolves around her family problems rather than her having her own identity. Kit's problems intensify when her mother has to have surgery to have a brain tumor removed. Although Kit doesn't win the short story contest, she does gain a lot of knowledge about who she is.

1.10.   Danziger, Paula. (1988). *The cat ate my gymsuit*. New York: Dell Laurel-Leaf. 119 pp. (ISBN: 0-440-91612-7)

Marcy Lewis is an introverted, overweight 13-year-old who is alienated from everyone at school because of her weight. She thinks of many excuses to skip P.E., the title of this book being one of them. Ms. Finney, her new English teacher, is instrumental in helping Marcy respect herself as an individual. When Ms. Finney is suspended by the school board for her controversial teaching methods, Marcy must decide if she will fight for Ms. Finney and the values she stands for in spite of the repercussions she will experience at school and at home. Along the way, Marcy realizes that being fat does not stop you from having friends and being a human being. Anyone who has ever felt less than what they want to be, both physically and socially, will enjoy this book.

1.11.   Gauch, Patricia Lee. (1985). *The green of me*. New York: Putnam. 156 pp. (ISBN: 0-339-20647-7)

At 17, Jennifer is doing some soul-searching while riding on a train, from Ohio to Virginia, to see her boyfriend. Just as there are many interpretations as to what "green" means, Jennifer wonders "what is the real green of me?" Jennifer recalls, in vignette style, many of her childhood experiences, from age six, that have influenced her personality. She also reflects on the behaviors of others and what it all means.

1.12.   Godden, Rumer. (1990). *Thursday's children*. New York: Dell Laurel-Leaf. 272 pp. (ISBN: 0-440-98790-3)

Doone Penny may be a guy, but he has a dream to become a famous ballet dancer. Unfortunately, it's his sister, Crystal, who gets the dancing lessons and the support of the family. Only Doone's teachers are aware of his talents and pay attention to his determination to become a star. (an American Library Association Best Book for Young Adults)

1.13.   Greene, Constance C. (1988). *Monday I love you*. New York: Harper & Row. 170 pp. (ISBN: 0-06-022183-6)

Grace Schmitt has a problem some girls dream about: At 15, she wears a size 38D bra. Being so overly endowed has its problems, and Grace has to endure the cruel pranks played on her by her classmates. Grace, as an escape, often dreams of having a rich, wonderful life. Interspersed in these dreams are memories of her childhood which offer insight into Grace's feelings of low self-esteem. A caring teacher, Ms. Govoni, helps Grace to stand up for herself and develop a better self-concept.

1.14.   Halvorson, Marilyn. (1990). *Let it go*. New York: Dell Laurel-Leaf. 240 pp. (ISBN: 0-440-20053-9)

Not only is Red's father a cop, but they've just moved to a small, rural town where Red fears his acceptance. Things get better after he meets Lance, but there is a hidden secret about Lance's family. This is a powerful story of friendship between these two teenage boys. (an NCSS-CBC Notable Children's Book in the Field of Social Studies)

1.15.   Hinton, S.E. (1989). *Rumble fish*. 122 pp.

See Dropouts and Delinquency

1.16.   Kerr, M.E. (1981). *Little Little*. 183 pp.

See Youth with Disabilities

1.17.   Koertge, Ron. (1991). *Mariposa blues*. Boston: Little, Brown, & Company. 171 pp. (ISBN: 0-380-71761-1)

Each summer Graham helps his father train race horses at Mariposa Downs, and each summer Graham is known around the track as his father's son. This summer Graham is set on being known as a person with his own merits, but first he must discover what those are. Along the way, he notices that he is having different feelings for his best friend, Leslie.

1.18.   Levinson, Nancy Smiler. (1990). *Annie's world*. 97 pp.

See Youth with Disabilities

1.19.   McGuire, Jesse. (1990). *Crossing over*. New York: Ivy Books. (ISBN: 0-8041-0446-8)

This novel centers on the topic of alienation as felt by a group of teenagers as they deal with their parents and themselves. Problems occur for everyone because of the teens' inability to express their true feelings. Elements of relationships are viewed and problems are eventually resolved through mutual respect, honesty, and effective communication. The subject of teen sex is also addressed when two characters decide to make love, one for the first time.

1.20.   Murphy, Claire Rudolf. (1992). *To the summit*. New York: Lodestar/Dutton. 156 pp. (ISBN: 0-525-67383-0)

Sarah Janson goes on an Alaskan mountain climbing expedition where she must prove her independence yet need of her father. Living with a father who never talks to her about his feelings has been difficult, but Sarah has a lot to learn about herself first before she can get into the needs of others. "The High One" offers the physical and emotional challenge that Sarah is ready to accept.

1.21.   Newton, Suzanne. (1986). *A place between*. New York: Viking Kestrel. 201 pp. (ISBN: 0-670-80778-8)

At 13 years of age, Arden Gifford experiences some big lessons of life. After her Grandpa's death and her father's loss of his job, their family moves in with Grandma in a new town. Although Arden makes a new friend, Tyrone, she longs for her old house and friends back in Haverlee.

1.22.   O'Neal, Zibby. (1985). *In summer light*. New York: Viking-Kestrel. 149 pp. (ISBN: 0-670-80784-2)

Kate, a 17-year-old self-described English major, is trying to recover from mono and is home for the summer on her parents' island. Her father is a famous artist who works in a studio next to the house, and her mother is a typical housewife. Besides being prone to naps, lacking energy and being idle, something else is wrong with Kate but she's not sure what. Things improve when Ian, a 25-year-old graduate student, comes to catalog her father's art. The closer Kate and Ian become, the more interested she becomes in her own art. As a youngster, she had loved to paint and had even won an award. As she got older, she stopped painting and Ian gets her to explore her inner self to find out why. Evidently, she has a block centered around her relationship, or lack of one, with her father. Gradually, she realizes that she needs to overcome the bitterness she feels towards her egotistical father and doesn't need to disappear into the background from her father's "genius" as her mother has. Her rediscovery of her own talent and love of painting prompts her to discover who she is and what she would like to become. (a *School Library Journal* Best Book of the Year, an American Library Association Notable Children's Book and Best Book for Young Adults, *Boston Globe-Horn Book* Award, and a *Christian Science Monitor* Best Children's Book)

1.23.   Paterson, Katherine. (1981). *Jacob have I loved*. New York: Avon Flare. 175 pp. (ISBN: 0-380-56499-8)

Sara Louise Bradshaw believes that she is the despised Esau and her adored twin, Caroline, is the beloved Jacob. Louise feels that she lives in the shadow of her beautiful and talented sister who's been pampered since birth due to fragile health. Louise, the heartier one of the two, is skilled in catching crabs and oysters. Caroline, on the other hand, has a beautiful voice and is a talented piano player. Louise's feelings of alienation and lack of identity stem from jealousy. She is in constant conflict with her hatred of her sister and the guilt which accompanies it. With the help of her mother and a friend, Louise finds the courage to find a place where she can be herself and seek her own dreams and independence. (1981 Newbery Honor Book)

1.24.   Paterson, Katherine. (1987). *The great Gilly Hopkins*. 156 pp.

See Adopted and Foster Families

1.25.   Paterson, Katherine. (1987). *Bridge to Terabithia*. New York: Thomas Y. Crowell. 144 pp. (ISBN: 0-690-04635-9)

Jess Aarons, a lonely 5th grader, has an incredible talent for drawing and running. His artistic talent is discouraged by his family because his parents feel it is a waste of time. On the first day of school, he loses a footrace to a new student, a 10-year-old girl named Leslie. Although their friendship does not form immediately, they eventually become inseparable. Leslie opens up a new world for Jess, the world of imagination. Together, they create their own imaginary kingdom in the woods which they call Terabithia. At their secret place, they can reign as king and queen and are able to lock out their worst fears and nightmares. The two have a wonderful, loving friendship until a tragedy shatters their lives. The novel explores the anger, frustration, and loneliness that often accompanies a death and shows that even in the most trying of circumstances, we have the ability to be who and what we want to be. (a Newbery Medal Winner)

1.26.   Petersen, P.J. (1990). *Goodbye to good ol' Charlie*. New York: Dell Laurel-Leaf. 160 pp. (ISBN: 0-440-20162-4)

Charlie is tired of his image--boring, reliable "Good Ol' Charlie." When his family announces that they are going to move to a new town, he decides he will change his image and is determined to be part of the in crowd. (an International Reading Association Young Adults' Choice)

1.27.   Pfeffer, Susan Beth.   (1988).   *Turning thirteen*.   New York: Scholastic. 144 pp. (ISBN: 0-590-40764-3)

Becky and Dina have been best friends forever. Everything is fine until the new girl comes to school and threatens their friendship. Becky feels desperate and decides to become Jewish so she can be more like Dina which excludes the new girl who is not Jewish. Along the way, new problems emerge for Becky who begins to question her own faith.

1.28.   Platt, Kin. (1990). *The boy who could make himself disappear.* 256 pp.

See Youth with Disabilities

1.29.   Powell, Padgett. (1984). *Edisto.* New York: Farrar, Straus, & Giroux. 183 pp. (ISBN: 0-374-14651-9)

Twelve-year-old Simons (pronounced Simmons) finds himself in a dilemma: He is more comfortable in the presence of blacks who accept him as he is than he does in the company of his parents who only look at him in terms of what he might (or will) become.

1.30.   Salinger, J.D. (1945). *The catcher in the rye.* New York: Bantam Books. 214 pp. (ISBN: 0-553-25025-6)

This classic novel presents three days in the life of Holden Caulfield, a troubled 16-year-old who has been kicked out of three different boys' schools. Holden, at first, appears to be a confident, cocky adolescent, but the reader soon learns that this is all a facade. Through Holden's humorous but moving narration, the reader finds Holden is actually a sensitive, insecure youth who is experiencing the pains of growing up and his impending adulthood.

1.31.   Samuels, Gertrude. (1989). *Yours, Brett.* New York: New American Library. (ISBN: 0-451-15977-2)

Brett Jayson is a lonely 12-year-old who is having problems coping with being alienated by parents who don't want her. Brett spends six years in different foster homes, all the while seeking the love of her natural parents. Brett's mother is too in love with herself and her many male friends to pay attention to her daughter. Brett's father is too weak to stand up to his present wife and be a father to his daughter. It is through the love of Brett's paternal grandparents that she is able to find the happiness that she would have never known without them.

1.32.   Scott, Virginia M. (1986). *Belonging.* 200 pp.

See Youth with Disabilities

1.33. Swarthout, Glendon. (1990). *Bless the beasts and children*. New York: Simon & Schuster Trade. 205 pp. (ISBN: 0-671-72644-7)

Six adolescent misfits, rejected by uncaring parents, are sent off to rodeo summer camp where they learn what it means to be men. Each has his own history of parental neglect, psychological feelings of inadequacy, and difficulty coping with a macho image. Unable to join other camp groups such as the "Commanches" or the "Sioux," this group of outcast boys forms the "Bedwetters" and learn to cope with reality and themselves. The novel takes the reader through a moving set of circumstances and the adventures of these boys as they struggle to achieve independence and a sense of positive identity. The final triumph is a risk-all effort to free buffaloes that are scheduled to be shot which results in a surprise ending. (an American Library Association Best of the Best Books for Young Adults)

1.34. Townsend, Sue. (1987). *The secret diary of Adrian Mole. Age 13 3/4*. New York: Avon Books. 185 pp. (ISBN: 0-380-86876-8)

Set in England, this book is based on Adrian Mole's diary entrees for a little over a year. Adrian records his worries about the spots on his face, his size, and his future while he contends with his mother leaving his father for the man next door, his father losing his job, his problems with the school bully, and his first love. Full of wonderful characters, this story captures the emotional highs and lows of adolescence. (nominated for an American Library Association Best Book for Young Adults in 1985)

1.35. Ure, Jean. (1985). *What if they saw me now?* New York: Dell. 150 pp. (ISBN: 0-440-99467-5)

An athletic teenager, Jamie Carr, goes to pick up his little sister at ballet practice and becomes enthralled with the ballet show for a local charity. His problems begin when he cannot successfully juggle the time demands placed on him by dance rehearsals and baseball practice and his friends find out. The desire of Jamie to participate in something he finds he does well and appreciates is tested by his friends and a society that does not readily accept male ballet dancers. The story also covers the phenomenon that new interests mean new friends which often places strains on old friendships.

1.36. Wartski, Maureen Crane. (1979). *My brother is special*. 153 pp.

See Youth with Disabilities

1.37. White, Edmund. (1983). *A boy's own story*. 224 pp.

See Homosexuality

1.38.   Zindel, Paul. (1983). *The pigman*. New York: Bantam Books. 176 pp. (ISBN: 0-553-26321-8)

John Conlan and Lorraine Jensen, both products of unhappy homes, are struggling through life. Mr. Angelo Pignati, "the pigman," is a lonely old man who helps make Lorraine's and John's life more meaningful. The two teens recount how they first set out to take advantage of the old man but wind up developing a heartwarming friendship instead. The three of them are happy sharing each other's company until tragedy strikes, and John and Lorraine must own up to reality and the consequences of their actions. (an American Library Association Best of the Best Books for Young Adults and a *New York Times* Outstanding Book of the Year)

1.39.   Zindel, Paul. (1980). *The pigman's legacy*. New York: Harper & Row. 183 pp. (ISBN: 0-060-26853-0)

The Pigman' Legacy is the delightful sequel to *The Pigman*. Four months after the death of "the pigman," Lorraine and John are still missing him and the good times they shared. Unexpectedly, they meet another lonely, old man who makes them feel as though their beloved pigman is still with them and looking out for their welfare. During one of their adventures with the Colonel in Atlantic City, however, John gambles with the old man's money and loses. This disaster makes John and Lorraine wonder whether or not the Pigman's legacy is a blessing or a curse. Eventually, John and Lorraine come to terms with their feelings of alienation as they make a very important contribution to the Colonel's life. (an American Library Association Best Book for Young Adults and a *New York Times* Outstanding Book of the Year)

1.40.   Zindel, Paul. (1983). *Pardon me, you're stepping on my eyeball!* New York: Bantam Books. 199 pp. (ISBN: 0-553-26690-X)

Marsh Mellow and Edna Shinglebox meet at a group therapy session where they are both frantically trying to cope with life and are trying to find themselves. Marsh's main problem is that he lies and hates everything. Edna is very insecure, and her parents try to take the blame for her lack of popularity with the boys. Edna reluctantly agrees to go out on a date with Marsh but eventually becomes determined to help Marsh find himself and his father. Their relationship takes them on numerous outrageous adventures, some with tragic consequences. (an American Library Association Best Book for Young Adults and a *New York Times* Outstanding Book of the Year)

Annotated Young Adult Nonfiction Dealing with Alienation and Identity

1.41.   Bauman, Lawrence & Riche, Robert.   (1986).   *The nine most troublesome teenage problems and how to solve them*.   Secaucus, NJ: Lyle Stuart.   223 pp.   (ISBN: 0-818-40392-6)

Bauman, a psychologist, noticed that there were common themes for all parent-teen relationships. After an introductory chapter, he focuses on nine of these themes including adolescents' anger, lying, doing poorly in school, non-communication, sex, and peer relationships. Most chapters begin with a discussion of the problem followed by case study examples and "creative synthesis," a specific problem solving technique.

1.42.   Blume, Judy.   (1987).   *Letters to Judy: What kids wish they could tell you*. New York: Pocket Books. 302 pp. (ISBN: 0-671-62696-5)

Judy Blume has compiled a series of letters that young adults have written to her which reveal their concerns about abuse, drugs, families, friendships, illness, sexuality, suicide, and other problems. In return, the author shares personal experiences as a child and as a parent to help the reader not feel so alone. She includes a "Resources" section which lists books for additional reading and addresses of special interest groups.

1.43.   Craig, Eleanor.   (1985).   *If we could hear the grass grow*. New York: New American Library. 285 pp. (ISBN: 0-451-13619-5)

This true story is based on Craig's actual experiences with 12 severely disturbed teens during one summer at Camp Hopewell, a camp she instituted for such children at her country home.

1.44.   Nida, Patricia Cooney & Heller, Wendy M.   (1985).   *The teenager's survival guide to moving*. New York: Atheneum. 136 pp. (ISBN: 0-689-31077-3)

In an easy-to-read, friendly style, the authors provide teenagers with useful tips to help them adjust to a family move.

1.45.   Powledge, Fred.   (1986).   *You'll survive*. New York: Charles Scribner's Sons. 88 pp. (ISBN: 0-684-18632-2)

Adolescence is a wonderful, horrible, and memorable time that most adults would not care to repeat. This book discusses the physical and emotional stages of adolescence; explores the relationships between teenagers and parents, peers, and society; and suggests ways of coping with common problems.

Nonfiction References Dealing with Alienation and Identity

Journal Articles

Beane, J.A. (1991, September). Sorting out the self-esteem controversy. *Educational Leadership, 49* (1), p. 25 ff.

Byrne, B.M. & Shavelson, R.J. (1987, Fall). Adolescent self concept: Testing the assumption of equivalent structure across gender. *American Educational Research Journal, 24* (3), p. 365 ff.

Calabrese, R.L. (1989, October-November). The effects of mobility on adolescent alienation. *High School Journal, 73* (1), p. 41 ff.

Calabrese, R.L. (1989, February). Alienation: The secondary school at risk. *NASSP Bulletin, 73* (514), p. 72 ff.

Chance, P. (1985, October). Fast track to puberty. *Psychology Today, 19* (10), p. 26 ff.

Chandler, T.A. (1985, January). What's negative about positive self concept? *Clearing House, 58* (5), p. 225 ff.

Eitzen, D.S. (1992, April). Problem students: The sociocultural roots. *Phi Delta Kappan, 73* (8), p. 584 ff.

Flake, C.L. (1990, December). Academic failure, alienation, the threat of extinction: A global perspective on children at risk. *Journal of Humanistic Education and Development, 29* (2), p. 50 ff.

Frymier, J. & Gansneder, B. (1989, October). The Phi Delta Kappa study of students at risk. *Phi Delta Kappan, 71* (2), p. 142 ff.

Grant, W.T. Foundation Commission on Work, Family, and Citizenship. (1988, December). The forgotten half: Pathways to success for America's youth and young families. *Phi Delta Kappan, 70* (4), p. 280 ff.

Hendrix, V.L., Sederberg, C.H., & Miller, V.L. (1990, Spring). Correlates of commitment/alienation among high school seniors. *Journal of Research and Development in Education, 23* (3), p. 129 ff.

Ianni, A.J. (1989, May). Providing a structure for adolescent development. *Phi Delta Kappan, 70* (9), p. 673 ff.

Johannessen, L.R. & Lindley, D.A., Jr. (1991, September). For teachers of the alienated. *English Journal, 80* (5), p. 72 ff.

Mackey, J. & Appleman, D. (1984, September-October). Broken connections: The alienated adolescent in the '80s. *Curriculum Review, 24* (1), p. 14 ff.

McKinney, C. (1991, Spring). Breaking down the walls. *The ALAN Review, 18* (3), p. 35 ff.

Nielson, L. (1983). Decreasing adolescents' feelings of powerlessness. *American Secondary Education, 13* (1), p. 5 ff.

Petersen, L. (1987, September). Those gangly years. *Psychology Today, 21* (9), p. 28 ff.

Pfeffer, S.B. (1990, Spring). Basic rules of teenage life. *The ALAN Review, 17* (3), p. 5 ff.

Tucker-Ladd, P.R. (1990, November-December). Alienated adolescents: How can schools help? *Clearing House, 64* (2), p. 112 ff.

Wooden, W.S. (1985, January). The flames of youth. *Psychology Today, 19* (1), p. 22 ff.

Workman, B. (1990, April). The teenager and the world of work: Alienation at West High? *Phi Delta Kappan, 71* (8), p. 628 ff.

Journal Themes

Emerging Adolescents: Their Needs and Concerns. (1985, March-April). *Childhood Education, 61* (4).

Books

Csikzentmilhaly, M. & Larson, R. (1984). *Being adolescent: Conflict and growth in teenage years.* New York: Basic Books. 332 pp. (ISBN: 0-465-00646-9)

Curtis, Robert H. (1986). *Mind and mood: Understanding and controlling your emotions.* New York: Charles Scribner's Sons. 138 pp. (ISBN: 0684185717)

Kuklin, S. (1993). *Speaking out: Teenagers take on race, sex and identity.* New York: G.P. Putnam's Sons. 138 pp. (ISBN: 0-399-22343-6)

CHAPTER 2

Youth with Disabilities

In 1975, the Education for All Handicapped Children Act (P.L. 94-142) mandated that all special needs school-aged children were entitled to receive a free, appropriate public education in the least restrictive environment. Since that time, much has happened to prepare our youth with disabilities with the skills necessary for successful community living and working. Amended in 1990, the Individuals with Disabilities Education Act (P.L. 101-476) changed the language and extended services for people with disabilities. Such efforts have included more funding, instructional technology and computers, more available personnel and materials, adaptive equipment, vocational involvement, and public awareness. Unfortunately, many special needs children enter our schools feeling defective when compared to other adolescents. Most build invisible walls to protect themselves, and their self-confidence is almost nonexistent. In spite of our efforts to help, the results have been disheartening since most graduates are unsuccessful in finding jobs. Many more drop out of school and are disconnected from mainstream America. There is much to be done to improve the quality of life for special needs children, but it will take a special commitment from all of us.

STARTLING INFORMATION ABOUT YOUTH WITH DISABILITIES

- There are approximately 43 million disabled person in the United States. (Wagner, 1992)

- Twenty-five percent of pregnant mothers receive no physical care of any sort during the crucial first trimester of pregnancy. About 20% of handicapped children would not be impaired if their mothers had had one physical exam during their first trimester of pregnancy, which could have detected potential problems. (Hodgkinson, 1991)

- During the 1987-1988 school year, about 250,000 students with disabilities exited the educational system under the category of either "drop out" (27%) or "other or unknown" (16.8%). (12th Annual Report of Congress on the Implementation of the Handicapped Act)

- Only 55% of special education students graduate from high school. (Wagner, 1989)

- A national longitudinal study revealed that two years after high school, only 30% of special education students were working full-time and 17% were working part-time. (Wagner, 1989)

- Special education students have a 35% chance of obtaining full-time employment after leaving school. (Browning, Brown, & Dunn, 1993)

WHAT TO DO AND WHERE TO GO FOR HELP

- Be patient, positive, and consistent.

- Encourage special needs students to stay in school.

- Help special needs students learn how to make informed choices regarding the services they receive, set goals regarding their lives, and develop action plans to attain those goals.

- Get professional help: Call Handicapped Services, Goodwill Industries, crisis intervention centers, mental health clinics, hospitals, a family physician, a clergy, a guidance counselor, or a teacher. If you need immediate help, call the National Crisis Alert Hotline at 1-800-231-1295. For more information, write to the American Academy of Child and Adolescent Psychiatry, 3615 Wisconsin Avenue, NW, Washington, D.C., 20016-3007.

Annotated Young Adult Novels Dealing with Youth with Disabilities

2.01.   Bach, Alice. (1980). *Waiting for Johnny Miracle*. New York: Harper & Row. 240 pp. (ISBN: 0-060-20348-X)

Twins Becky and Theo Maitland are bright, athletic, and identical in every way but one--Becky develops cancer in her leg.

2.02.   Blume, Judy. (1973). *Deenie*. New York: Dell Laurel-Leaf. 144 pp. (ISBN: 0-440-93259-9)

Deenie Fenner is a beautiful girl, the one who got all of the looks in the family. Deenie's mother has pressured her to stand tall for years because she has aspirations for Deenie to be a model. At 13, however, Deenie is diagnosed with adolescent idiopathic scoliosis, a lateral curvature of the spine. With the help of her father and friends as well as her own personal fortitude, Deenie is able to face the challenge of the prescribed treatment--Deenie must wear a brace for four years or risk being permanently crippled. Deenie is able to find internal strength to cope with the limitations, both real and imagined, that the brace places on her.

2.03.   Brancato, Robin. (1988). *Winning*. New York: Alfred A. Knopf. 211 pp. (ISBN: 0-394-80751-0).

Gary Madden, the star of the football team, is paralyzed from the shoulders down after a routine tackle. Gary becomes angered and depressed and takes a lot of his frustration out on his family and friends. He is faced with having to accept his fate and building a different life for himself, but his family and friends are not always there to give him the emotional support he needs. He gets help and insight from an understanding, sympathetic, English teacher who's also just recovering from her own, personal tragedy. Together they discover what winning is all about. (an American Library Association Best of the Best Books for Young Adults)

2.04.   Bridgers, Sue Ellen. (1990). *All together now*. New York: Bantam Books. 192 pp. (ISBN: 0-553-24530-9)

Dwayne Pickens is a 33-year-old man with a mind of a 12-year-old. When Casey, a tomboy, comes to stay the summer with her grandparents, she meets Dwayne who changes her life forever. Knowing that Dwayne dislikes girls, she allows him to think she is a boy. After playing a lot of baseball with him and getting to know him as a person, Casey, the mature young lady, comes to his defense when his brother threatens to have Dwayne institutionalized. (an American Library Association Notable Children's Book and Best Book for Young Adults, a *Boston Globe-Horn Book* Honor Book, a Booklist Reviewers' Choice, and The Christopher Award)

2.05.   Byars, Betsy. (1970). *The summer of the swans*. New York: Viking. 142 pp. (ISBN: 0-670-68190-3)

Sara is a 14-year-old girl with a younger brother, Charlie, who is mentally retarded. When Sara takes him to the park one day, Charlie becomes fascinated by some swans. The next day Charlie asks to go see the swans again, but Sara is too busy to take him. Charlie wanders off to the park by himself and gets lost. The rest of the story deals with Sara's search for her brother and how Charlie survives the night in the forest. (a Newbery Award Winner)

2.06.   Cleaver, Vera and Bill. (1973). *Me too*. Philadelphia: J.B. Lippincott Company. 158 pp. (ISBN: 0-397-31485-X)

Lornie and Lydia are identical twins in every respect but one--Lornie is severely mentally retarded. Lydia reacts with anger and confusion when her father abandons the family. Without his income, Lornie can no longer stay at the residential school for the retarded and Lydia will have to take care of her for the summer. Lydia decides that she will do what the school couldn't. She will teach Lornie so much that their father will be unable to tell them apart. In the end, the reader must also try to understand what Lydia is forced to accept.

2.07.   Colman, Hila. (1980). *Accident*. New York: William Morrow. 154 pp. (ISBN: 0-688-22238-2)

When Adam DeWitt asks Jenny for a date, he has no idea it will turn out so drastically. They both are involved in a motorcycle accident that leaves Jenny paralyzed and Adam traumatized. After a year in rehabilitation, they manage to develop their relationship again.

2.08.   Covington, Dennis. (1991). *Lizard*. New York: Delacorte Press. 198 pp. (ISBN: 0-385-30307-6)

Lucius Sims has been deformed since birth with eyes that look in different directions and a nose that lies down on its side. He's nicknamed Lizard when, at 13, his caretaker has him institutionalized in a home for retarded boys. After a theatrical presentation, he begs the troupe to take him with them. The troupe leader sneaks him out, and they hide in a park to escape authorities. There they meet Rain and her brother, Sammy, two deserted children with problems of their own. (winner of the Delacorte Press Prize for a First Young Adult Novel).

2.09.   Crutcher, Chris. (1987). *The crazy horse electric game*. New York: Greenwillow Books. 215 pp. (ISBN: 0-688-06683-6)

Sixteen-year-old Willie Weaver was the star of his baseball team until a freak boating accident leaves him hurt and brain damaged. After feeling betrayed by his father and girlfriend and becoming extremely frustrated by his situation, he runs away from home and finds himself in more trouble. Surrounded by street people and pimps, Willie finally enrolls in a special school for the handicapped where he learns coping strategies and finds strength to go home. (an American Library Association Best Book for Young Adults)

2.10.   Crutcher, Chris. (1986). *Running loose.* New York: Dell Laurel-Leaf. 192 pp. (ISBN: 0-440-97570-0)

Louie Banks has good friends, a starting spot on the football team, and a terrific girlfriend. Unfortunately when tragedy strikes and starts robbing him of these things, he must learn how to release his anger and find something else to believe in. (an American Library Association Best Book for Young Adults)

2.11.   DeClements, Barthe. (1985). *Sixth grade can really kill you.* New York: Viking Penguin/Viking Kestrel. 146 pp. (ISBN: 0-670-80656-0)

To draw people away from her real problem of not being able to read, "Bad Helen" resorts to a series of practical jokes during her 6th grade year. Eventually she admits and accepts her problem and channels her energies into solving it instead of producing the distractions she was known for.

2.12.   Engebrecht, Pat. (1983). *The promises of moonstone.* New York: Ballantine Books. 182 pp. (ISBN: 0-449-70093-3)

Sixteen-year-old Kristina and her mother have a wonderful relationship and both are ballet dancers. Their happy lives are challenged when Anna gets hurt in a beach accident that leaves her paralyzed and depressed. In an effort to understand her mother better, Kristina volunteers to work in a crippled children's hospital. Two new friends help her to accept the tragedy even in the face of her mother's two suicide attempts.

2.13.   Feuer, Elizabeth. (1990). *Paper doll.* New York: Farrar, Straus, & Giroux. 185 pp. (ISBN: 0-374-35736-6)

It's been ten years since Leslie Marx lost her legs in a tragic car accident. Since that time, her father has pushed her to excel in playing the violin. Leslie begins to question whether or not she is playing music for herself or because it's her father's wish. Her music loses her special touch until she meets Jeffrey, another student who has cerebral palsy. Jeffrey thinks Leslie is talented and encourages her to perform for an audience. Not only does Leslie play her violin for all of the right reasons, but she finds a loving relationship is possible for her in spite of her handicap.

2.14.   Garrigue, Sheila. (1986). *Between friends.* New York: Scholastic. 156 pp. (ISBN: 0-590-40773-2)

Jill is lonely after her family moves to a small town in Massachusetts from San Diego. She befriends Dede, a retarded girl, but finds her new friendship causes problems with some other friends and her mother.

2.15. Girion, Barbara. (1986). *A handful of stars*. New York: Dell Laurel-Leaf. 192 pp. (ISBN: 0-440-93642-X)

Julie Meyers begins high school with everything going her way until it is discovered that she has epilepsy. At first, Julie is angry and resentful about her illness and then despair sets in. Eventually, through much struggle, she adjusts and is able to approach her future with a positive attitude. (an ALA Best Book for Young Adults and a Children's Book of the Year)

2.16. Glenn, M. (1989). *Squeeze play*. New York: Ticknor & Fields. (ISBN: 0-899-19859-7)

A 6th grader must face the unnecessary teasing from his classmates when he is accidentally hit in the eye with a baseball. Wearing an eye patch to school has got to be the most humiliating thing possible, but he soon learns that his science teacher's experience as a survivor of the Holocaust was much worst. Rather than let the teasing continue, he decides to confront his classmates and tell them about his injury.

2.17. Gould, Marilyn. (1986). *The twelfth of June*. Philadelphia: J.B. Lippincott. 183 pp. (ISBN: 0-397-32130-9)

In this sequel to *Golden Daffodils*, Janis is now 12 years old and in junior high school. In spite of the fact that she has cerebral palsy, she wants to be like other girls and wants a boyfriend. Janis eventually concludes that she is not as handicapped by her illness as those who respond by trying to protect her.

2.18. Greenberg, Joanne. (1989). *Of such small differences*. New York: Signet Books. 272 pp. (ISBN: 0-451-16419-9)

John's world is unimaginable to those who can see and hear. Being blind and deaf is bad enough but not as bad as trying to love someone who is not handicapped too. This poignant novel allows the reader to appreciate the daily things we take for granted, especially when compared to the handicapped experience. (an ALA Best Book for Adults and Young Adults)

2.19. Hall, Lynn. (1985). *Just one friend*. New York: Charles Scribner's Sons. 118 pp. (ISBN: 0-684-18471-0)

Dory is a mentally handicapped 16-year-old who is leaving her school for "special children" to be mainstreamed into a regular high school. She is terrified and desperately wants a friend to ride the bus with her on her first day of school. She decides that Robin, a former friend when she was a little girl, should be that person. Because Robin is usually picked up by Meredith, Dory decides to stop Meredith from picking up Robin in her car. Dory's plans go awry and there is a tragedy. (an ALA Best Book for Young Adults)

2.20.   Hall, Lynn. (1990). *Halsey's pride*. New York: Macmillan. 128 pp. (ISBN: 0-684-19155-5)

Not only does March Halsey have to deal with being 13, but she also has to deal with being an epileptic who has a mother who can't deal with her illness. It is decided that March should live with her father, and she is determined to hide her seizures from her new teachers and classmates. Meanwhile, her father owns a kennel and has a prize show dog that he hopes will become a champion breeder. Unfortunately, Pride has a genetic defect which precludes March's father's dream from becoming a reality. March, through help from her friends and a neighbor, maintains a positive outlook in spite of the anguish and emotional isolation she feels from her parents.

2.21.   Hamilton, Dorothy. (1982). *Last one chosen*. Scottdale, PA: Herald Press. 112 pp. (ISBN: 0-8361-3306-4)

Eleven-year-old Scott Hardesty has one leg that is shorter than the other due to a tragic farm accident that his father feels responsible for. The two of them have problems associated with the accident: His father carries his guilt silently, and Scott wishes he could play ball like other kids so he will not always be the last one chosen.

2.22.   Holland, Isabelle. (1989). *The unfrightened dark*. Boston: Little, Brown, & Company. 120 pp. (ISBN: 0-316-37173-4)

Jocelyn Hunter has had to make several adjustments in her life, especially since the tragic car accident that killed her parents and left her blind. The simplest of tasks are difficult and walking to and from school are dangerous excursions. Thankfully, she has a terrific guide dog, Brace, who helps her and keeps her company. Unfortunately, Aunt Marian dislikes Brace, and someone with an accent is threatening to steal her dog. When Brace is stolen, Jocelyn and some of her school friends try to find the thief.

2.23.   Hunt, Irene. (1985). *The everlasting hills*. New York: Charles Scribner's Sons. 192 pp. (ISBN: 0-684-18340-4)

Jeremy Tyding not only suffers from brain damage as a result of a difficult birth, but also has to deal with a father who has nothing but contempt for him. After his mother's death, the only love and attention he ever got was from his older sister, Bethany. Things change when a young man falls in love and marries Bethany. Ishmael, an old recluse in the mountain community, invites Jeremy to live with him. Because Ishmael believes in Jeremy's powers to learn, he is able to help Jeremy overcome some of his handicaps. By the time Ishmael dies, Jeremy has a kind of reconciliation with his father whose respect he has earned.

2.24.   Hyland, Betty. (1987). *The girl with the crazy brother*. New York: Franklin Watts. 137 pp. (ISBN: 0-531-10345-5)

While a high school sophomore, Dana Miller is having to adjust to a recent move, a new school and friends, and an older brother who's starting to act really weird. Bill confides in her that he has to eat oranges so that he won't turn blue and that he's hearing voices. One night, Bill pleads for her help but all she can do is watch the hospital attendants take him away. Bill is diagnosed with schizophrenia, and Dana starts worrying about him, her family, and what the kids will think about all of this at her school.

2.25.   Kellogg, M. (1984). *Tell me that you love me, Junie Moon*. New York: Farrar, Straus, & Giroux. 216 pp. (ISBN: 0-374-51825-4)

Having had enough of institutionalized life, three handicapped individuals try to live together in mainstream America.

2.26.   Kent, Deborah. (1978). *Belonging*. New York: Ace Books. 200 pp. (ISBN: 0-448-05385-3) (Out of Stock)

Despite the misgivings of her parents, Meg decides she no longer wants to attend the special school for the blind but wants to attend the regular high school. This is the story of her first year there where Meg shares her fears and motivation, her problems and triumphs, with the reader. Meg longs for independence and wants acceptance as a total person, not as an object of pity. Yet, at its heart, this is not really just a story about a blind teenager with problems, but rather is a story about a teenager with problems and decisions not unlike most intelligent girls her age.

2.27.   Kent, Deborah. (1989). *One step at a time*. New York: Scholastic. 208 pp. (ISBN: 0-590-41580-8) (Out of Print)

Tracy Newberry is told during her freshman year of high school that she is going blind from Retinitis Pigmintosa. She does the best she can do to adjust to the terrible news in order to get on with her life.

2.28.   Kerr, M.E. (1981). *Little Little*. New York: Harper & Row. 183 pp. (ISBN: 0-06-023184-X)

This is the story about two dwarfs in search of their place in the world. Little Little Labelle is a 17-year-old dwarf. Her wealthy parents decide that Little Little ought to marry a midget T.V. minister, Little Lion, but she is interested in "The Roach," a dwarf who stars in the Palmer Pest Control television commercials. Not only must the three of them deal with their handicaps, they also have to contend with typical teenage identity problems. Adolescents who feel alienated by some problem or handicap they possess will enjoy this story told with sensitivity and great doses of therapeutic humor.

2.29.   Kingman, Lee. (1985). *Head over wheels.* New York: Dell Laurel-Leaf. 224 pp. (ISBN: 0-440-93129-0)

Seventeen-year-old twin boys must face the fact that one of them will never be able to walk again after a crippling car accident.

2.30.   Klein, Norma. (1987). *My life as a body.* New York: Alfred A. Knopf. 247 pp. (ISBN: 0-394-99051-X) (Out of Print)

This is the story of the unusual love-relationships of two couples. Augie Lloyd becomes involved with the boy she tutors, Sam Feldman. What makes their relationship different is that Sam is partially paralyzed. Augie helps Sam accept his handicap, and Sam helps Augie accept sex. The other relationship involves Augie's friend, Claudia, and her involvement with another woman. The latter relationship closely parallels the sexual identity issues experienced by Augie.

2.31.   Lee, Mildred. (1980). *The people therein.* New York: Clarion Books. 271 pp. (ISBN: 0-395-29434-7)

In spite of Lanthy's crippling handicap, she knows what she wants. A naturalistic teacher, Drew, helps her achieve her goals.

2.32.   L'Engle, Madeleine. (1989). *The young unicorns.* New York: Dell Laurel-Leaf. 224 pp. (ISBN: 0-440-99919-7)

The Austin family has just moved to New York City and is having a hard time adjusting to urban life. Their situation isn't that bad after they meet their teenage neighbor, Emily, who has just lost her sight. The Austins try to help her through her adjustment period. Through Emily, they unknowingly find themselves involved with an ex-gang member and become caught up in a terrifying gang plot to rule the city.

2.33.   Levinson, Nancy Smiler. (1990). *Annie's world.* Washington, D.C.: Kendall Green. 97 pp. (ISBN: 0-930323-65-3)

When Annie finally gets to go to public school, she is greeted by taunts and teasing about her deafness. Her family tries to offer her help, but Annie feels even more alienation with their involvement.

2.34.   Levy, Marilyn. (1982). *The girl in the plastic cage*. New York: Ballantine Books. 190 pp. (ISBN: 0-449-70030-5)

Things change for 13-year-old Lori when she learns she has scoliosis, a curvature of the spine. She had aspirations of being a gymnast, but now all of those dreams seem foolish. She does meet someone at the doctor's office who manages to make things better for awhile. She and Kurt start to develop a nice relationship just when she's getting into her body brace and he's getting out of his. Not only is her gymnastic future threatened, but Lori worries that her relationship with Kurt and her friends will be lost too.

2.35.   Marsden, John. (1989). *So much to tell you. . .* Boston: Joy Street Books. 117 pp. (ISBN: 0-316-54877-4)

Marina's life was fine until her parents' bitter divorce and the accident that left her disfigured. Now, she must learn to get along with others at her new boarding school--and herself.

2.36.   Mathis, Sharon Bell. (1990). *Listen for the fig tree*. New York: Puffin Books. 175 pp. (ISBN: 0-14-034364-4)

Muffin Johnson, a black teenager, is remarkably level-headed for a girl who is blind. Her life becomes more complicated when her mother resorts to alcohol to escape the approaching anniversary of her husband's murder at Christmas time.

2.37.   McDaniel, Lurlene. (1992). *Will I ever dance again?* Worthington, OH: Willowisp Press. 127 pp.

Rachel used to be a normal, happy, healthy, and very talented ballerina until she gets sick with diabetes. Thinking that her disease has made her a freak, Rachel stops dancing and spends every waking hour filled with self pity. Finally, with the help of her family and friends, she starts dancing again and becomes a professional ballerina despite her physical problems.

2.38.   Meyer, Carolyn. (1990). *Killing the kudu*. New York: Margaret K. McElderry Books. 208 pp. (ISBN: 0-689-50508-6)

Eighteen-year-old Alex is a paraplegic who has mixed feelings about his upcoming summer visit with his grandmother. Alex is looking forward to it since he will be away from his overprotective mother but also is anxious since his cousin, Scott, will be there too. It was Scott who accidentally shot him years ago and was responsible for Alex's handicap, and the boys haven't seen each other since the tragedy. At first, the boys are very uncomfortable about the situation, and then, with the help of a young housekeeper, the boys eventually come to terms with what happened.

2.39.   Naylor, Phyllis R. (1986). *The keeper*. New York: Atheneum. 212 pp. (ISBN: 0-689-31204-0)

Nick is forced to make an agonizing decision when his father's mental illness begins to destroy the family. (an American Library Association Best of the Best Books for Young Adults)

2.40.   Neufeld, John. (1971). *Twink*. New York: Signet Books. 128 pp. (ISBN: 0-451-15955-1)

Harry Walsh, a preppy, is 16 before he meets his stepsisters, Twink and Whizzer, for the first time. Harry is aware that Twink has cerebral palsy and is blind, but the sight of her shakes him up at first. Harry is determined to find out all that he can about her from Whizzer and his stepmother. As Harry learns more about her, he finds that she is a brave and wonderful person. Through Twink's inner strength and will to survive, Harry learns the meaning of being human and the joy of being alive.

2.41.   Peck, Robert Newton. (1979). *Clunie*. New York: Alfred A. Knopf. 124 pp. (ISBN: 0-394-84166-2)

Clunie, a mentally retarded girl, lives with her father who is a recovered alcoholic. He is consumed with guilt and is extremely protective of her. She attends a small town high school where two boys, Braddy and Leo, affect her life. Although the boys have a lot in common--both are poor, both are extremely interested in doing well on the varsity baseball team, and both are infatuated with the beautiful, rich Sally--Braddy and Leo exemplify polar attitudes toward the mentally handicapped. Braddy befriends Clunie and finds pleasure in the innocent way she sees the world. Leo, on the other hand, sees Clunie as an outlet for his sexual frustrations. Since he can't get Sally's attention, he leads others in cruelly chasing and taunting Clunie to a tragic end.

2.42.   Pfeffer, Susan Beth. (1989). *Claire at sixteen*. New York: Bantam Books. 180 pp. (ISBN: 0-553-05819-3)

Claire Sebastian exploits an opportunity to help her recently crippled sister. Some judge Claire as being a cold-blooded manipulator, while others view her as a devoted sister willing to take inordinate responsibility for the crisis.

2.43.   Platt, Kin. (1990). *The boy who could make himself disappear*. New York: Dell Laurel-Leaf. 256 pp. (ISBN: 0-440-90837-X)

This is the story of a 12-year-old boy who suffers from the rejection by both of his parents. Roger was seriously burned in an accident when he was very young, and his parents' divorce contributes to his feelings of worthlessness. He withdraws into himself and tries to make himself disappear. (an American Library Association Best Book for Young Adults)

2.44.   Richmond, Sandra. (1988). *Wheels for walking*. New York: Signet Books. 176 pp. (ISBN: 0-451-15235-2)

This novel details the physical and emotional experiences of Sally, an 18-year-old girl, who's paralyzed from the chest down after a car accident. She's finding it as difficult to hold her life together as she does trying to control her body. Several people are there for her during her struggle: her boyfriend, Brian; a fellow quadriplegic, Jake; and her therapist, Michael. Although they are there for her support, she learns that she must somehow pull it together from within. She ultimately gets over her bitterness and begins to adjust to her life as a quadriplegic. (Children's Book Council Notable Book and IRA Young Adult Choice)

2.45.   Rodowsky, Colby F. (1989). *What about me?* New York: Farrar, Straus, & Giroux. 144 pp. (ISBN: 0-374-48316-7)

Dorie's brother, Fred, is mentally retarded. Although she loves him, Dorie also finds that she resents all of the extra attention he gets from their parents. This novel movingly presents the extra demands placed upon a family with a retarded child.

2.46.   Sallis, Susan. (1980). *Only love*. New York: Harper & Row. 250 pp. (ISBN: 0-060-25174-3)

Although Fran Adamson is a paraplegic with numbered days, she is the life of Thornton Hall. When another patient falls in love with her, she is both elated and frightened because she knows that in all fairness she must tell him that her life will be very short.

2.47.   Scott, Virginia M. (1986). *Belonging*. Washington, D.C.: Gallaudet College Press. 200 pp. (ISBN: 0-930323-14-9)

Before the summer of her 15th birthday, Gustie Blaine was the model teenager. As a cheerleader and honor student, she was well liked at school and got along well with her parents and thought nothing of it. Things drastically change for Gustie when she loses her hearing from meningitis. She suffers the loss of friends who do not understand her deafness, fails several classes, and experiences a strained relationship with her parents. Gustie does not understand why she feels so isolated from all that she used to know and do. Gradually, Gustie begins to make new friends. With the help of Lenore and Jack, and a special education teacher, Mr. Tate, Gustie realizes that she still has choices in life, and she still can communicate with others. Although her ordeal is sad, Gustie learns a lot more about people and herself than the average teen. She learns what it really means to belong.

2.48.   Shyer, Marlene Fanta. (1988). *Welcome home, Jellybean.* New York: Aladdin Books. 152 pp. (ISBN: 0-689-71213-8)

Neil is the 12-year-old brother of Gerri Oxley, a retarded child who comes home after spending her first 13 years of life in an institution. Neil tells how each family member must learn how to deal with their new life with a retarded member. At first, it's an unbelievable disaster but eventually Gerri manages to win their love and approval.

2.49.   Slepian, Jan. (1980). *The Alfred summer.* New York: Macmillan. 119 pp. (ISBN: 0-027-82920-0)

Three teenagers, Alfred, Lester, and Myron, decide to build a boat together. What makes their project so extraordinary is that Alfred is mentally retarded, Lester has cerebral palsy, and Myron is apparently normal. This novel is both moving and funny.

2.50.   Slepian, Jan. (1981). *Lester's turn.* New York: Macmillan. 139 pp. (ISBN: 0-027-82940-5)

This novel is the sequel to *The Alfred Summer.* After Alfred is institutionalized, Lester (cerebral palsy and all) scts out to rescue him.

2.51.   Snyder, Carol. (1990). *Dear Mom and Dad, don't worry.* New York: Bantam Books. 160 pp. (ISBN: 0-553-05801-0)

At 13 years of age, Carly Stern injures her back in a freak fall. Because Carly's parents are worry-warts, Carly feels guilty that she has created another crisis for them to worry about. Eric, a special person at school, helps Carly to deal with her parents and her injury. She learns to accept the limitations not only in herself but in others too.

2.52.   Taylor, Theodore. (1991). *The weirdo.* San Diego: Harcourt, Brace, & Jovanovich. 289 pp. (ISBN: 0-152-94952-6)

Chip Newt, a 17-year-old burn victim, lives in the Powhatan Swamp with his father. It is through his involvement with nature, a researcher, and a new friend that Chip learns to value his life by protecting the lives of the animals of the swamp.

2.53.   Teague, Sam. (1987). *The king of hearts' heart*. Boston: Little, Brown, & Company. 186 pp. (ISBN: 0-316-83427-0)

Harold and Billy have a lot in common: They were born in the same month, in the same hospital, and are neighbors. They used to do everything together until a tragic fall leaves Billy brain damaged but Harold okay when they were four years old. Now, at 13 years of age, Harold thinks Billy is an aggravation, especially since he's found companionship with Kate and fun in track. Fortunately, Harold has a change of heart and decides he will help Billy to train for a track championship in the International Summer Special Olympics.

2.54.   Voigt, Cynthia. (1987). *Izzy, willy-nilly*. New York: Fawcett Juniper. 262 pp. (ISBN: 0-449-70214-6)

Pretty and popular, 15-year-old Isobel "Izzy" Lingard accepts a date with a senior which her parents reluctantly allow her to keep. This seemingly small, unimportant decision becomes the biggest regret of Izzy and her parents' lives. Her right leg has to be amputated below the knee after a car accident caused by a drunk driver, her date. Many of her friends knew that Marco was too drunk to drive but did nothing to stop him. Her new life completely changes her relationships with family and friends. Izzy slowly comes to the realization that most of her friends are really shallow; they were unquestioned friendships from childhood. When new friends emerge from unexpected places, Izzy redefines and learns to accept herself again. This novel deeply examines Izzy's feelings about her disability as well as the feelings of her family and friends. (an American Library Association Best of the Best Books for Young Adults, the Horn Book Fanfare List, a Parents' Choice Remarkable Book for Literature, and a Library of Congress Children's Book of the Year)

2.55.   Voigt, Cynthia. (1988). *Tree by leaf*. New York: Macmillan. 192 pp. (ISBN: 0-689-31403-5)

Twelve-year-old Clothilde Speer inherits Speer Point from a great aunt who she didn't even know. Her family moves there the day before her father joins the cavalry of World War I. After her father's face is disfigured, he returns to Speer Point but insists on living in the boathouse. There he can escape from his family's looks and won't feel like he's inflicting his pain on his family. Clothilde does feel the pain and comes to realize that being handicapped or hurt doesn't mean you run away from those who love you.

2.56.   Wartski, Maureen Crane.   (1979).   *My brother is special.*
         Philadelphia: Westminster Press. 153 pp. (ISBN: 0-664-32644-7)

This story deals with the problems and situations a family faces while establishing themselves in a new community. Noni spends a lot of time helping her 9-year-old brother get ready for the Special Olympics. This novel points out the ridicule handicapped people encounter and explores the subtle nuances of the effects a retarded child has on family dynamics.

2.57.   Windsor, M.A. (1986). *Pretty Saro.* New York: Atheneum. 208 pp.
         (ISBN: 0-689-31277-6) (Out of Stock)

Sarah Jean Banks has a pretty nice life considering her family is mega-wealthy.   At 14, Sarah's favorite pastime is showing horses for her mother's farm.   Most of the kids at school think she is a snob, but Sarah changes when two tragedies beset her: First, her best pony, Moonlight Rhythm, goes lame right before the Kentucky Grand Championship; and second, she discovers she has to wear a hearing aid which completely alters how she reacts to people. Because of her handicap, Sarah completely changes her outlook and expectations of life.

2.58.   Wood, June Rae. (1992). *The man who loved clowns.* New York:
         G.P. Putnam's Sons. 224 pp. (ISBN: 0-399-21888-2)

Delrita Jensen is having to deal with the typical adolescent concerns of an 8th grader while dealing with the not-so-typical concerns of a brother who has Down's syndrome.

2.59.   Young, Alida. (1988). *Never look back.*   Worthington, OH:
         Willowisp Press. 144 pp. (ISBN: 0-874-06286-1)

Heather Ames, a high school bowler and long distance runner, discovers during a race that her body is unexplainably racked with searing pain. She and her family consult with a few doctors who are unable to diagnose her problem. She continues her high school activities, hobbling from class to class, unable to understand why her growing pains are so much more severe than other teens'. Heather endures the humiliation of others who see her as a hypochondriac. Finally, after consultation with a medical specialist, Heather is diagnosed with J.R.A., Juvenile Rheumatoid Arthritis.   After therapeutic treatment, Heather returns to school determined that the arthritis won't beat her.

Annotated Young Adult Nonfiction Dealing with Youth with Disabilities

2.60.   Bernstein, J. (1988). *Loving Rachel: A family's journey from grief.* Boston: Little, Brown, & Company. 279 pp. (ISBN: 0-316-09204-5)

Rachel is blind and her family has to learn how to appreciate her for what she is, not for what she could have been.

2.61.   Craven, Margaret. (1990). *Again calls the owl.* New York: Dell. 128 pp. (ISBN: 0-440-30074-6)

This is the author's inspirational story of how she battled against her blindness, struggled to become a writer, and how she managed to write her first novel, *I Heard the Owl Call My Name* which won international acclaim.

2.62.   Deford, F. (1986). *Alex: The life of a child.* New York: New American Library. 205 pp. (ISBN: 0-451-14545-3)

The author shares what it is like for a child growing up with Cystic Fibrosis.

2.63.   Eareckson, Joni & Musser, Joe. (1990). *Joni.* New York: Bantam Books. 192 pp. (includes a 16 page photo insert) (ISBN: 0-553-27786-3)

At 17, Joni became a quadriplegic as a result of a diving accident. This autobiography details her struggle to accept and adjust to her handicap and how she became a successful artist who draws with a pen held in her teeth.

2.64.   Jones, Ron. (1990). *The acorn people.* New York: Bantam Books. 96 pp. (ISBN: 0-553-27385-X)

This true story about a group of handicapped boys at summer camp is based on the journal of the author, Ron Jones. The two week camp begins with inexperienced counselors meeting five handicapped children for the first time at Camp Wiggin. Benny B., a peanut-sized black boy, may have lost his legs to polio but he didn't lose his spirit. Spider, nicknamed because he has no arms or legs, loves to talk; what his eyes don't capture, his mouth tries to trap. Thomas Stewart, age 15, has muscular sclerosis and weighs only 35 pounds. Martin, the most able-bodied member, is tall, red-haired, outgoing, and blind. Finally, there is Aaron Gerwalski, nicknamed Arid because of his smell, who has clammy skin and no bladder. Camp Wiggin, a summer camp for boy scouts, is obviously not equipped for the special needs of these children. The first few days are tense and trying for everyone, but both counselors and boys wind up having an unforgettable summer full of joys, experiences, and accomplishments. In essence, these five boys defy everyone's notion of what handicapped children ought to do or not do. Each one of these characters discovers personal strengths and talents, and the counselors learn even more.

2.65.   Jones, Ron. (1990). *B-Ball: The team that never lost a game*. New York: Bantam Books. 160 pp. (ISBN: 0-553-05867-3)

Ron Jones describes his experiences as a basketball coach for a Special Olympics team. He describes his players' unyielding courage and determination and how they all felt like victorious winners after every game.

2.66.   Keller, Helen. (1988). *The story of my life*. New York: New American Library. 213 pp. (ISBN: 0-451-52245-1)

This is Helen Keller's autobiographical account of her life before, during, and after her involvement with Anne Sullivan. Readers gain insight into the nature and importance of language and the need to communicate.

2.67.   Killilea, Marie. (1990). *Karen*. New York: Dell Laurel-Leaf. 304 pp. (ISBN: 0-440-94376-0)

This is the true story about Karen, a girl with cerebral palsy who learns how to walk, talk, read, and write in spite of her handicap. There is a sequel, *With Love From Karen*, which is the author's responses to thousands of letters received after the publication of *Karen*. (the Golden Book Award and two Christopher Awards)

2.68.   Little, Jean. (1991). *Little by Little: A writer's education*. New York: Viking Penguin/Puffin. 240 pp. (ISBN: 0-14-032325-2)

Jean Little, the noted children's author, describes what she had to go through while growing up in Canada. These memoirs specifically address her struggle with her blindness and her pursuit of her writing career.

2.69.   Meyers, Robert. (1980). *Like normal people*. New York: Signet Books. 203 pp. (ISBN: 0-451-09112-4) (Out of Print)

The author writes about his brother, Roger, who is mentally retarded. This is the story of Roger's marriage to Virginia Hensler, who is also retarded, and their struggle to make their marriage work against enormous odds. Their story was initially presented as a newspaper series years ago.

2.70.   Nolan, Christopher. (1990). *Under the eye of the clock: The life story of Christopher Nolan.* New York: Delacorte Press. 176 pp. (ISBN: 0-385-29774-2)

Christopher Nolan was both paralyzed and mute at birth. Now a 22-year-old Irish poet, the author shares his struggle to fit into a "normal" school and his unyielding drive to master writing so he could express his vision to others. (Whitbread Award)

2.71.   Roy, Ron. (1985). *Move over, wheelchairs coming through! Seven young people in wheelchairs talk about their lives.* New York: Clarion Books. 96 pp. (includes photographs) (ISBN: 0-89919-249-1)

Ron Roy interviewed seven teenagers who are confined to wheelchairs for their only means of movement. The most severe case is Lizzy who can speak and move her head but must rely on a computerized wheelchair that she operates with her chin. The author focuses on how these teens get along in their daily lives. The book also includes information about the disease each of the teens has and a list of further readings.

2.72.   Seldon, Bernice. (1987). *The story of Annie Sullivan, Helen Keller's teacher.* New York: Dell. 96 pp. (ISBN: 0-440-48285-2)

Annie Sullivan has her own tragic beginnings which prompted her to become Helen Keller's teacher. When she was eight years old, she could barely see. When her mother died, she was left to care for her younger two siblings and an alcoholic father. When that situation became unbearable, the children were sent to live with some relatives. Before long, their aunt and uncle could no longer care for the children and they were separated. Her younger sister went to live with another aunt, while she and her brother went to live in the poorhouse. There, her brother dies of tuberculosis, leaving Annie all alone. Finally, some kind people help her get corrective surgery for her eyes and she acquires employment with the Kellers. The rest is history.

2.73.   Siegel, Dorothy. (1978). *Winners: Eight special young people.* New York: Julian Messner. 192 pp. (ISBN: 0-671-32861-1)

This is a collection of eight stories, each about a different teenager who is handicapped and manages to live an independent and useful life in spite of physical problems.

2.74.   Sullivan, T. & Gill, D. (1989). *If you could see what I hear.* New York: Harper & Row. 184 pp. (ISBN: 0-060-80961-2).

Tom Sullivan, blind from birth, refuses to accept the limits of his handicap. This story tells how Tom manages to become an athlete, composer, T.V. personality, husband, and father.

2.75.   Valens, Evans G. (1988). *Other side of the mountain*. New York: Perennial Library. 313 pp. (ISBN: 0-060-80948-5)

This is the inspiring story of Olympic skiing contender Jill Kinmont's triumph over permanent paralysis.

Nonfiction References Dealing with Youth with Disabilities

Journal Articles

Browning, P., Brown, C. & Dunn, C.   (1993, February-March).   Another decade of transition for secondary students with disabilities. *High School Journal, 76* (3), p. 190 ff.

Brunner, C.E. & Majewski, W.S.   (1990, October).   Mildly handicapped students can succeed with learning styles. *Educational Leadership, 48* (2), p. 21 ff.

Chapman, J.W.   (1988, Fall).   Learning disabled children's self-concepts. *Review of Educational Research, 58* (3), p. 347 ff.

Farnsworth, L. (1985, August). Jason was handicapped...But he knew how to get his own way. *Learning, 14* (1), p. 44 ff.

Hodgkinson, H. (1991, September). Reform versus reality. *Phi Delta Kappan, 73* (1) p. 9 ff.

Kuipers, J. (1992, May). Not yet a mile in their moccasins and already my feet hurt. *Phi Delta Kappan, 73* (9), p. 718 ff.

McCarthy, M.M. (1991, September). Severely disabled children: Who pays? *Phi Delta Kappan, 73* (1), p. 66 ff.

O'Connor, T. (1984, December). Adolescent development and the learning disabled teenager: Implications for the classroom teacher. *English Journal, 73* (8), p. 33 ff.

Ohanian, S. (1990, November). P.L. 94-142: Mainstream or quicksand? *Phi Delta Kappan, 72* (3), p. 217 ff.

Wagner, C.G.   (1992, May-June).   Visions: Enabling the 'disabled':
    Technologies for people with handicaps. *The Futurist, 26* (3), p. 29 ff.

Journal Themes

Learning with the 'Learning Disabled.' (1989, March). *English Journal, 78* (3).

Books

Quicke, J. (1985). *Disability in modern children's fiction.* Brookline, MA:
    Brookline Books. 176 pp. (ISBN: 0-914-79709-3)

Wagner, M. (1989). *Youth with disabilities during transition: An Overview of
    descriptive findings from the national longitudinal transition study.*
    Stanford, CA: SRI International.

CHAPTER 3

Homosexuality

Gay and lesbian youth are in our society, but many have not acknowledged their identities because of their fear of rejection. Although homosexuality is now portrayed more positively in the media, people's feelings on the subject are often uncomfortable, negative, and intense. At the federal level, for example, there are no laws that protect homosexuals from discrimination based on sexual orientation. Although the March on Washington in April 1993 promoted gay awareness, those who attempt to help adolescents need to be aware of the national, state, and local laws as they relate to the issues of homosexuality and their right to advocate, encourage, or promote homosexuality.

STARTLING INFORMATION ABOUT TEENAGE HOMOSEXUALITY

- Objective data on homosexual teens has failed to verify the "pathology" assumed to underlie homosexual affiliation; hence, a gay or lesbian orientation is defensible as an acceptable alternative lifestyle to a straight identity. (Cates, 1992)

- Being attracted to one's own sex is as natural for someone who is homosexual as being attracted to the opposite sex is for someone who is heterosexual (Eichberg, 1990); in fact, the real issue with regard to homosexuality is not what causes sexual orientation but how society reacts to it. (Mallon, 1992)

- It is commonly accepted that 5 to 15% of our population, including adolescents, is homosexual. (Krysiak, 1987)

- The average age of homosexual awareness occurs for males between 13-15 years of age; for females, the average age is twenty. (Powell, 1987)

• The suicide rate for gay and lesbian teenagers is two to six times higher than that of heterosexual teens. (Krueger, 1993)

• Gay and lesbian teenagers are more likely than their heterosexual peers to drop out of schools, become runaways, and abuse alcohol and other drugs. (Krueger, 1993)

• Contrary to the myth that gay men are child molesters, 93% of all child molestation is perpetrated by heterosexual male family members. (Harris, 1990)

WHAT TO DO AND WHERE TO GO FOR HELP

• An important consciousness-raising first step for any well-intentioned individual is to examine their own knowledge, beliefs, and values about homosexuality.

• The health education needs of adolescent gays and lesbians are seldom met as a result of homophobia. Don't preach to adolescents about sex but do be specific. A more realistic strategy is to encourage the restraint for high risk behaviors with an emphasis on condom use during intercourse.

• Parents usually need assistance in coping when they find out that their son or daughter is gay.

• Get professional help: Call a family planning clinic, hospital, a mental health facility, a counselor, or a teacher. For more information, write to the American Civil Liberties Union (ACLU), Lesbian and Gay Rights Project, 132 West 43rd Street, New York, New York, 10036; or the National Federation of Parents and Friends of Gays, 5715 Sixteenth Street, NW, Washington, D.C., 20026.

Annotated Young Adult Novels Dealing with Homosexuality

3.01. Benard, Robert. (1987). *A Catholic education.* New York: Dell Laurel-Leaf. 288 pp. (ISBN: 0-440-91124-9)

Nick Manion's last three years of high school and first year of college has been male dominated. He has attended an all-boys Catholic school and now thinks he wants to be a Jesuit priest. During seminary, Nick's world takes a turn that is unexpected. Could he be gay? Nick's personal and religious conflicts are treated sensitively.

3.02.   Brown, Rita Mae. (1983). *Rubyfruit jungle*. New York: Bantam Books. 246 pp. (ISBN: 0-553-23813-2)

Molly knows at a very young age that she is different than her friends; she is homosexual. Her family and friends have a hard time dealing with it, but Molly manages to accept herself and eventually reconciles with her family. There are some graphic scenes in this classic book.

3.03.   Chambers, Aidan. (1983). *Dance on my grave*. New York: Harper & Row. 251 pp. (ISBN: 0-060-21253-5)

Hal Robinson and Barry Gorman are typical teenage friends with one exception; they are gay. Hal is sure that he has found the perfect person for himself, but Barry doesn't want to have a committed relationship. After a bitter fight, Barry rushes off and dies in a fatal motorcycle accident.

3.04.   Chesire, Jimmy. (1990). *Home boy*. New York: Plume. 320 pp. (ISBN: 0-452-26441-3).

Franklin Gamble, a 17-year-old boy, lives at Father McFlaherty's Home for Boys. While living in this rural setting, Franklin painfully admits that he is gay and confronts what that means both sexually and socially.

3.05.   Childress, Alice. (1989). *Those other people*. New York: Putnam. 186 pp. (ISBN: 0-399-21510-7)

Seventeen-year-old Jonathan Barnett is trying to figure out who he is, especially after his ended affair with Harp. Harp was more concerned that Jonathan "come out of the closet" than their relationship. In the midst of this confusion, Jonathan decides to put his life on hold for a while, including college, and moves to a small town where he acquires a job as a computer instructor at a local high school. He witnesses inappropriate behaviors by the physical education teacher to a sexually confused female student, and Jonathan is confronted with a major decision which may force him "out" in the long run.

3.06.   Colman, Hila. (1986). *Happily ever after*. New York: Scholastic. 156 pp. (ISBN: 0-590-33551-0) (Out of Print)

When Melanie and Paul were in the 2nd grade, they became fast friends and Melanie would often announce that they would marry someday. Now that they are about to graduate from high school, Melanie is ready for marriage but Paul definitely is not. Melanie thinks it's peculiar when Paul decides to go to Mexico rather than attend his own graduation. In Mexico, he meets Andrew, a young man from England who captures his interest. When he returns, Melanie senses that things are different and manages to get him to come out to her.

3.07. Garden, Nancy. (1982). *Annie on my mind*. New York: Farrar, Straus, & Giroux. 233 pp. (ISBN: 0-374-30366-5)

When 17-year-old Liza Winthrop meets Annie Kenyon at the New York's Metropolitan Museum of Art, it is love at first sight. After several problems, Liza stays away from her for six months before they are reunited. Two gay teachers serve as role models for the girls. When they are fired because of their sexuality, the two women react without shame and guilt which teaches Liza and Annie a valuable lesson. Adolescents who have gay tendencies will enjoy this non-sensational story told with great sensitivity. (an American Library Association Best of the Best Books for Young Adults)

3.08. Greene, Bette. (1991). *The drowning of Stephan Jones*. New York: Bantam Books. 217 pp. (ISBN: 0-553-07437-7)

Carla is crazy about Andy Harris, a cute boy from a highly respected family, but Andy hardly notices her. Instead, he is preoccupied, in a negative way, with two gay men who have moved into their town. Because Carla is so infatuated with Andy, she fails to see the hatred that Andy displays for these two men. Andy's hatred gets increasingly worse and ends in the death of Stephan Jones. The young people involved are put on trial, and Carla must choose between telling the truth or standing up for her friends.

3.09. Hautzig, Deborah. (1978). *Hey, Dollface*. New York: Greenwillow. 160 pp. (ISBN: 0-688-84170-8)

While attending the Garfield School for Girls, Val Hoffman and Chloe Fox befriend each other out of loneliness. The two girls admittedly feel out of place and find themselves doing everything together including cutting classes. Although their loneliness issue is resolved through one another, they have another issue to contend with: Are they becoming more than friends?

3.10. Holland, Isabelle. (1987). *The man without a face*. 157 pp.

See Divorced and Single Parents

3.11. Homes, A.M. (1989). *Jack*. New York: MacMillan. 220 pp. (ISBN: 0-02-744831-2)

When Jack finds out that his father is a homosexual, he learns that he has a lot to deal with for a 14-year-old: spouse abuse, divorce, an obnoxious best friend, and meeting and falling for his first girlfriend.

3.12.   Kerr, M.E. (1986). *Night kites.* 216 pp.

See AIDS

3.13.   Klein, Norma. (1987). *Breaking up.* 174 pp.

See Divorced and Single Parents

3.14.   Klein, Norma. (1987). *My life as a body.* 247 pp.

See Youth with Disabilities

3.15.   Klein, Norma. (1989). *Now that I know.* New York: Bantam Books. 165 pp. (ISBN: 0-553-28115-1)

Thirteen-year-old Nina has grown accustomed to the three years of joint custody, but now she is faced with dealing with her father's secret life and the reason for her parents' divorce. Finding out that her father is a homosexual has put her in a difficult situation: Not only does she have to resolve her own conflict with her father, but she also has to deal with the frustration of her mother. Two of her friends, Dara and Damian, help Nina work through her confusion, lack of understanding, and anger. Nina eventually learns to accept her father's alternate lifestyle.

3.16.   Levy, Marilyn. (1990). *Rumors and whispers.* New York: Fawcett Juniper. 160 pp. (ISBN: 0-449-70327-4)

Due to a recent move, Sarah is upset that she has to spend her senior year in California. Before long, she wishes that's all she has to be upset about. Suddenly, her brother Doug is thrown out of the house and is no longer welcomed by their father. When Sarah finally figures out that it's because he is gay, she offers Doug the loving support he needs. To complicate matters, it is uncovered that there is an AIDS-infected teacher at Sarah's school which triggers a volatile, community debate about the issue. Things get better for Sarah when she develops a relationship with a sensitive classmate.

3.17.   Meyer, Carolyn. (1990). *Elliot and Win.* New York: Macmillan. 208 pp. (ISBN: 0-020-44702-7)

Win is excited that he is going to get a "Big Brother" but is disappointed when the person he gets is a man who likes opera and gourmet cooking rather than the great outdoors. Win gets even more upset when his best friend, Paul, suggests that this caring man is a homosexual.

3.18.   Russell, Paul. (1991). *Boys of life*. New York: E.P. Dutton. 307 pp. (ISBN: 0-525-93327-1)

Tony Blair is trying to figure out his sexual identity at a time of life when everything is confusing.

3.19.   Salat, Cristina. (1993). *Living in secret*. New York: Bantam Books. 192 pp. (ISBN: 0-553-08670-0)

When 11-year-old Amelia's parents get a divorce, her father is awarded custody because it would be inappropriate for her to be raised in a lesbian environment. Amelia thinks differently and persuades her mother and her mother's partner to take her to California to start a new life; Amelia informs her dad that she is running away. In California, Amelia changes her name to Julie and so begins a number of secrets that must be kept in order to protect her new family.

3.20.   Scoppettone, Sandra. (1991). *Trying hard to hear you*. Boston: Alyson Publications. 264 pp. (ISBN: 1-555-83196-6)

Camilla loves Phil but Phil loves Jeff, her close friend for years. This novel centers around the problems experienced by gay males and the peer cruelty they endure. In a tragic ending, the couple's former friends have to live with the knowledge that cruelty can have disastrous effects on people's lives.

3.21.   Scoppettone, Sandra. (1991). *Happy endings are all alike*. Boston: Alyson Publications. 202 pp. (ISBN: 1-555-83177-X)

Two high school senior girls, Jaret Taylor and Peggy Denziger, are in love with each other. Even though they are both good students from good homes, their situation is very delicate. If anybody in their small town found out, problems would be created for all. Unfortunately, an angry friend of Jaret's younger brother discovers the girls' secret. He brutally rapes Jaret in order to teach her a lesson, then blackmails her into keeping the rape silent or else he will tell the entire town about her love affair. The rape, however, eventually brings everything out in the open.

3.22.   Shannon, George. (1989). *Unlived affections*. New York: Harper & Row. 135 pp. (ISBN: 0-06-025305-3)

Willie Ramsey has had a lot to deal with for a young man of 18 years. He was raised by his grandmother who did not offer him a lot of information about his mother and father, only that his mother was dead and his unfit father died before he was born. Now that his grandmother has passed away, the responsibility of selling her house and cleaning out its contents is on him.

While sorting through some things, Willie discovers some letters written by his father to his mother. These letters provide insight into Willie's own confusion about himself and his inability to completely love his girlfriend.

3.23.   Snyder. Anne. (1987). *The truth about Alex*. New York: Signet Books. 176 pp. (ISBN: 0-451-14996-3)

Facing pressure from adults and classmates, a high school senior must decide whether to reject the friendship of a friend and football teammate who is gay. An appointment to West Point is at stake.

3.24.   White, Edmund. (1983). *A boy's own story*. New York: E.P. Dutton. 224 pp. (ISBN: 0-452-26352-2)

According to the *New York Times*, this novel "is not exclusively a homosexual boy's story. It is any boy's story to the marvelous degree that it evokes the inchoate longings of late childhood and adolescence, the sense that somehow, someday, somewhere, life will provide a focus for these longings, and the agonizing length of time that life seems to take in getting around to this particular piece of business."

3.25.   Wieler, Diana. (1992). *Bad boy*. New York: Doubleday. 184 pp. (ISBN: 0-385-30415-3)

Things have been going great for A.J.. He and his best friend, Tulley, have made the Triple A ice-hockey league, and A.J. has been holding his own on the ice. When A.J. takes out an opponent during a play, A.J. gets some fame around his school and acquires the nickname "Bad Boy." A.J.'s developed an interest in Tulley's younger sister, Summer, and isn't getting any help from his friend. Instead, Tulley seems to be very withdrawn lately. When Summer asks A.J. to find her brother one night, A.J. is upset when he sees Tulley walking arm-in-arm with another hockey player into a gay bar. A.J. is afraid he'll be labeled gay, since Tulley has been his long-time best friend. A.J. avoids Tulley with everything he's worth until an attack on Summer makes him confront his own prejudice.

3.26.   Woodson, J. (1991). *The dear one*. 145 pp.

See Teenage Pregnancy

3.27.   Young, Alida E. (1988). *I never got to say goodbye*. 128 pp.

See AIDS

Annotated Young Adult Nonfiction Dealing with Homosexuality

3.28.   Alyson, Sasha. (Ed.). (1991). *Young, gay, and proud.* Boston: Alyson Publications. 96 pp. (ISBN: 1-55583-001-3)

Facts, letters, and anecdotes, make this a valuable read for any adolescent experiencing homosexual tendencies. Chapters include "You're Not the Only One," "Telling Other People," "Why Are We Hassled?" "Gays and Health," and others.

3.29.   Bell, Ruth et.al. (1988). *Changing bodies, changing lives: Revised and updated.* New York: Vintage Books. 272 pp. (ISBN: 0-394-56499-5)

Although this reference book isn't solely about AIDS or homosexuality, there is an excellent unit on both of these topics. The rest of the text provides teens with straightforward, non-preachy information about questions teenagers often have about their bodies, emotions, and sex. Throughout, teenagers share their own experiences concerning several issues.

3.30.   Blake, Jeanne. (1990). *Risky times: How to be AIDS-smart and stay healthy: A guide for teenagers.* 158 pp.

See AIDS

3.31.   Cohen, Daniel & Cohen, Susan. (1992). *When someone you know is gay.* New York: Dell. 162 pp. (ISBN: 0-440-21298-7).

This book is designed to provide insights to heterosexual teens about their homosexual friends. A gay teen will also find this book helpful and informative.

3.32.   Fricke, Aaron. (1981). *Reflections of a rock lobster.* Boston: Alyson Publications. 116 pp. (ISBN: 0-93287-009-0)

The author has had frequent national attention as a gay spokesperson. He made his first appearance when he took a boyfriend to his high school prom in Cumberland, Rhode Island. He has also appeared on several talk shows speaking about what it is like growing up gay in America.

3.33.   Hawkes, Nigel. (1987). *AIDS.* 32 pp.

See AIDS

3.34. Heron, Ann. (Ed.). (1986). *One teenager in ten: Testimony by gay and lesbian youth*. New York: Warner Books. 128 pp. (ISBN: 0-446-32653-4) (Out of Stock)

Parent-teenage discussion about sex is often difficult at best, but for a teen struggling with homosexual issues it can be a disaster. The title of the book is based on research done at the Kinsey Institute that suggests that "one teenager in ten" is probably gay. Rita Mae Brown's introduction supports the testimonies of 28 homosexuals, 11 women and 17 men between the ages of 15 and 24, who share their "coming out" experiences.

3.35. Holbrook, Sabra. (1987). *Fighting back: The struggle for gay rights*. New York: E.P. Dutton/Lodestar Books. 89 pp. (ISBN: 0-525-67187-0)

It is estimated that 10% of the population is gay, and yet there are many homosexuals who are denied basic freedoms because of their sexual orientation. Holbrook provides an historical look at the attitudes of this country regarding homosexuality and traces the progress of civil rights for all Americans. The author also presents some interesting information that may link the cause of homosexuality to a person's body's chemical composition.

3.36. Hyde, Margaret O. & Forsyth, Elizabeth H. (1992). *AIDS: What does it mean to you?* (4th Ed.). 128 pp.

See AIDS

3.37. Meyer, Caroline. (1979). *The center: From a troubled past to a new life*. 193 pp.

See Alcohol and Drugs

3.38. Monette, Paul. (1990). *Borrowed time*. 342 pp.

See AIDS

3.39. Rench, Janice E. (1990). *Understanding sexual identity: A book for gay teens and their friends*. New York: Lerner. 56 pp. (ISBN: 0-822-50044-2)

In a straight-forward, matter-of-fact style, the author attempts to dispel some of the myths associated with homosexuality in an attempt to eliminate unnecessary hatred and violence.

3.40.   Rofes, Eric E. (1985). *Socrates, Plato, and guys like me: Confessions of a gay schoolteacher*. Boston: Alyson. 163 pp. (ISBN: 0-932870-67-8).

Eric Rofes describes certain aspects of his personal and professional life between 1976 and 1978. In particular, Rofes shares his thoughts about being a new teacher and the conflicts experienced because of his sexuality. He basically "stayed in the closet" because of fear of losing his job. At the same time, he felt like a hypocrite because of pretending to be someone he wasn't. Rofes shares his struggle to become secure with himself.

3.41.   Ruskin, Cindy. (1988). *The quilt: Stories from the NAMES Project*. 160 pp.

See AIDS

Nonfiction References Dealing with Homosexuality

Journal Articles

Cates, J.A. (1987, July-August). Adolescent sexuality: Gay and lesbian issues. *Child Welfare, 66* (4), p. 353 ff.

Coleman, E., Remafedi, G. (1989, September-October). Gay, lesbian, and bisexual adolescents: A critical challenge to counselors. *Journal of Counseling and Development, 68* (1), p. 36 ff.

Dunham, K. (1989, June). Educated to be invisible: The gay and lesbian adolescent. *Psychology Today*.

Flax, E. (1990, May). Reaching out to homosexual teens. *Teacher Magazine*, p. 34 ff.

Gonsiorek, J.C. (1988). Mental health issues of gay and lesbian adolescents. *Journal of Adolescent Health Care, 9*, p. 114 ff.

Hanckel, F. & Cunningham, J. (1976, March). Can young gays find happiness in YA books? *Wilson Library Bulletin, 50* (7), p. 528 ff.

Hart, E.L. & Parmeter, S.H. (1992). 'Writing in the margins': A lesbian and gay-inclusive course. In Mark Hurlbert & Samuel Totten's *Social Issues in the English Classroom*. Urbana, Illinois: National Council of Teachers of English, p. 154 ff.

Herdt, G. (1989). Introduction: Gay and lesbian youth, emergent identities, and cultural scenes at home and abroad. *Journal of Homosexuality, 14* (1/2), p. 1 ff.

Hunter, J. & Schaecher, R. (1987, Spring). Stresses on lesbian and gay adolescents in school. *Social Work in Education, 9* (3), p. 180 ff.

Krueger, M.M. (1993, March). Everyone is an exception: Assumptions to avoid in the sex education classroom. *Phi Delta Kappan, 74* (7), p. 569 ff.

Krysiak, G. (1987). A very silent and gay minority. *The School Counselor, 34* (4), p. 304 ff.

Mallon, G. (1992, November-December). Gay and no place to go: Assessing the needs of gay and lesbian adolescents in out-of-home care settings. *Child Welfare, 71* (6), p. 547 ff.

Martin, A.D. (1982). Learning to hide: The socialization of the gay adolescent. *Adolescent Psychiatry, 10,* p. 52 ff.

Martin, A.D. & Hetrick, E.S. (1988). The stigmatization of the gay and lesbian adolescent. *Journal of Homosexuality, 15* (3), p. 163 ff.

Powell, R.E. (1987, January). Homosexual behavior and the school counselor. *The School Counselor, 34* (3), p. 202 ff.

Reiter, L. (1989). Sexual orientation, sexual identity, and the question of choice. *Clinical Social Work Journal, 17,* p. 138 ff.

Remafedi, G. (1987). Homosexual youth: A challenge to contemporary society. *Journal of the American Medical Association, 258* (2), p. 222 ff.

Rofes, E. (1989, November). Opening up the classroom closet: Responding to the educational needs of gay and lesbian youth. *Harvard Educational Review, 59* (4), p. 444 ff.

Schneider, M. & Tremble, B. (1986). Training service providers to work with gay or lesbian adolescents: A Workshop. *Journal of Counseling and Development, 65,* p. 98 ff.

Schneider, M. & Tremble, B. (1985). Gay or straight: Working with the confused adolescent. *Journal of Social Work and Human Sexuality, 4,* p. 631 ff.

Sears, J.T. (1991, September). Helping students understand and accept sexual diversity. *Educational Leadership, 49* (1), p. 54 ff.

Selverstone, R. (1989). Adolescent sexuality: Developing self-esteem and mastering developmental tasks. *Siecus Report, 18*, p. 1 ff.

Weisner, T.S. & Garnier, H. (1992, Fall). Nonconventional family life-styles and school achievement: A 12-year longitudinal study. *American Educational Research Journal, 29* (3), p. 605 ff.

Williams, R.F. (1993, Spring). Gay and lesbian teenagers: A reading ladder for students, media specialists and parents. *The ALAN Review, 20* (3), p. 12 ff.

Wolf, V.L. (1989). The gay family in literature for young people. *Children's Literature in Education, 20* (1), p. 51 ff.

Books

Barrett, M.B. (1989). *Invisible lives.* New York: William Morrow. 349 pp. (ISBN: 0-688-07730-7)

Blumenfeld, W.J. (1992). (Ed.). *Homophobia: How we all pay the price.* Boston: Beacon Press. 308 pp. (ISBN: 0-807-07919-7)

Blumenfeld, W.J. & Raymond, D. (1989). *Looking at gay and lesbian life.* Boston: Beacon Press. 416 pp. (ISBN: 0-807-07907-3)

Eichberg, R. (1990). *Coming out: An act of love.* New York: E.P. Dutton. 281 pp. (ISBN: 0-525-24909-5)

Hanckel, F. & Cunningham, J. (1979). *A way of love, a way of life: A young person's introduction to what it means to be gay.* New York: Lothrop, Lee, & Shepard. 188 pp. (ISBN: 0-688-41907-0)

Harris, S. (1990). *Lesbian and gay issues in the English classroom: The importance of being honest.* Milton Keynes, PA: Open University Press. 146 pp. (ISBN: 0-335-15194-9)

Kramer, L. (1985). *The normal heart.* New York: New American Library. 123 pp. (ISBN: 0-453-00506-3)

Reid, John. (1986). *The best little boy in the world.* New York: Ballantine. 213 pp. (ISBN: 0-345-34361-1)

CHAPTER 4

Divorced and Single Parents

Many of America's youth are living apart from their complete biological families, and a new stepfamily faces many challenges. Stepfamily members have experienced many losses and have no shared family histories, ways of doing things, and beliefs. The days of Ward and June Cleaver--a working father, a housewife mother, and children who are all related--are practically over except for a small percentage of families still hanging on to the traditional family commonly found in the Fifties.

STARTLING INFORMATION ABOUT DIVORCED AND SINGLE PARENTS

• In 1987, almost 50% of all marriages ended in divorce. (Hofferth, 1987)

• More than one million children each year experience the divorce of their parents, up from about 300,000 a year in 1950. (Eitzen, 1992)

• Children often believe they have caused the conflict between their mother and father, and many assume the responsibility for bringing their parents back together again. (American Academy of Child & Adolescent Psychiatry, *Facts for Families*, 1992)

• In 1988, 4.3 million children were living with a mother who had never married--up 678% since 1970. (Hodgkinson, 1991)

• In 1990, one-fourth of all women having babies were not married and two-thirds of teenagers were not. (U.S. Census Bureau, 1991)

• At any given time, 25% of American children live with one parent, usually a divorced or never-married mother. (Edwards & Young, 1992)

- Almost 50% of America's youth will spend some years before they reach age 18 being raised by a single parent. (Hodgkinson, 1991)

- Most children living with one or two parents do not have any parents at home full time. (Population Reference Bureau, Center for the Study of Social Policy, 1990)

WHAT TO DO AND WHERE TO GO FOR HELP

- Divorce can be misinterpreted by children unless they are clearly told what is happening, how they are involved and not involved, and what will happen to them; avoid technical jargon and excess information.

- Get professional help: Call crisis intervention centers, mental health clinics, hospitals, a family physician, a clergy, a guidance counselor, or a teacher. For more information, write to the National Institute for the Family, 3019 Fourth Street, NE, Washington, D.C., 20017; Single Parent Resource Center, 1165 Broadway #504, New York City, New York, 10001; or Stepfamily Association of America (SAA), 602 East Joppa Road, Baltimore, Maryland, 21202.

Annotated Young Adult Novels Dealing with Divorced and Single Parents

4.01. Abercrombie, Barbara M. (1981). *Cat man's daughter*. New York: Harper & Row. 160 pp. (ISBN: 0-060-20030-8)

Katie's father is the Cat Man, a T.V. star who's looking for fun and perpetual youth. Her mother is a modern interior decorator, the executive woman with little time for the family. Katie's grandmother kidnaps her in an attempt to bring her newly-divorced parents to an understanding of their selfish neglect of Katie. While living with grandmother Riley, 13-year-old Katie learns about friendship, neighboring, and caring.

4.02. Ames, Mildred. (1978). *What are friends for?* New York: Charles Scribner's Sons. 145 pp. (ISBN: 0-684-15991-0)

Amy and Michelle develop a strong relationship based on their shared experiences involving their parents' divorces. Amy can really relate to Michelle, but things go awry when Amy has problems understanding Michelle's shoplifting behavior.

4.03.   Angell, Judie. (1981). *What's best for you: A novel*. Scarsdale, NY: Bradbury Press. 187 pp. (ISBN: 0-878-88181-6)

It's really awful that Lee's parents are filing for a divorce, but it's downright unfair that they're intending to split up the three children between them; Lee is the oldest at 15 years, Allison is 12, and Joel is seven.

4.04.   Auch, Mary Jane. (1988). *Mom is dating weird Wayne*. New York: Holiday House. 146 pp. (ISBN: 0-8234-0720-9)

Being a 7th grader is hard enough for Jenna without having to deal with a 1st grade brother and her parents' divorce. Now her mother is dating the television weatherman, Weird Wayne. Jenna has a hard time of it, especially since she feels obligated to stay loyal to her father. When her father acts as though he has forgotten her, Jenna begins to see that she must accept her new situation as best as she can.

4.05.   Bauer, Marion Dane. (1991). *Face to face*. New York: Clarion Books. 192 pp. (ISBN: 0-395-55440-3)

Michael has been unable to accept his stepfather even though it has been eight years since his real father deserted his family. The main problem is that Michael lives in the fantasy that his father would want him back if he were to meet him again "face to face." Michael gets a big dose of reality when he goes on a whitewater rafting trip with his biological father and learns that this man is too shallow and self-centered to want to bother with his teenage son.

4.06.   Betancourt, Jeanne. (1986). *Puppy love*. New York: Avon Books. 96 pp. (ISBN: 0-380-89958-2)

Aviva has adjusted to her parents' divorce and the living arrangements established by their joint custody. Now, at the start of her 8th grade year, they expect her to adjust to two new developments: Her remarried mother is pregnant, and her father is moving in with his girlfriend.

4.07.   Blume, Judy. (1979). *It's not the end of the world*. New York: Bantam Books. 167 pp. (ISBN: 0-553-13628-3)

Karen Newman is a 12-year-old girl whose been keeping a journal where she scores every one of her parents' fights and gives each day a letter grade. After her parents announce that they are getting a divorce, Karen becomes preoccupied with trying to get them back together again. Karen plots and schemes many situations that will bring them to the realization that they really do love each other. It's during a family crisis that she finally realizes that her parents are happier apart. After seeing her parents unable to comfort one another in an awful situation, Karen finally accepts the divorce and learns to adjust to her new life. After all, parents can still love their children even when they stop loving each other.

4.08.   Blume, Judy. (1987). *Just as long as we're together*. New York: Dell. 296 pp. (ISBN: 0-440-40075-9)

Stephanie is basically a happy-go-lucky 7th grader. She spends most of her time with her two best friends, Rachel and Alison. Rachel never has to study much to get good grades, and Alison is both Vietnamese and adopted. These two friends help Stephanie return to her happy nature when Stephanie learns the real reason why her father is in Los Angeles--a trial separation.

4.09.   Bonham, Frank. (1980). *Gimme an H, gimme an E, gimme an L, gimme a P*. New York: Charles Scribner's Sons. 210 pp. (ISBN: 0-684-16717-4)

Kate was abandoned by her mother when she was only nine years old. To make matters worse, her father marries a woman only nine years older than Kate who resents and mistreats her when her father is away. Unfortunately, he is becoming increasingly absent and it is no wonder that Kate is emotionally distraught while trying to cope with her situation.

4.10.   Bridgers, Sue Ellen. (1989). *Notes for another life*. New York: Bantam Books. 208 pp. (ISBN: 0-553-27185-7)

Two teenagers, Kevin and Wren, live with their grandparents because their parents are incapable of taking care of them properly. Their father is in a mental institution, and their mother lives in Atlanta and only bothers to visit a couple of times a year. Kevin suffers from depression and Wren is withdrawn. When Kevin's girlfriend breaks up with him, he "goes off the deep end" and overdoses on his grandparents' medication. Although he survives that ordeal, everything comes to a head when their father is released from the hospital. After learning that his wife has filed for divorce, he ends up having to be reinstitutionalized. Through all of this turmoil, Kevin and Wren find comfort in one another. (an American Library Association Best of the Best Books for Young Adults)

4.11.   Brooks, Bruce. (1984). *The moves make the man*. New York: Harper & Row. 280 pp. (ISBN: 0-060-20679-9)

Jeremy, the narrator of this story, is a bright, happy, well-adjusted, black boy who lives alone with his mother. Bix, on the other hand, is having a difficult time living alone with his stepfather while his mother is in a mental hospital. There is a sharp contrast between the happiness of Jeremy's home and the struggles present for Bix.

4.12.   Byars, Betsy. (1983). *The animal, the vegetable, and John D. Jones.* New York: Dell Yearling. 160 pp. (ISBN: 0-440-40356-1)

Clara and Deanie are really looking forward to spending some time with their father at his beach house. The girls are surprised to find that they will be sharing their father with his widowed friend and her son, John D. Jones.

4.13.   Cleary, Beverly. (1984). *Dear Mr. Henshaw.* New York: Dell. 133 pp. (ISBN: 0-440-41794-5)

Leigh Botts is an average 12-year-old boy living with his mother, a single working woman. Because of a class assignment, Leigh winds up forming a writing relationship with Mr. Henshaw, the author of his favorite book. Mr. Henshaw responds to Leigh's questions concerning his dad, his school, his dog, and his problems. With the help of Mr. Henshaw, Leigh gains confidence and a better understanding of himself, his dad, and his mom. Written as a series of flashbacks and memories in diary and journal entry form, this story accurately reflects the problems young adolescents face regarding parents and school. (a Newbery Honor Book)

4.14.   Cleary, Beverly. (1991). *Strider.* New York: William Morrow. 192 pp. (ISBN: 0-688-09900-9)

In this sequel to *Dear Mr. Henshaw,* Leigh Botts is now 14 years old and is still keeping his diary. In it, Leigh records his feelings and lessons learned through Strider, a stray dog he and a friend find on the beach. Leigh and Barry decide to have joint custody, but Leigh eventually wants sole ownership as he grows increasingly more fond of his pet. Strider not only helps him with his relationship with his father but also is somewhat instrumental in his joining the track team.

4.15.   Cole, Brock. (1989). *Celine.* New York: Farrar, Straus, & Giroux. 216 pp. (ISBN: 0-374-31234-6)

Sixteen-year-old Celine is more mature, in some ways, than her new stepmother. Her stepmother goes on a trip leaving Celine alone to take care of her younger stepbrother while her father is in Europe and her biological mother is in South America. Celine and Jacob bond together as "siblings" while Celine helps him come to terms with his parents' divorce and its effect on their lives.

4.16.   Colman, Hila. (1978). *Tell me no lies.* New York: Crown. 74 pp. (ISBN: 0-517-53229-8)

Angela is a 13-year-old who has never met her real father. Her mother has always told her that her father, Jose, left for a far away country several years ago; in actuality, he lives in a nearby town. Angela manages to persuade her mother to let her visit a friend who lives approximately three blocks from her father. By accident, Angela is introduced to her two stepbrothers. One of the boys invites her to go fishing with him and his father. While on the fishing trip, Jose realizes that he is Angela's father but explains to her that he has another family of his own. Angela returns home a different and more mature person.

4.17.   Colman, Hila. (1980). *What's the matter with the Dobsons?* New York: Crown Publishers. 122 pp. (ISBN: 0-517-53406-6)

Lisa and Amanda Dobson's parents are getting a divorce, and their parents have arranged for split custody of the sisters.

4.18.   Colman, Hila. (1984). *Just the two of us.* New York: Scholastic. 168 pp. (ISBN: 0-590-32512-4) (Out of Print)

Fourteen-year-old Samantha, or Sammy, has adjusted quite well with living with her father after her mother's death. She and her father, Lenny, travel all over the country because his job requires him to open new restaurants in various new locations. When Lenny decides to settle down and manage his own restaurant, Sammy is confronted with having to make real friends for the first time. To make matters worse, Lenny is talking about getting remarried, and Sammy doesn't know if she can deal with all of these new feelings that she's experiencing.

4.19.   Colman, Hila. (1985). *Weekend sisters.* New York: William Morrow. 170 pp. (ISBN: 0-688-05785-3)

Life for 15-year-old Amanda changes drastically after the divorce of her parents. Not only does she have to deal with her father and his new wife, but now her boyfriend has taken an interest in Fern, her new stepsister. Fern lies, steals, and is interfering with Amanda's relationship with her father. Although Amanda is convinced that life is sometimes unfair, she is determined to get through this mess.

4.20.   Conrad, Pam. (1987). *Holding me here.* New York: Bantam Starfire. 147 pp. (ISBN: 0-553-26525-3)

Robin's parents go through a friendly divorce when she is 14 years old. To earn some extra money, her mother rents Robin's old playroom to Mrs. Mary Walker, an abused wife who has just left her husband and children. Robin takes it upon herself to reunite Mary with her family, but her plan blows up in her face and she learns some painful realities.   Robin learns that sometimes divorce is necessary, and it is unfortunate that children often suffer in the process.

4.21.   Cooney, Caroline B. (1990). *Family reunion*. New York: Bantam Starfire. 176 pp. (ISBN: 0-553-285-73-4)

Shelley cannot believe that her perfect relatives, the Preffyns, have invited her and her Dad to a family reunion. It's not her fault that her father has remarried--again, and their attitudes make her crazy.   (a YASD Recommended Book for Reluctant Readers)

4.22.   Corcoran, Barbara. (1978). *Hey, that's my soul you're stomping on*. New York: Atheneum. 122 pp. (ISBN: 0-689-30617-2)

Rachel's parents send her to live with her grandparents in Palm Springs while they finalize the details of their divorce. Although Rachel's grandparents try to help her with her feelings, she finds more help from talking to newly-made friends who have faced similar problems. Rachel eventually learns to love the town and her grandparents.

4.23.   Corcoran, Barbara. (1985). *Face the music*. New York: Atheneum. 204 pp. (ISBN: 0-689-31139-7) (Out of Stock)

Marcie's mother has become very dependent upon her since the divorce. Marcie is confronted with trying to break away from her smothering mother without damaging their mother-daughter relationship, especially when Marcie's outside interest in music is presenting her with an awesome opportunity.

4.24.   Cottonwood, Joe. (1992). *Danny ain't*. New York: Scholastic. 288 pp. (ISBN: 0-590-45067-0)

Danny's mother died when he was very young. He was left in the care of his father, a man who's now being hospitalized for emotional problems and Vietnam flashbacks. Because of a prior negative experience with foster care, Danny decides to try it alone this time relying on the help of a few friends and a couple of coyotes. During his struggles, Danny learns who is as well as who he "ain't."

4.25.   Dana, Barbara. (1987). *Necessary parties*. New York: Bantam Books. 320 pp. (ISBN: 0-553-26984-4)

Christopher Mills feels his family is falling apart and he's right; his parents are getting a divorce. With the help of an attorney, his grandfather, and a copy of *The Rights of Young People*, Chris forces a situation that changes the course of all of their lives.

4.26.   Danziger, Paula. (1988). *The divorce express*. New York: Dell Laurel-Leaf. 148 pp. (ISBN: 0-440-92062-0)

Phoebe Brooks isn't sure that she can handle 9th grade in a new town as well as her parents have adjusted to living their separate lives. Phoebe's parents divorced in order to pursue their separate careers. Her mother lives in New York City and is an interior decorator. Her mother's job requires her to travel so Phoebe lives with her father in the Woodstock area. She rides the bus most weekends in order to visit her mother. While riding the "Divorce Express" she meets Rosie, a girl whose mother is white and Jewish and father is black and Christian. Like Phoebe, she too is a child of divorce but lives with her mother in Woodstock and visits her father in New York City. They share the problems and frustrations they mutually experience because of their parents' divorces. As Phoebe says, "you take the letters in the word 'divorce,' rearrange them, and they spell 'discover.'"

4.27.   Danziger, Paula. (1986). *It's an aardvark eat turtle world*. New York: Dell Laurel-Leaf. 144 pp. (ISBN: 0-440-94028-1)

Rosie and Phoebe, two characters from *The Divorce Express*, have been best friends for a long time. Rosie's divorced mom and Phoebe's divorced dad fall in love, and they decide to all try to live together. Phoebe, however, has a hard time adjusting and makes life difficult for the entire family. Rosie experiences her first love and also experiences her first bout with prejudice. (an IRA/CBC Children's Choice)

4.28.   Foley, June. (1989). *Falling in love is no snap*. New York: Dell Laurel-Leaf. 144 pp. (ISBN: 0-440-20349-X)

Alexandra and her divorced mother have had a "super kid" and "super mom" relationship until her mother laughs at her choice of boyfriends. At that point, Alexandra begins to see herself as an individual apart from her mother's image. (a YASD Recommended Book for Reluctant Readers)

4.29.   Forman, James. (1981). *The pumpkin shell*. 156 pp.

See Death and Dying

4.30.   Forshay-Lunsford, Cin. (1986). *Walk through cold fire*. 205 pp.

See Dropouts and Delinquency

4.31.   Fosburgh, Liza. (1990). *The wrong way home*. 192 pp.

See Death and Dying

4.32.   Fox, Paula. (1980). *A place apart*. 183 pp.

See Death and Dying

4.33.   Fox, Paula. (1988). *The moonlight man*. New York: Dell Laurel-Leaf 179 pp. (ISBN: 0-440-20079-2)

This novel is about a 15-year-old girl who's still dealing with her emotions about her parents' divorce when she was three years old. Her father has always been elusive, tenuous, and undependable, yet he has a charismatic personality that keeps her involved with him. (an American Library Association Notable Children's Book)

4.34.   Gerber, Merrill Joan. (1982). *Please don't kiss me now*. New York: New American Library. 176 pp. (ISBN: 0-451-11575-9) (Out of Print)

At 15, Leslie is trying hard to deal with her mother's new lifestyle and odd behavior since the divorce. Unfortunately, Leslie and her mother are fighting regularly, and she's having difficulty adjusting to her father's new family. Brian, a new boyfriend, offers Leslie some comfort but is not really interested in her real, everyday problems. Leslie learns to value her mother and "family" when a tragedy happens to a friend and her family.

4.35.   Gerson, Corinne. (1981). *How I put my mother through college*. New York: Atheneum. 136 pp. (ISBN: 0-689-30810-8)

Thirteen-year-old Jessica has had to make a lot of adjustments since her parents' divorce. Now her mother wants to return to college. Jessica feels more like the parent than the child, especially when her mother keeps asking for her advice about clothes, dates, and college life.

4.36.   Gibbons, Faye. (1985). *Mighty close to heaven*. 183 pp.

See Death and Dying

4.37.   Gilmore, H.B. (1985). *Ask me if I care*. 180 pp.

See Alcohol and Drugs

4.38.   Goldman, Katie. (1982). *In the wings.* New York: Dial Press . 166 pp. (ISBN: 0-803-73968-0)

Jessie's parents are separated and a divorce seems imminent. Even having a big part in the school play isn't easing the pain this 15-year-old is experiencing. Her grades are dropping and she's having difficulty relating to Andrea, her best friend. Jessie's in a downward, negative spiral which will not change until she is able to accept the divorce situation for what it is.

4.39.   Gregory, Diana. (1981). *The fog burns off by 11 o'clock.* New York: Harper Collins. 155 pp. (ISBN: 0-201-04139-1) (Out of Print)

Dede Applegate, a 13-year-old, adjusts to her parents' divorce after spending her summer vacation with her father and his new girlfriend.

4.40.   Guest, Elissa Haden. (1987). *Over the moon.* 208 pp.

See Death and Dying

4.41.   Harris, Mark J. (1989). *Come the morning.* 176 pp.

See Poverty

4.42.   Hinton, S.E. (1979). *Tex.* 194 pp.

See Poverty

4.43.   Holland, Isabelle. (1987). *The man without a face.* New York: Harper. 157 pp. (ISBN: 0-694-05611-1)

Charles Norstadt is a 14-year-old boy who lives without a father. His older sister, Gloria, is always mean to him, so he much prefers his little sister, Meg. While he and his family are vacationing in an affluent area near the sea, Charles finds out that Gloria is not going away to boarding school as was planned. Dreading the thought of another year of her abuse, he decides to reapply to take St. Mathew's Boarding School's entrance exam so that he can go away. Since he already failed the entrance exam once, he asks Justin McLeod, the community recluse whose face had been severely burned, to tutor him so he can pass the entrance exam on his second try. What follows is the most rigorous studying Charles has ever known. Gradually, Charles learns to appreciate hard work. More importantly, he learns about friendship and love as he and McLeod slowly tear down the emotional walls each had built around himself. With his mother about to marry her fifth husband, Charles looks for affection and reassurance from McLeod. In the end, Charles becomes confused about the nature of his love for his scarred and sensitive tutor. (an American Library Association Best of the Best Books for Young Adults)

4.44.   Howe, Norma. (1986). *God, the universe, and hot fudge sundaes.* 160 pp.

See Death and Dying

4.45.   Hunt, Irene. (1987). *Up a road slowly.* 100 pp.

See Death and Dying

4.46.   Hunter, Evan. (1978). *Me and Mr. Stenner.* New York: Dell Laurel-Leaf. 128 pp. (ISBN: 0-440-95551-3)

Not only must Abby adjust to her parents' divorce, she must also adjust to her mother's remarriage with Mr. Stenner. Although Mr. Stenner tries especially hard to be nice to her, Abby cannot show any feelings for him or that would betray her real father. Abby eventually learns that it is possible to love a stepparent without dismissing one's love for the natural parent.

4.47.   Hurwitz, Johanna. (1984). *DeDe takes charge!* New York: William Morrow. 121 pp. (ISBN: 0-688-03853-0)

While Dede is in the 5th grade, she has to adjust to the reality of her parents' divorce. Soon she's not only dealing with her own feelings but is finding it necessary to help her mother cope with life without Dad.

4.48.   Irwin, Hadley. (1988). *Bring to a boil and separate.* New York: Signet Books. 159 pp. (ISBN: 0-451-14825-8) (Out of Print)

Separation best characterizes Katie's 13th year. Not only does she spend her summer at camp in a different session than her best friend, but when she returns home, she finds that her parents have separated their veterinary practice and are living apart. Katie feels as though her parents are divorcing her even though they try to reassure her of their love. Without her best friend, Katie must rely on inner strength to help her deal with the breakup.

4.49.   Irwin, Hadley. (1992). *The original Freddie Ackerman.* New York: Margaret K. McElderry. 183 pp. (ISBN: 0-698-50562-0)

Trevor "Freddie" Ackerman has quite an extended family. Besides his biological parents, he has an assortment of stepparents and siblings who he comically calls "its" and "thems." It's not until his mother remarries and she ships him off to stay with a couple of aunts during her long honeymoon, that

Freddie learns about the meaning of family. Initially, Freddie's aunts believe he can take care of himself. When he befriends Ariel and the two get into mischief, his aunts are there to help him sort things out.

4.50.   Kerr, M.E. (1988). *Love is a missing person*. New York: Harper & Row. 164 pp. (ISBN: 0-694-05634-0)

   Suzy and Chicago are sisters who are separated after their parents' divorce; Suzy lives with her mother, and her sister lives with her father. Suzy attempts to deal with many problems that occur after the divorce: Chicago starts dating a black boy and is beaten up by a gang of black girls, her father starts dating a girl younger than Chicago, and the librarian where Suzy works is having a pretty obvious love affair. Suzy tries to figure where she fits in all of their lives.

4.51.   Klass, Sheila Solomon. (1981). *To see my mother dance*. New York: Charles Scribner's Sons. 154 pp. (ISBN: 0-684-17227-5)

   On Jessica's 1st birthday, her mother deserted her and her father. Throughout her childhood, Jessica has fantasized that her beautiful mother, Karen, will one day return to be her loving mother once again. Jessica's grandmother has been filling the void left by Karen, but her grandmother has maintained a low opinion of her ex-daughter-in-law since the desertion. Jessica's fantasy is challenged when her dad announces that his lawyer friend, Martha, is going to be his new wife. Jessica's search for her mother is filled with deep insights into a teenager's life without mother and the adjustments that need to be made when a stepmother is introduced to the family. Jessica and Martha eventually become friends after Martha helps to locate Karen, and Jessica sees for herself that her biological mother has no love or concern for her at all.

4.52.   Klass, Sheila Solomon. (1988). *Page four*. New York: Bantam Books. 176 pp. (ISBN: 0-553-26901-1)

   When David takes an assessment of his life during his senior year of high school, he decides that he pretty much has it all: a happy family, good friends, decent grades, and a position on the varsity basketball team. Suddenly, David's perfect world nearly falls apart when his father announces his plans to leave the family and move to Alaska with a younger woman. David nearly destroys his own life out of spite and bitterness. David, seeing his mother's grief, begins to help her. As she begins to heal, David does too.

4.53.   Klaveness, Jan O'Donnell. (1990). *Ghost island*. New York: Dell Laurel-Leaf. 224 pp. (ISBN: 0-440-93097-9)

In three years, Delia Pearce's life has changed considerably. Not only has her father died, but she has to adjust to her mother's new marriage. Delia decides that the only place that can bring her happiness is the Canadian lake and the island her father willed to her. She decides to go there in hopes that she can feel how she used to feel. When she gets there, however, nothing is the same. Poachers are endangering the wildlife and shattering any peace Delia had hoped to find.

4.54.   Klein, Norma. (1976). *Mom, the Wolf Man and me*. New York: Avon Books. 160 pp. (ISBN: 0-380-00791-6)

Brett, an 11-year-old girl, is very happy and secure with being raised by her single mother. Although her unconventional mother was never married to her father, the two of them get along rather well. Brett never knew her father but is not particularly upset by that fact. Actually, Brett would prefer that her mother stay unmarried. In contrast, Brett's best friend is obsessed with finding a new father for herself and a husband for her mother. As fate would have it, the Wolf Man meets and falls in love with Brett's mother, they decide to marry, and Brett has to learn to accept him.

4.55.   Klein, Norma. (1976). *Taking sides*. New York: Avon Books. 144 pp. (ISBN: 0-380-00528-X)

After the divorce of Nell's parents, she finds she must learn to adjust to different living arrangements. Nell and her little brother are confused because they are going to live with their father and not their mother like most of their divorced friends. While living with her father, Nell now must share a room with her younger brother. Living with her father, however, is not the problem: It's the guilt she experiences because she finds she likes him better than she does her mother. Maturity helps her to cope with her feelings better, especially when it is revealed that their father is ill.

4.56.   Klein, Norma. (1981). *Robbie and the leap year blues*. New York: Dial Press. 154 pp. (ISBN: 0-803-77437-0)

Robbie, an only child, feels like he is in the middle of his parents' upcoming divorce. His parents are dating other people, and he cannot figure out why they cannot work out their problems. His thoughts lead him to question why people get married in the first place at a time when girls, who mature faster than boys, are outperforming him in just about everything.

4.57.   Klein, Norma. (1985). *Family secrets*. New York: Dial Press. 262 pp. (ISBN: 0-803-70221-3)

Peter and Leslie are enjoying their boyfriend and girlfriend relationship until things get complicated. As it turns out, Peter's father and Leslie's mother have been having an affair with each other. When their respective parents decide to marry, this makes Peter and Leslie stepbrother and stepsister. Everyone concerned has to work out what this new marriage means.

4.58.   Klein, Norma. (1987). *Angel face*. New York: Fawcett Juniper. 245 pp. (ISBN: 0-449-70282-0)

At 15, Jason Lieberman, the youngest of four children, finds himself shouldering most of the brunt of their parents' recent divorce. Jason finds himself having to console his unhappy mother regarding his father's leaving her for another woman. His mother's emotional demands increase when Jason's father remarries. Suddenly, Jason finds he is having his own relationship problems with Vicki, his girlfriend. No longer his mother's "Angel Face," Jason tries to alleviate his mother's suspicions while maintaining his first sexual romance.

4.59.   Klein, Norma. (1987). *Bizou*. New York: Fawcett Juniper. 144 pp. (ISBN: 0-449-70252-9)

Bizou's father, a famous French photographer, died when she was very young. For 13 years, she has lived in Paris with her mother, a free-spirited black fashion model. After inquiring about family in the United States, her mother reluctantly takes Bizou to the U.S. for a visit. Bizou's mother is under obvious strain and leaves her with a friend for a couple of weeks. The friend helps Bizou find her family and reunites her with her mother.

4.60.   Klein, Norma. (1987). *Breaking up*. New York: Avon Books. 174 pp. (ISBN: 0-380-55830-0)

Fifteen-year-old Alison Rose's parents are divorced and are fighting over who should raise her. Ali's father would have her believe that the divorce was all of her mother's fault. After all, Ali's father contends that her mother is being more than a friend to another woman. Both parents want custody, and Ali is emotionally torn between her parents as she tries to decide on her own what to do.

4.61.   Klein, Norma. (1987). *It's okay if you don't love me*. New York: Fawcett Juniper. 256 pp. (ISBN: 0-449-70236-7)

Jody's values come into question when she starts dating Lyle, a guy whose morals are in direct conflict with hers. Jody, a New Yorker, has grown accustomed to her mother's divorces and live-in boyfriends. Lyle, on the other hand, is a Midwesterner with more conventional values of love and fidelity.

4.62.   Knudsen, James. (1987). *Playing favorites*. New York: Avon
         Books. 121 pp. (ISBN: 0-380-89736-9)

Evan, a high school sophomore, has to learn to deal with his father's
"here today, gone tomorrow" lifestyle. Not only does Evan have to deal with
his father, but he also must deal with his first true romance, Teddy. The story
covers numerous problems that Evan and Teddy encounter in their unlikely
relationship.

4.63.   Koertge, Ron. (1990). *Where the kissing never stops*. New York:
         Dell Laurel-Leaf. 224 pp. (ISBN: 0-440-20167-5)

Not only does Walker find himself dealing with his father's death, but
now he has to confront his mother's new job as a stripper.   Walker tries
desperately to keep his mother's job a secret, but a new romance for him
complicates his life even further. (an American Library Association Best Book
for Young Adults)

4.64.   Latiolais, Michelle. (1990). *Even now*. New York: Farrar, Straus, &
         Giroux. 211 pp. (ISBN: 0-374-14993-3)

Lisa's parents have been divorced for six years, but the problems still
remain for this 16-year-old. Lisa's mother is seeing an old boyfriend, and her
father has a new girlfriend. Lisa feels guilty and tense regardless of which
parent she is with, and Lisa is at a point where she has to do some soul-
searching to find peace within herself.

4.65.   Levy, Marilyn. (1986). *Summer snow*. New York: Fawcett Juniper.
         171 pp. (ISBN: 0-449-70188-3)

Sixteen-year-old Leslie Bishop is devastated by her parents' divorce
and blames her father for it. She decides to never see him again but relents
when her mother convinces her to spend the summer with him at his new home
in California. She is surprised by the carefree, liberal lifestyle of her "new"
father and his girlfriend and compounds her problems by getting involved with
drugs in order to be accepted by some new "friends."

4.66.   Luger, Harriett. (1983). *The un-dudding of Roger Judd*. New York:
         Viking Press. 137 pp. (ISBN: 0-670-73886-7)

Sixteen-year-old Roger Judd does not like his current living situation.
After his parents' divorce, he goes to live with his father, his new wife, and a
new half sister who he can't stand; problems abound. Roger finds that he's
having trouble at school, is having a difficult time relating to girls, and misses
his mother. After an unpleasant scene, it is mutually decided that he should go

and live with his mother for awhile, even though she is a recovering alcoholic. Roger resents the rules she imposes, until he learns that acceptance of reasonable rules and responsibility is part of growing up.

4.67.   MacLachlan, Patricia. (1985). *Sarah, plain and tall*. New York: Harper & Row. 58 pp. (ISBN: 0-06-024101-2)

Anna and her younger brother, Caleb, live on a frontier farm with their father, Jacob. Their mother had died the day after Caleb's birth, and the children all miss having a mother. One day their father announces that he is sending for a mail-order bride from Maine. The family corresponds with Sarah and eagerly wait for her arrival, for the children long for a mother. When Sarah arrives, the family introduces her to frontier life on the farm while she reminisces about her brother, her aunts, and life by the sea. As summer draws near and the time for the preacher to come approaches, the family anxiously awaits Sarah's decision: Will she stay or return to her life by the sea? (a Newbery Medal winner)

4.68.   Maloney, Ray. (1987). *The impact zone*. New York: Dell Laurel-Leaf. 256 pp. (ISBN: 0-440-94013-3)

Jim Nichols is struggling with his life with his mother and stepfather in California. He convinces himself that he can get his life in order by running away to his real father in Hawaii. Unfortunately, when he gets there his surfing father gives him some disturbing news. (the Third Annual Delacorte Press Prize for Outstanding First Young Adult Novel)

4.69.   Marsden, John. (1989). *So much to tell you. . .* 117 pp.

See Youth with Disabilities

4.70.   Martin, Ann M. (1986). *With you and without you*. 179 pp.

See Death and Dying

4.71.   Mazer, Harry. (1990). *Guy Lenny*. New York: Dell Laurel-Leaf. 144 pp. (ISBN: 0-440-93311-0)

Guy's life is very complicated for a 12-year-old. He's been living with his father after his parents' divorce, but now his father thinks he needs a new mother. Meanwhile, Guy's real mother comes back and wants him to live with her and her new husband. Is running away a solution?

4.72.   Mazer, Harry. (1991). *Someone's mother is missing.* 166 pp.

See Death and Dying

4.73.   Mazer, Norma Fox. (1983). *Taking Terri Mueller.* New York: William Morrow. 212 pp. (ISBN: 0-688-01732-0)

Thirteen-year-old Terri always thought her mother was dead. After she learns that her father kidnapped her after their divorce, Terri's search for her missing mother begins. (Edgar Award Prize)

4.74.   Mazer, Norma Fox. (1986). *A, my name is Ami.* New York: Scholastic. 153 pp. (ISBN: 0-590-40054-1)

Growing up is painful enough, but things are worse for Ami whose parents aren't living together anymore. Ami's grateful for her best friend, Mia, who is always there to listen as Ami tries to cope with her changing feelings about her parents. Mia is also there when Ami talks to her about her brother, her mother's desertion, her father's "new friend," and the boys at school.

4.75.   McDaniel, Lurlene. (1984). *Sometimes love just isn't enough.* Worthington, OH: Willowisp Press. 143 pp. (ISBN: 0-87406-049-4)

Andrea Manetti, a 13-year-old, blames herself and her little brother, Timmy, for their parents' divorce. Andrea thinks, "If only I had been a better daughter, then my parents would still be together." As for Timmy, Andrea always felt that his being mentally retarded deeply affected her father because he is the only son. Andrea eventually comes to terms with her own feelings about divorce. She is fortunate to have two parents who still love her in spite of their troubles.

4.76.   McDonnell, Christine. (1988). *Count me in: A novel.* New York: Viking Kestrel. 173 pp. (ISBN: 0-140-31856-9)

At 13, Katie is finding it difficult adjusting to her new family situation after her parents' divorce. After her mother remarries, she has to learn how to get along with her new stepfather and then the news that her mother is pregnant.

4.77.   Miller, M.J. (1992). *Me and my name.* New York: Puffin Books. 128 pp. (ISBN: 0-140-34374-1)

Erin lives with her mother and step-father. Everything is just fine until Erin's mother is expecting twins, and her step-father wants to adopt her and change her last name. Her natural father says she may choose what she wants, but the decision isn't easy.

4.78.   Miner, Jane Claypool. (1982). *Split decision: Facing divorce.* Mankato, MN: Crestwood House. 63 pp. (ISBN: 0-896-86170-8)

From the Crisis Series, Ann is determined to alter her parents' decision to get a divorce.

4.79.   Morgenroth, Barbara. (1981). *Will the real Renie Lake please stand up.* New York: Atheneum. 164 pp. (ISBN: 0-689-30820-5)

After her parents' divorce and the emotional turmoil associated with it, Renie develops identity problems of her own as she tries to figure out her new role in a broken family. After a period of delinquency while living in the Bronx, she finally goes to live with her father and his new family.

4.80.   Myers, Walter Dean. (1990). *Hoops.* 192 pp.

See Poverty

4.81.   Myers, Walter Dean. (1992). *Somewhere in the darkness.* New York: Scholastic. 168 pp. (ISBN: 0-590-42411-4)

Jimmy Little's mother died when he was just a baby so home has always been with Mama Jean. His father, a man called Crab, was imprisoned years ago for killing two security guards during a robbery. Now when Jimmy is 15 years of age, Crab shows up unexpectedly and wants to take Jimmy with him on a cross-country trek. Mama Jean who's been both mother and father to Jimmy is hurt when Jimmy decides that he must get to know this stranger who is his biological father. Unbeknownst to Jimmy, Crab has a limited amount of time to convince Jimmy of his innocence.

4.82.   Naylor, Phyllis Reynolds. (1983). *The Solomon system.* New York: Atheneum. 210 pp. (ISBN: 0-689-30991-0) (Out of Stock)

Fourteen-year-old Ted has always been close to his older brother, Nory. They go to summer camp as usual, but it feels different to Ted this year for some reason. Ted figures that it must be because their parents are separating, and he finds himself reevaluating his relationship with his brother and their expectations of one another.

4.83.   Nelson, Theresa. (1986). *The 25 cent miracle.* New York: Bradbury Press. 214 pp. (ISBN: 0-02-724370-2)

At 11 years of age, Ellie seems to have more than her fair share of problems. Her mother is dead, and her father is unemployed most of the time. There is talk about the possibility of her being shipped off to go to live with her Aunt Darla, a fat woman who Ellie doesn't particularly care for. To prevent that from happening, Darla decides to play matchmaker and find her father a new wife. Unfortunately, her matchmaking efforts often cause a chain reaction of unexpected and undesirable events.

4.84.   Neufeld, John. (1977). *Sunday father.* New York: New American Library. 160 pp. (ISBN: 0-451-07292-8) (Out of Print)

Allie is 11 and Tessa is 15 years old. The only thing these two have in common, besides being brother and sister, is that their parents have recently divorced. Allie adjusts quickly to the idea of seeing his father only on weekends and accepts his father's new-wife-to-be with ease. Tessa, on the other hand, becomes determined to prevent their wedding. For Tessa, her whole world is falling apart, and she finds life to be quite painful. This story is told from two points of view. First the reader "sees" a situation through an objective third person, and then it is followed by Tessa's point of view of the same scene. The reader will find Tessa's interpretation and reasoning behind her behavior interesting.

4.85.   Nixon, Joan Lowery. (1986). *And Maggie makes three.* New York: Harcourt, Brace, & Jovanovich. 112 pp. (ISBN: 0-15-250355-2)

Maggie is pretty upset with her father when he doesn't show up to see her perform. Now, for no reason, he is coming to visit and expects her to be nice to his new wife. Maggie definitely does not want to meet her.

4.86.   Okimoto, Jean Davies. (1979). *My mother is not married to my father.* New York: Putnam. 109 pp. (ISBN: 0-399-20664-7) (Out of Stock)

Cynthia and Sara's parents get a divorce, and the readjustment period for them is difficult. Their father moves into an apartment and dates the what's-her-name receptionist. When the girls visit him, they feel uncomfortable and awkward and don't know what's expected of them. Meanwhile, their mother is frequently calling Uncle Melvin, a psychiatrist, who helps them talk out their feelings. Cynthia, a 6th grader, tells the story from her point of view.

4.87.   Okimoto, Jean Davies. (1980). *It's just too much.* New York: Putnam. 126 pp. (ISBN: 0-399-20737-6)

Cynthia thinks that adjusting to junior high school is difficult but not as difficult as adjusting to her new stepfather and two stepbrothers.

4.88.   O'Neal, Zibby. (1982). *A formal feeling.* New York: Viking Press. 162 pp. (ISBN: 0-670-32488-4)

See Death and Dying

4.89.   Orgel, Doris. (1985). *Risking love.* New York: Dial Press. 185 pp. (ISBN: 0-8037-0131-4)

Dinah Moskowitz, now 20, is still troubled over the fact that her mother did not insist that she live with her after the divorce six years ago; instead, Dinah was allowed to choose which parent to live with. At the time, she chose to live with her father and had to learn to adjust to a stepmother. Now she is dating Gray, a young man who wants her to move with him after his graduation. For Dinah, that means that she will have to give up her college education--at least for the time being. For a girl whose parents are divorced, the decision to forego her education for the love of a guy is too much for her to handle alone. Dinah seeks the help of a psychiatrist who gets her to come to terms with her feelings and make sound decisions. The story is about these sessions.

4.90.   Osborne, Mary Pope. (1984). *Love always, Blue.* New York: E.P. Dutton. 183 pp. (ISBN: 0-8037-0031-8)

For the life of her, Blue cannot understand why her parents have separated and blames her mother for the breakup. Finally, after much heartache and pleading, her mother allows her to go and visit her father in his new place in Greenwich Village. Blue is not only upset by the dinginess of his apartment but is saddened to discover that her father suffers from an illness that even her love can't penetrate.

4.91.   Osborne, Mary Pope. (1986). *Last one home.* New York: Dial Books. 148 pp. (ISBN: 0-803-70219-1)

Bailey is a 12-year-old girl whose parents are divorced. Because her brother is leaving for the army and her father's remarriage is imminent, Bailey attempts to prevent the changes. She refuses to accept Janet, her future stepmother, and attempts a reunion with her natural mother. Bailey decides to run away to her mom's but is found just in time by Janet. Without explanation, Bailey decides that Janet is probably okay after all.

4.92.   Park, Barbara. (1983). *Don't make me smile.* New York: Avon Books. 132 pp. (ISBN: 0-380-61994-6)

Charlie Hickle gets into some self-destructive behavior after his parents' divorce: He intentionally makes poor grades in school and then runs away. Things get better after he finds a confidant in Dr. Girard.

4.93.   Paulsen, Gary. (1987). *Hatchet*. New York: Bradbury Press. 195 pp. (ISBN: 0-02-770130-1).

Due to Brian Robeson's parents' recent divorce, he will spend his summers with his father in the Canadian Wilderness. Brian knows why his mother left his father, and he constantly thinks about "the secret." Tragedy besets this teenager as he leaves for his first summer in a single engine plane. Due to an unforeseen heart attack and death of the pilot, Brian manages to crash land the plane in the middle of nowhere. Although not badly hurt, Brian must learn how to survive using only his wits and a hatchet his mother gave him as a going away gift. Not only does Brian survive this ordeal for many months, but he also learns how to come to terms with his parents' broken relationship. (Literary Merit)

4.94.   Peck, Richard. (1991). *Unfinished portrait of Jessica*. New York: Delacorte Press. 162 pp. (ISBN: 00-385-30500-1)

The novel centers around Jessica Ferris, a teenager who is processing her parents' divorce. Jessica blames her mother for the divorce and shuts her out of her life. Even though she's living with her mother, Jessica puts all of her energy into what becomes adoration of her father. Jessica's great uncle, Lucius Pirie, is the artist who painted a portrait of Jessica's grandmother, her namesake. Like the portrait, Jessica is "unfinished" but is doing the reflective work necessary to become "whole." When Jessica is sent to Mexico to stay with her father for Christmas vacation, she has a rude awakening and returns home with a new attitude about her relationship with her mother.

4.95.   Peck, Richard. (1988). *Father figure*. New York: Dell. 182 pp. (ISBN: 0-440-20069-5)

When Jim Atwater was nine and his brother was just a baby, their father deserted them. Jim, Bryon, and their mother went to live with their stern, unmoving grandmother. Jim is a junior in high school and Bryon is eight when their mother commits suicide to escape the ravages of cancer, and grandma sends the boys to Florida to live with a father they don't know. Jim has been the father figure for his little brother since their parents' divorce eight years ago, and he resents Bryon's immediate attachment to their father. Jim must cope with his own grief for his mother, his worries about Bryon, and his resentment for his father. The story is told from Jim's point of view and reflects the growing up he does over the summer with "Dad." (an American Library Association Best Book for Young Adults)

4.96.   Pfeffer, Susan Beth. (1985). *Marly the kid.* New York: Dell Laurel-Leaf. 112 pp. (ISBN: 0-440-95424-X)

Fifteen-year-old Marly runs away to live with her father and second wife after she finds she just cannot get along with her mother. Life with dad takes her on a journey of self discovery.

4.97.   Pfeffer, Susan Beth. (1985). *Starting with Melodie.* New York: Scholastic. 128 pp. (ISBN: 0-590-41213-2) (Out of Print)

Elaine is jealous of her best friend, Melodie, because Melodie's life is so exciting in comparison to hers. Melodie's mother is an actress, her father makes movies, and she lives in a cool house with servants and all. As with anything, things are not as they seem. Elaine sees another side to all of this when Melodie's parents get a separation, and Melodie is the pawn in a custody battle.

4.98.   Platt, Kin. (1975). *Chloris and the freaks.* New York: Bradbury. 217 pp. (ISBN: 0-878-88089-5)

Chloris and Jennifer are two sisters who suddenly find themselves having to deal with the difficult aspects of marriage and divorce. Twelve-year-old Jennifer feels powerless and frustrated, and she views adults as childish and unpredictable. When her attempts to keep Fidel and her mother together fail, Jennifer becomes angry, depressed, and helpless. Chloris cannot adjust to her new stepfather and tries to convince her sister, Jennifer, to resist him too. Finally, their stepfather speaks up and expresses an adult view of marriage and divorce.

4.99.   Platt, Kin. (1978). *Chloris and the weirdos.* New York: Bradbury. 231 pp. (ISBN: 0-878-88137-9)

Chloris and Jenny are now old enough to date. Their mother, two divorces later, is now dumping her dating problems onto them. Jenny chronicles her life with her messed up mother, mixed up sister, and a new boyfriend who is a top skateboarder.

4.100.   Platt, Kin. (1990). *The boy who could make himself disappear.* 256 pp.

See Youth with Disabilities

4.101.   Rinaldi, Ann. (1985). *But in the fall I'm leaving.* New York: Holiday House. 250 pp. (ISBN: 08234-0560-5)

Although Brieanna McQuade's mother deserted the family when Brie was two years old, she chooses to idolize her mother because of her father's high expectations of her. When her mother rejects her again now that Brie is a teenager, Brie acts out and is destructive. Through a series of events, Brie gets a job working for Miss Emily who discloses some painful, family secrets.

4.102. Roos, Stephen. (1989). *You'll miss me when I'm gone.* 208 pp.

See Alcohol and Drugs

4.103. Roth, David. (1984). *A world for Joey Carr.* New York: Ballantine/Fawcett Juniper. 149 pp. (ISBN: 0-449-70048-8)

Joey's mother has been dead for two years, a victim of a street mugging. Since that time, Joey's father has withdrawn into a world of booze and women, leaving Joey without support. At 14, Joey decides to hitchhike to Vermont to find his grandparents. He is given a ride by Hannah who is on a quest of a different kind. Joey's quest is successful in that he gets his father's attention, establishes contact with his grandparents, and learns to accept the fact that love brings pain. The reader is left to decide if Hannah's quest is successful.

4.104. Rylant, Cynthia. (1990). *A kindness.* 128 pp.

Sec Teenage Pregnancy

4.105. Salat, Cristina. (1993). *Living in secret.* 192 pp.

See Homosexuality

4.106. Schwartz, Sheila. (1978). *Like mother, like me.* New York: Pantheon. 166 pp. (ISBN: 0-394-83755-X)

After Jen's father leaves the family, she not only has her own feelings to deal with but also must help her mother adjust to life without Dad.

4.107. Sebestyen, Ouida. (1982). *IOU's.* Boston: Little, Brown, & Company. 188 pp. (ISBN: 0-316-77933-4)

Thirteen-year-old Stowe Garrett lives with his divorced mother but is feeling torn between his loyalty to her and his desire to seek the love of his other relatives.

4.108. Sharmat, Marjorie. (1989). *He noticed I'm alive . . . and other hopeful signs*. New York: Dell Laurel-Leaf. 160 pp. (ISBN: 0-440-93809-0)

Two years ago, Jody's mother left a note saying she had to go and "find herself," leaving Jody and her father to fend for themselves. Now, at 15 years of age, Jody has met a boy who she thinks she is crazy about. She really wishes her mother were there to help her sort out her feelings for Matt, but there is a big problem--her father is dating Matt's mother.

4.109. Sharmat, Marjorie. (1989). *Two guys noticed me . . . and other miracles*. New York: Dell Laurel-Leaf. 160 pp. (ISBN: 0-440-98846-2)

In this sequel to *He Noticed I'm Alive . . . and Other Hopeful Signs*, Jody's father has asked Matt's mother to marry him. Things get more complicated when Jody's mother, a woman who left for two years to find herself, returns and wants them to resume their family. If that's not enough, Jody has met a new boy but she still likes Matt. Jody is all confused and for all good reason.

4.110. Stolz, Mary. (1979). *Go and catch a flying fish*. New York: Harper & Row. 213 pp. (ISBN: 0-060-25867-5)

Life for Taylor, Jem, and B.J. Reddick is great until they have to face the reality of their parents' impending divorce. Living on the idyllic Gulf Coast of Florida provides a sharp contrast to the emotional ugliness they all experience.

4.111. Talbert, Marc. (1991). *Pillow of clouds*. New York: Dial Books. 204 pp. (ISBN: 0-8037-0901-3)

After Chester's parents' divorce, he's faced with a tough decision: Which parent will he choose to live with? His mother is an alcoholic businesswoman in Iowa, and his father is a boring bookstore owner in New Mexico. After he makes his decision, he's left with the uncomfortable task of informing his mother that he's decided to live with his father.

4.112. Terris, Susan. (1981). *No scarlet ribbons*. New York: Farrar, Straus & Giroux. 154 pp. (ISBN: 0-374-35532-0)

Rachel is initially happy about her mother's new marriage and the good times a new stepfather and stepsiblings would bring. She eventually becomes upset with the situation when her mother actually spends time with these other children. Rachel decides to take her resentment out on her mother's new marriage. Through various schemes, she tries to sabotage their relationship and almost succeeds.

4.113. Voigt, Cynthia. (1983). *A solitary blue*. New York: Atheneum. 189 pp. (ISBN: 0-689-31008-0)

Jeff Greene was abandoned by his mother and was left in the care of his remote, perfectionist father when he was seven. His mother left him because she felt she had more important work to do like raising funds to feed homeless and motherless children or preserving endangered species. While living with his father, Jeff is always careful to keep things just the way his father likes them; he often wonders who is taking care of whom. When Jeff visits his mother for a summer four years later, two things happen: He discovers that this woman who he has adored for years doesn't love him, and she widens the gap that already exists between him and his father. Until Brother Thomas, a wise monk who befriends Jeff's father, and Dicey, a young girl, enter his life, Jeff "walks through life" much the way a robot might. With the help of these two people, Jeff is able to find happiness, friendship, and, most important of all, the love and acceptance of his father. (an American Library Association Best of the Best Books for Young Adults, an ALA Notable Children's Book, a Newbery Honor Book, a Boston Globe/Horn Book Honor Book, a Notable Children's Trade Book in the Field of Social Studies, and a Children's Book of the Year)

4.114. Voigt, Cynthia. (1983). *Homecoming*. New York: Ballantine Books. 318 pp. (ISBN: 0-449-70254-5)

Dicey Tillerman's story begins in a parking lot of a large shopping mall. Her mother has brought the fatherless family from Providencetown, Massachusetts, to a mall north of Phillip's Beach, Connecticut, in an effort to bring them to their Aunt Cilla in Bridgeport. During the trip, Dicey's mother loses her will to live and deserts them at the mall. Dicey, who is the oldest, takes charge and finishes the trip to Bridgeport with her two younger brothers and sister. Unfortunately, Aunt Cilla does not prove to be a desirable parent so Dicey resumes the trek to Crisfield, Maryland, where their grandmother lives. They are not openly received and find they must prove their worth to their grandmother in order to stay. (an American Library Association Best of the Best Books for Young Adults)

4.115. Voigt, Cynthia. (1984). *Dicey's song*. New York: Ballantine Books. 211 pp. (ISBN: 0-449-70071-2)

Dicey's Song is the sequel to *Homecoming*. Four children find a home with their grandmother away from their unbalanced mother. Dicey has difficulty letting go of the responsibility she has had in raising her younger siblings. While adjusting to the living arrangements with her grandmother, Dicey stays aloof from the students in her new class. She refuses to "play the game" by the social rules which might help her ease her way into the mainstream of the high school milieu. Dicey admires a certain black girl but cannot imagine that they could ever be friends. Wilhelmina, on the other hand, is determined to be friends with Dicey even though her overtures are generally rebuffed. Dicey comes to greater understanding of herself and others when she and "Gram" face the death of her mother in a mental hospital. (an ALA Notable Children's Book, a Boston Globe/Horn Book Honor Book, a Notable Children's Trade Book in the Field of Social Studies, and a 1983 Newbery Award Winner)

4.116.   Voigt, Cynthia. (1987). *Sons from afar*. New York: Atheneum. 212 pp. (ISBN: 0-689-31349-7)

The two Tillerman boys set off to find their father, the man who deserted their mother and four children some years before she died. James and his younger brother, Sammy, come to their decision to search for their dad for different reasons. The boys leave for Baltimore to seek information from the Merchant Marines where their father was last employed. They are unable to locate any useful information about his whereabouts, but they do uncover some interesting information about his character. Much of the story revolves around James's effort to overcome his self doubt and desire to establish a good self image. The boys learn something about their own characters and their care for one another in the passing of events. (an SLJ Best Book of the Year)

4.117.   Wagner, Robin S. (1975). *Portrait of a teenage alcoholic*. 120 pp.

See Alcohol and Drugs

4.118.   Walker, Mildred Pitts. (1986). *Justin and the best biscuits in the world*. New York: Lothrop, Lee, & Shepard. 122 pp. (ISBN: 0-688-06645-3)

After Justin's father died, Justin has been raised in a home full of women. His mother and two older sisters do their best to care for him, but he often feels inadequate in caring for himself even if he is only ten years old. Relief comes when Grandpa lets him stay on the ranch for a few days where he learns about his family's history. There he lives like a cowboy and discovers that things get easier the more often you do them.

4.119.   White, Ellen Emerson. (1987). *Life without friends*. 250 pp.

See Death and Dying

4.120. Wolkoff, Judie. (1984). *Happily ever after . . . almost.* New York: Dell Yearling. 224 pp. (ISBN: 0440-43366-5)

Kitty and Sarah are glad that their parents got a divorce. Now they don't have to listen to all of their fighting. But, when both parents remarry, their extended families become so large that it is comical.

4.121. Woodson, Jacqueline. (1991). *The dear one.* 145 pp.

See Teenage Pregnancy

4.122. Wortis, Avi. (1983). *Sometimes I think I hear my name.* 144 pp.

See Dropouts and Delinquency

4.123. Zindel, Paul. (1989). *The amazing and death-defying diary of Eugene Dingman.* New York: Bantam Books. 208 pp. (ISBN: 0-553-27768-5)

Fifteen-year-old Eugene Dingman spends his summer working as a waiter in a ritzy resort in upper New York state. During the summer, Eugene learns to deal with a number of problematic situations in his life. While away from home for the first time, he develops a love-at-first-sight crush for a waitress whose boyfriend despises him. At the same time, he is trying to cope with knowledge about a situation at home: His mother's first romantic interest, since his parents' divorce several years ago, is sleeping in his now vacant bedroom. For some reason, he feels a desperate need to reestablish a relationship with his estranged father who has since remarried. Eugene is able to survive the summer with the help of an Indian kitchen worker, his sister, and his journal. (an *American Bookseller* Pick of the Lists and a New York Library Books for the Teen Age)

Annotated Young Adult Nonfiction Dealing with Divorced and Single Parents

4.124. Anderson, Hal W. & Anderson, Gail S. (1981). *Mom and dad are divorced, but I'm not: Parenting after divorce.* Chicago: Nelson Hall. 258 pp. (ISBN: 0-882-29522-5)

Acknowledging throughout that children are not responsible for their parents' divorces, the book offers solutions to typical problems encountered by children in divorced situations. The authors stress that when counseling children, avoid excess detail and avoid technical jargon.

4.125. Boeckman, Charles. (1980). *Surviving your parents' divorce*. New York: Franklin Watts. 133 pp. (ISBN: 0-531-02869-0)

Written for the middle school child, this book objectively explains the various aspects of divorce: child support, custody, visitation rights, the child's feelings about the process, etc. Information addressing the normal feelings of guilt and fear is also included. The book is positive in its approach to changing family structures and includes actual case histories.

4.126. Booher, Dianna Daniels. (1979). *Coping. . .When your family falls apart*. New York: Julian Messner. 126 pp. (ISBN: 0-671-33083-7)

Booher explores the emotional responses older teenagers experience as a result of their parents' divorce. She offers hope and suggestions to help with the adjustment period until acceptance can be achieved.

4.127. Diamond, Susan Arnsberg. (1986). *Helping children of divorce: A handbook for parents and teachers*. New York: Schocken. 130 pp. (ISBN: 0-805-20821-6)

Besides providing help for parents on how to handle their children after a divorce, the author suggests ways in which teachers can be more sensitive to students whose parents are divorced. She provides examples of insensitive remarks that have been made and how the situation could have been handled more positively.

4.128. Dolmetsch, Paul & Shih, Alexa. (Eds.). (1985). *The kids' book about single-parent families*. New York: Doubleday Books. 193 pp. (ISBN: 0-385-19279-7)

The authors interview several children and capture their stories about what it is like living with a single parent, including unmarried mothers, divorced parents, widows, and widowers.

4.129. Fayerweather Street School. (1981). *The kids' book of divorce by, for, and about kids*. Lexington, MA: Lewis Publishing Company. 123 pp. (ISBN: 0-866-16003-5) (Out of Stock)

Written by children between the ages of 11 to 14, this book is a compilation of their personal testimonials about how they found out about their parents' divorces and their adjustments to custody arrangements, parental dating, remarriage, stepparents, and living with gay parents.

4.130. Gilbert, Sara. (1981). *Trouble at home*. New York: Lothrop, Lee & Shepard. 191 pp. (ISBN: 0-688-41995-X)

Separation and divorce are issues of great concern to children. In this guide, Gilbert examines the positive responses children can make to their troubles.

4.131. Gilbert, Sara. (1982). *How to live with a single parent*. New York: Lothrop, Lee & Shepard. 128 pp. (ISBN: 0-688-00633-7)

It's tough for children to adjust from a two parent to a single parent household. In this book written for middle school-aged children, Gilbert provides advice and reassurances to help teenagers cope during the transition period. She includes a list of children's organizations and addresses as well as a list for parents.

4.132. Goldzband, Melvin G. (1985). *Quality time: Easing the children through divorce*. New York: McGraw-Hill. 193 pp. (ISBN: 0-070-23693-3)

Looking at what's best for children through the divorce process, Goldzband emphasizes quality versus quantity time spent with the children.

4.133. Hausslein, Evelyn B. (1983). *Children and divorce: An annotated bibliography and guide*. New York: Garland. 130 pp. (ISBN: 0-824-09391-7)

This book is a collection of annotated articles and books available to professionals, parents, and children on the topics related to divorce. The collection spans from 1975 to 1980.

4.134. Horner, Catherine Townsend. (1988). *The single-parent family in children's books: An annotated bibliography*. Metuchen, NJ: Scarecrow. 339 pp. (ISBN: 0-810-82065-X)

Horner includes 215 annotations of children's fiction dealing with one-parent families. The books are categorized by the causes of single parent status: divorce, unwed mothers, orphans, widows, and the chosen absence of one parent. Some nonfiction books are also included.

4.135. Hyde, Margaret O. (1981). *My friend has four parents*. New York: McGraw Hill. 120 pp. (ISBN: 0-070-31644-9)

In very simple language, Hyde explains a lot of the legal aspects associated with divorce and addresses some of the emotional problems a young person might experience. This book also offers excellent help to parents who are trying to assist their children in their acceptance of a stepfamily. A section on custody and parental kidnapping is also included.

4.136. Jackson, Michael & Jackson, Jessica. (1981). *Your father's not coming home anymore*. New York: Richard Marek. 320 pp. (ISBN: 0-399-90109-4)

The Jacksons interviewed more than 30 young people, between the ages of 13 and 21, whose parents had divorced and captured their experiences and reactions to the situation. The book was written when the authors were teenagers themselves.

4.137. Krementz, Jill. (1984). *How it feels when parents divorce*. New York: Alfred A. Knopf. (includes photographs) 115 pp. (ISBN: 0-394-54079-4)

Krementz captures the individual stories of 19 teenagers and reveals their feelings about their parents' divorce and how it affected their lives. Topics include the pre- and post-divorce fighting, custody battles, stepfamilies, financial concerns, and their experiences with counselors and therapists.

4.138. LeShan, Eda. (1986). *What's going to happen to me? When parents separate or divorce*. New York: Macmillan. 144 pp. (ISBN: 0-689-71093-3)

This book, written for 10 to 13-year-olds, explains the feelings a child must go through when dealing with a divorce: before it happens, when it happens, and after it happens.

4.139. List, Julie A. (1980). *The day the loving stopped: A daughter's view of her parents' divorce*. New York: Seaview Books. 215 pp. (ISBN: 0-872-23559-9)

Through letters and journal entries, the author shares what it was like for her and the rest of her family when her parents decided to get a divorce, and her everyday father became a weekend one.

4.140. McGuire, Paula. (1987). *Putting it together: Teenagers talk about family breakup*. New York: Delacorte Press. 167 pp. (ISBN: 0-440-50242-X)

After interviewing more than 20 children, teenagers, and counselors about the effects of divorce, the author points out the amazing resiliency of young people. Some kids manage to get their lives back together even when their parents' lives have broken up.

4.141.   Richards, Arlene Kramer & Willis, Irene. (1986). *How to get it together when your parents are coming apart*. Summit, NJ: Willard Press. 170 pp. (ISBN: 0-961-53490-7)

Although most older teenagers have a lot more questions concerning the divorce process, they often have more difficulty asking these questions than younger children do. Through the case study approach, the authors present the problems associated with divorce and suggests reasons why outside help is often necessary and beneficial.

4.142.   Robson, Bonnie. (1979). *My parents are divorced, too: What teenagers experience and how they cope*. Toronto: Dorset. 211 pp. (ISBN: 0-888-93010-0)

Being a child psychiatrist has enabled the author to share the feelings expressed by 28 youngsters, age 12 to 17, who are struggling with the problems of custody, remarriage, and visitation.

4.143.   Rosenberg, M.B. (1990). *Talking about step families*. New York: Bradbury Press. 160 pp. (ISBN: 0-027-77913-0)

Through interviews, the author reveals the feelings and attitudes of several step-children, step-parents, and natural parents. When two members of the same family share their views, the perspectives are often quite different.

4.144.   Rowland, Peter. (1980). *Saturday parent: A book for separated families*. New York: Continuum. 143 pp. (ISBN: 0-826-40026-4)

The author compiled many interviews he conducted with parents who only see their children on weekends. The message is clear: It is important for noncustodial parents to keep in touch with their children even though they no longer live together.

4.145.   Salk, Lee. (1978). *What every child would like his parents to know about divorce*. New York: Harper & Row. 149 pp. (ISBN: 0-060-13764-9)

This guide for parents covers such topics as the effects of divorce on children, what to tell children when it's decided that divorce is inevitable, questions of custody, and dealing with legal matters.

4.146.   Sobol, Harriet Langsam. (1979). *My other mother, my other father*. New York: Macmillan. 34 pp. (ISBN: 0-027-85960-6)

This book is a 12-year-old's story about what it was like for her when her parents divorced and remarried.

4.147. Troyer, Warner. (1980). *Divorced kids*. New York: Harcourt, Brace & Jovanovich. 175 pp. (ISBN: 0-151-25748-5)

Troyer presents the child's view of divorce and how they had to cope with being lied to, new stepfamilies, and various other conflicting emotions.

4.148. Walker, Glynnis. (1986). *Solomon's children: Exploding the myths of divorce*. New York: Arbor House. 218 pp. (ISBN: 0-877-95748-7)

Walker used the information obtained from the responses of 368 children of divorced parents to questionnaires she gave them and made these conclusions: Children are eager to talk about their feelings, opinions, and conflicts about divorce and believe that parents should have equal rights regarding custody.

4.149. Wallerstein, Judith S, & Kelly, Joan Berlin. (1980). *Surviving the breakup: How children and parents cope with divorce*. New York: Basic Books. 341 pp. (ISBN: 0-465-08341-2)

The authors followed 60 families for five years after divorce in order to examine the short and long term effects on children. The researchers discovered that these children, between the ages of 3 and 18, valued their relationships with their fathers, although, in most cases, his contact was less than the mother's. Additionally, they found that these children's anger and desires for resolution last for many years.

Nonfiction References Dealing with Divorced and Single Parents

Journal Articles

Barney, J. (1990, October). Stepfamilies: Second chance or second-rate? *Phi Delta Kappan, 72* (2), p. 144 ff.

Barney, J. & Koford, J. (1987, October). Schools and single parents. *Education Digest, 53* (2), p 40 ff.

Berman, C. (1985, February). When he has kids and she doesn't . . . yet. *Ms, 13* (8), p. 36 ff.

Conant, J. (1987, August 24). You'd better sit down, kids. *Newsweek, 110* (8), p. 58 ff.

Crosby, E.A. (1993, April). The at-risk decade. *Phi Delta Kappan, 74* (8), p. 598 ff.

Editors. (1985, August). Are family problems affecting your classroom? *Learning, 14* (1), p. 68 ff.

Edwards, P.A. & Young, L.S.J. (1992, September). Beyond parents: Family, community, and school involvement. *Phi Delta Kappan, 74* (1), p. 72 ff.

Eitzen, D.S. (1992, April). Problem students: The sociocultural roots. *Phi Delta Kappan, 73* (8), p. 584 ff.

Gallman, V. (1987, December). Holidays and single moms. *Essence, 18* (8), p. 102 ff.

Garvin, J.P. (1984, November). Children of divorce: A challenge for middle school teachers. *Middle School Journal, 16* (1), p. 6 ff.

Gelman, D. (1985, July 15). The single parent: Family albums. *Newsweek, 106* (3), p. 44 ff.

Glenn, N.D. (1985, June). Children of divorce. *Psychology Today, 19* (6), p. 68 ff.

Guttman, J., Geva, N., & Gefen, S. (1988, Winter). Teachers' and school children's stereotypic perception of 'the child of divorce.' *American Educational Research Journal, 25* (4), p. 555 ff.

Hirshey, G. (1988, August). What children wish their parents knew. *Family Circle*, p. 84 ff.

Hodgkinson, H. (1991, September). Reform versus reality. *Phi Delta Kappan, 73* (1), p. 9 ff.

Hofferth, S.L. (1987, February). Implications of family trends for children: A research perspective. *Educational Leadership, 44* (5), p. 78 ff.

Manning, D.T. & Wooten, M.D. (1987, January). What stepparents perceive schools should know about blended families. *Clearing House, 60* (5), p. 230 ff.

Midkiff, R.B. & Lawler-Prince, D. (1992, fall). Preparing tomorrow's teachers: Meeting the challenge of diverse family structures. *Action in Teacher Education, 14* (3), p. 1 ff.

Moore, D. & Hotch, D.F. (1982, April). Parent-adolescent separation: The role of parental divorce. *Journal of Youth and Adolescence, 11* (2), p. 115 ff.

Pierson, D.A. (1982, spring). Issues confronting adolescents in stepfamilies. *The ALAN Review, 9* (3), p. 31 ff.

Stansbury, G.W. (1985, summer). The hurting doesn't stop at 8:45: Divorced kids in the classroom. *Contemporary Education, 56* (4), p. 236 ff.

Strother, J & Jacobs, E. (1984, November). Adolescent stress as it relates to stepfamily living: Implications for school counselors. *The School Counselor, 32* (2), p. 97 ff.

Walton, S. (1985, March). Single-parent families: New script, same action. *Psychology Today, 19* (3), p. 79 ff.

Journal Themes

The American Family: The Shattered Dream. (1980, Winter). *American Educator, 4* (4).

When the Family Comes Apart: What Schools Need to Know. (1979, October). *National Elementary Principal, 59* (1).

Books

Allers, R.D. (1982). *Divorce, children, and the school.* New Jersey: Princeton Book Company. 158 pp. (ISBN: 0-916-62222-3)

Brogan, J.P. & Maiden, U. (1986). *The kids' guide to divorce.* New York: Fawcett Crest. (ISBN: 0-449-21242-4)

Cline, R.K.J. (1990). *Focus on families.* Santa Barbara, CA: ABC-CLIO. 233 pp. (ISBN: 0-87436-508-2)

Krementz, J. (1988). *How it feels when parents divorce.* New York: Alfred A. Knopf. 115 pp. (ISBN: 0-394-75855-2)

Wallerstein, J.S. & Blakeslee, S. (1989). *Second chances.* New York: Ticknor & Fields. 329 pp. (ISBN: 0-899-19648-9)

CHAPTER 5

Adopted and Foster Families

As more and more teenagers experience unwanted pregnancies, there is an increasing number of babies being given up for adoption or foster care. Sometimes when the mothers and fathers get older, they want to find the whereabouts of their children. Sometimes when the adoptees get older, they want to locate their biological parents. It is never guaranteed that all parties involved want to experience a reunion. Nonetheless, there are agencies available to assist in the relocation process. It is a highly emotional experience for all concerned when an adoptee is reunited with his or her natural parents.

STARTLING INFORMATION ABOUT ADOPTED AND FOSTER FAMILIES

- In 1983, there were 500,000 children in substitute family care in the United States and 20% of them were eligible for adoption. (Pardeck & Pardeck, 1987)

- If an adoptee first learns about his or her adoption intentionally or accidentally from someone other than the adoptive parents, the child may feel anger or mistrust for the parents and may view the adoption as bad because it was kept a secret. (American Academy of Child & Adolescent Psychiatry, *Facts for Families*, 1992)

- It is widely accepted that the adoptees' desire to know their biological roots is nearly a universal phenomenon, but adoptees vary in the intensity of their desire and their reasons for searching. (Sachdev, 1992)

- Adopted children are at increased risk for a variety of psychological and academic problems compared to their nonadopted peers. (Brodzinsky & Brodzinsky, 1992)

- Contrary to clinical opinion, the overrepresentation of young adoptees in counseling is not attributed solely to the fact that adoptees are more troubled; rather, adoptees do display more problems but they are also referred for counseling more often. (Warren, 1992)

- Almost four million school-age children are being reared by neither parent. (Hodgkinson, 1991)

WHAT TO DO AND WHERE TO GO FOR HELP

- Child and adolescent psychiatrists recommend that an adoptee should be told about the adoption by the adoptive parents in a way that the child can understand.

- The adolescent who asks for information about his or her biological family should be given the information with tact and supportive discussion.

- Get professional help: Call crisis intervention centers, mental health clinics, hospitals, a family physician, a clergy, a guidance counselor, or a teacher. For immediate help, call the Birth Hope Adoption Agency at 1-800-392-2121 or the National Adoption Hotline at 1-202-328-1200. For more information, write to the National Adoption Exchange, 1218 Chestnut Street, Philadelphia, Pennsylvania, 19107; or Operation Identity, 13101 Blackstone Road, NE, Albuquerque, New Mexico 87111.

Annotated Young Adult Novels Dealing with Adopted and Foster Families

5.01. Byars, Betsy. (1977). *Pinballs*. New York: Scholastic. 136 pp. (ISBN: 0-060-20917-8)

Three foster children slowly grow to realize that they can make choices about how they live their lives.

5.02. Calvert, Patricia. (1986). *Yesterday's daughter*. New York: Charles Scribner's Sons. 138 pp. (ISBN: 0-684-18746-9)

Leenie O'Brien was deserted by her unmarried mother and adopted by her grandparents when she was three months old. Now she is 16, and her mother is coming to visit. Leenie must struggle with her resentment of her mother in addition to her adolescent identity problems. This excellent novel contains significant insights about the meaning of life.

5.03.   Calvert, Patricia. (1989). *When morning comes*. New York: Charles Scribner's Sons. 153 pp. (ISBN: 0-684-19105-9)

Cat Kincaid has been warned that if she cannot adjust to her new foster home, one of many, then her next home will be the detention center. Annie Bowen, her foster caregiver, seems nice enough, but living on a bee farm is a far cry from the city streets that Cat enjoys. Cat befriends Hooter Lewis at her new school, and Hooter tries to get Cat to stop running from her troubles.

5.04.   Derby, Pat. (1986). *Visiting Miss Pierce*. New York: Farrar, Straus & Giroux. 133 pp. (ISBN: 0-374-38162-3)

Barry Wilson receives a class assignment during his freshman year of high school that changes his life. He is to befriend an 83-year-old woman, Miss Pierce, and visit her all semester in a convalescent home. Miss Pierce thinks that Barry is her dead brother, Willie. He listens attentively "as Willie" and learns the whole story, a story that hits Barry right in his heart. Their conversations help Barry get a new perspective on his own adoption.

5.05.   Guy, Rosa. (1978). *Edith Jackson*. New York: Viking Press. 187 pp. (ISBN: 0-670-28906-X)

Eighteen-year-old Edith sets out to find security for herself and her sisters. Along the way Edith learns that her sisters may not want what she wants or what she wants for them.

5.06.   Holland, Isabelle. (1991). *The house in the woods*. New York: Ballantine Books. 165 pp. (ISBN: 0-449-70410-6)

Bridget's mother died five years ago, and her adoptive father and the twins are always criticizing her about her weight. Only Morgan, her younger brother, seems to truly love her. But, Morgan doesn't talk and her father is threatening to send him to a hospital. Bridget finds happiness inside an empty, dilapidated country house where she finds time to think. She eventually discovers some surprising facts about her adoption, her biological parents, and her silent younger brother.

5.07.   Howard, Ellen. (1988). *Her own song*. New York: Atheneum. 160 pp. (ISBN: 0-689-31444-2)

Mellie has always been content living in Portland, Oregon, until she decides that it is time to find her natural mother. She eventually ends up in Chinatown where she learns about things totally foreign to her. This novel is set in the turn of the century.

5.08.   L'Engle, Madeleine. (1990). *Meet the Austins*. New York: Dell Laurel-Leaf. 192 pp. (ISBN: 0-440-95777-X)

Maggy Hamilton is an orphan who goes to live with the Austin family; they are a warm, fun-loving family.

5.09.   Levinson, Nancy Smiler. (1981). *Silent fear*. 63 pp.

See Abuse

5.10.   Lifton, Betty Jean. (1981). *I'm still me*. New York: Alfred A. Knopf. 224 pp. (ISBN: 0-394-84783-0)

Sixteen-year-old Lori is required to make a family tree for a class assignment. Being adopted makes it difficult: She doesn't have any information on her biological parents and doesn't think it's right to use the information of her adoptive parents. Lori wonders why teachers can't be more sensitive.

5.11.   Lowry, Lois. (1990). *Find a stranger, say goodbye*. New York: Dell Laurel-Leaf. 192 pp. (ISBN: 0-440-20541-7)

Natalie Armstrong has a loving family and is ready for college except for one thing: She knows she's adopted and is determined to find her natural mother. Natalie's seemingly well-rounded and perfect life becomes unsettling to her, and she is driven to find out the identity of her biological mother and her past. Her foster parents support her in her search for her real mother, but 17-year-old Natalie is not happy with what she discovers.

5.12.   Mills, Claudia. (1985). *Boardwalk with hotel*. New York: Macmillan. 131 pp. (ISBN: 0-02-767010-4)

Jessica's known for as long as she can remember that she's adopted, but it isn't until she's 11 years old that she finds out why. Her babysitter informs her that her parents adopted her because they thought they couldn't have children. Soon after her adoption, however, her mother gave birth to Julie and Brian. Jessica experiences feelings of being loved least, so she retaliates by gaining her parents' constant attention even if that means negative attention. She becomes fiercely competitive with Brian and takes her anger out on Julie.

5.13. Myers, Walter Dean. (1988). *Won't know till I get there*. New York: Viking Penguin/Puffin Books. 192 pp. (ISBN: 0-14-032612-X)

Steve, a 14-year-old who lives in Harlem, keeps a diary about his parents' decision to adopt Earl, a foster child. Things go awry when Steve learns that Earl has a criminal record. After committing vandalism, they are both assigned to do community service in an old folks home where they both learn some valuable lessons.

5.14. Nixon, Joan Lowery. (1987). *A family apart*. New York: Bantam Books. 162 pp. (ISBN: 0-553-05432-5)

This historical novel is based on an actual event in history--the 19th century practice of sending children out west on "orphan trains" to be adopted. The story is about how the mother of six children puts them on the Orphan Train to begin new, and hopefully better, lives. (an NCSS-CBC Notable Children's Book in the Field of Social Studies, a YASD Recommended Book for Reluctant YA Readers, & a Winner of the Golden Spur Award)

5.15. Nixon, Joan Lowery. (1989). *Caught in the act*. New York: Bantam Books. 150 pp. (ISBN: 0-553-05443-0)

This, the second of four novels dealing with the Orphan Train, is the story of 12-year-old Mike Kelly and his adoption by German immigrants. Mike is one of six Kelly children who were separated from their mother in New York and sent west, in the 1850's, to be adopted. Mike's new family situation is not pleasant, but Mike feels compelled to make it work because he runs the risk of being convicted if sent back to New York. Earlier, he had stolen to feed his siblings.

5.16. Nixon, Joan Lowery. (1990). *A place to belong*. New York: Bantam Books. 160 pp. (ISBN: 0-553-28485-1)

This, the final volume of the Orphan Train quartet, finds Danny and Peg trying to reunite their family again. This time the brother and sister are with a nice couple in St. Joseph, Missouri.

5.17. Okimoto, Jean Davies. (1990). *Molly by any other name*. New York: Scholastic. 257 pp. (ISBN: 0-590-42993-0)

When Molly turns 18, she fills out some application forms that make her deal with the fact that she is adopted. The forms ask for information regarding her family heritage and health tendencies, so Molly decides it is time to find out about her biological family. The book has three parts: her adoptive parents' perspective, her biological mother's perspective, and the meeting of the two families.

5.18.   Paterson, Katherine. (1987). *The great Gilly Hopkins*. New York: Avon Books. 156 pp. (ISBN: 0-380-45963-9)

Galadriel "Gilly" Hopkins has alienated herself from the whole world. If only her "idealized" mother would come and get her, then everything would be all right. Gilly is a wild, bright girl bent on displeasing everyone as she goes from one foster home to another. She succeeds at this until Trotter, a foster mother, finally makes her feel loved. As Gilly learns to love, she learns to accept many hard truths, including those about her real mother, and is able to go on with her life. (a Newbery Honor Book, Christopher Medal Winner, and Winner of the National Book Award)

5.19.   Roberts, Nadine. (1990). *With love from Sam and me*. New York: Fawcett/Juniper. 135 pp. (ISBN: 449-70368-1)

Fifteen-year-old Marylou Britten, a foster child, cares for Sam the new, two-year-old black foster child when he arrives at Uncle Ed and Aunt Bonnie's house. Because Uncle Ed and Aunt Bonnie are more concerned with the money they receive for the foster children rather than the children themselves, Marylou decides to run away from these abusive foster parents and takes Sam with her.

5.20.   Shyer, Marlene Fanta. (1980). *My brother, the thief*. New York: Charles Scribner's Sons. 138 pp. (ISBN: 0-684-16434-5)

This story is told from the point of view of Carolyn Desmond, a 12-year-old girl. Carolyn describes the relationship she and her father have with Richard, Dr. Desmond's 15-year-old adopted son. Dr. Desmond sets high goals for his children, but the children react differently to his demands. Richard, who already suffers from a poor self-image, reacts negatively. Dr. Desmond learns to be gentler with the children and learns to treat them according to their individual needs.

5.21.   Sommer, Sarah. (1984). *And I'm stuck with Joseph*. Scottdale, PA: Herald Press. 124 pp. (ISBN: 0-8361-3356-0)

Sheila Shenk has always wanted a little sister for as long as she can remember. She begs her parents to try and promises to help with the extra work that a baby requires. Sheila gets the shock of her life when her parents announce their plans to adopt--a three year old boy! Not only is Sheila disappointed by not getting a little sister, but her new "brother" is incorrigible and difficult to love.

5.22.   Thesman, Jean. (1992). *When the road ends.* Boston: Houghton
         Mifflin. 184 pp. (ISBN: 0-395-59507-X)

Mary Jack Jordan has been passed around from foster family to foster
family, and the Percy family will probably be no different from the others. It is
obvious from the onset that Mr. Percy loves children, but Mrs. Percy considers
them an aggravation. Mary Jack is 12 years old, and immediately she is the
middle child between 14-year-old Jack and 7-year-old Jane. Jack and Jane are
also foster children, but Jane doesn't talk. Mary Jack soon finds herself
genuinely caring for her new brother and sister, especially during troubling
times.

5.23.   Thomas, Joyce Carol. (1986). *Water girl.* New York: Avon Books.
         120 pp. (ISBN: 0-380-89532-3)

Amber Westbrook gets the shock of her life when she is 15 years old:
She accidentally finds a letter in the attic that discloses that she is adopted. She
runs away and spends a few days by herself in the woods to sort it all out. At a
time when she is troubled by man's inhumanity to man (i.e. slavery,
concentration camps, the treatment of the Indians, etc.), she is able to accept
the situation and realizes that nothing changes the love she and her parents
share unless she decides to mess it up.

5.24.   Voigt, Cynthia. (1987). *Sons from afar.* New York: Atheneum. 224
         pp. (ISBN: 0-689-31349-7)

James becomes obsessed with finding his biological father, thinking
that the discovery will help him with his own problems of adolescence. His
brother, Sammy, isn't all that interested but decides to help James with his
cause. The boys know virtually nothing about their father since he left when
they were both quite young. What they discover about him, they'd rather not
know. On the positive side, the boys become closer and learn about their own
inner strengths and weaknesses. (a *School Library Journal* Best Book of the
Year)

Annotated Young Adult Nonfiction Dealing with Adopted and
Foster Families

5.25.   Arms, Suzanne. (1983). *To love and let go.* New York: Alfred A.
         Knopf. 228 pp. (ISBN: 0-394-50319-8)

This book is the author's presentation, in narrative form, of the stories
of young women and their struggle to give their children up for adoption.
Several reasons are given for their decisions, but most are made out of love and
respect for the child's needs.

5.26.   Berman, Claire. (1974). *We take this child.* New York: Doubleday. 203 pp. (ISBN: 0-385-02476-2)

Based on interviews with families who have adopted children, this book looks at the various situations related to adoption: the handicapped child, the older child, the transracial child, and the intercountry child.

5.27.   Bunin, Catherine & Bunin, Sherry. (1976). *Is that your sister?* New York: Pantheon. 35 pp. (ISBN: 0-394-83230-2)

An adopted six-year-old girl tells about adoption and how she and her adopted sister feel about it.

5.28.   Caplan, Lincoln. (1990). *An open adoption.* New York: Farrar, Straus, & Giroux. 145 pp. (ISBN: 0-374-10558-8)

An open adoption is one where the mother meets the prospective parents before the adoption takes place. This is the story of a 20-year-old college student, Peggy Bass, who decides that Dan and Lee Stone should be the parents of her baby. They meet, make arrangements, and even become friends before the baby is born. The pros and cons of such an arrangement are frankly discussed.

5.29.   DuPrau, Jeanne. (1990). *Adoption: The facts, feelings and issues of a double heritage.* New York: Julian Messner. 129 pp. (ISBN: 0-671-69328-X)

DuPrau presents the legal and emotional aspects of the adoption process. She also discusses the movement that recommends giving adoptees free access to records concerning their biological origins.

5.30.   Dusky, Lorraine. (1979). *Birthmark.* New York: M. Evans. 191 pp. (ISBN: 0-87131-299-9)

Dusky shares her very personal view of adoption from the biological mother's perspective. She was all set to have a career as a journalist when she got pregnant by a married man. Ms. Dusky describes what it was like for her when she decided to search for the child she gave up for adoption.

5.31.   Feigelman, William & Silverman, Arnold R. (1983). *Chosen children: New patterns of adoptive relationships.* New York: Praeger. 261 pp. (ISBN: 0-275-90974-3)

The authors discuss the results they found based on research, from 1973 to 1976, on the changing patterns of adoption. Information is provided on the causes, issues, and questions associated with the adoption process, including transracial and single parent adoptions.

5.32. Hormann, Elizabeth. (1987). *After the adoption*. Old Tappan, NJ: F.H. Revell. (ISBN: 0-800-71516-0)

This book examines what to expect after an adoption actually takes place and offers suggestions on how to develop healthy, family relationships.

5.33. Jewett, Claudia. (1978). *Adopting the older child*. Harvard, MA: Harvard Common Press. 308 pp. (ISBN: 0-916-78208-5)

Claudia Jewett describes the life of her large family comprised of seven adopted children and three biological children.

5.34. Koh, Frances M. (1984). *Oriental children in American homes*. Minneapolis, MN: East-West Press. 132 pp. (ISBN: 0-960-60900-8)

The author investigated the outcomes and special concerns involved in the adoptions of Oriental children by American families.

5.35. Krementz, Jill. (1982). *How it feels to be adopted*. New York: Alfred A. Knopf. 107 pp. (includes photos) (ISBN: 0-394-52851-4)

Written for middle school children and older, Krementz interviewed several adopted children and their families to reveal the feelings, experiences, and concerns of all involved.

5.36. Ladner, Joyce A. (1977). *Mixed families: Adopting across racial boundaries*. New York: Anchor Press/Doubleday. 290 pp. (ISBN: 0-385-12792-8)

Through interviews with adopted black children and their white parents, Ladner presents information regarding interracial adoption in the United States.

5.37. Lifton, Betty Jean. (1975). *Twice born: Memoirs of an adopted daughter*. New York: McGraw-Hill. 281 pp. (ISBN: 0-070-37824-X)

Lifton, using the biography approach, reveals what adoption is like in the United States.

5.38. Lifton, Betty Jean. (1979). *Lost and found: The adoption experience*. New York: Dial. 303 pp. (ISBN: 0-803-75036-6)

Several adopted children offer personal insights into their relative situations.

5.39.   McRoy, Ruth G. & Zurcher, Jr., Louis A. (1983). *Transracial and inracial adoptees: The adolescent years.* Springfield, Illinois: Thomas. 155 pp. (ISBN: 0-398-04840-1)

Using the case study approach, the authors present a comprehensive discussion of transracial and interracial adoptions in the United States.

5.40.   Melina, Lois Ruskai. (1987). *Adoption: An annotated bibliography and guide.* New York: Garland. 292 pp. (ISBN: 0-824-08942-1)

This book is a compilation of adoption materials published between 1974 and 1987 about such issues as birth parents' rights, preadoption concerns for adoptive parents, special needs adoptions, search and reunion procedures, etc. The author also includes a list of children's resources, educational and audiovisual materials, an adoption directory by state, a guide to agencies, and a list of organizations.

5.41.   Musser, Sandra Kay. (1992). *I would have searched forever.* Cape Coral, FL: Adoption Awareness Press. 160 pp. (ISBN: 0-934-89600-3)

The author tells her story on what it was like searching for her natural parents.

5.42.   Nickman, Steven L. (1985). *Adoption experiences.* New York: Julian Messner. 192 pp. (ISBN: 0-671-50817-2)

Written specifically for adolescents, the author retells the stories of six adopted children and a young couple about to adopt a child. The book is not only informative but offers insights into what adoptees might feel throughout their adoption experiences.

5.43.   Powledge, Fred. (1982). *So you're adopted.* New York: Charles Scribner's Sons. 112 pp. (ISBN: 0-684-17347-6)

Besides a discussion of the social and legal aspects of adoption, the author includes a discussion of the personal concerns and questions that often trouble adopted children and their families.

5.44.   Rillera, Mary Jo. (1991). *The adoption searchbook: Techniques for tracing people.* Westminster, CA: Pure, Inc. 210 pp. (ISBN: 0-910-14300-5)

For the adoptee who is thinking about finding his or her natural parents, this book provides useful information on how to go about it.

5.45.   Sorosky, Arthur D., Baran, Annette, & Pannor, Reuben. (1984). *The adoption triangle: Sealed or open records, how they affect adoptees, birth parents, and adoptive parents.* New York: Anchor Books. 256 pp. (ISBN: 0-385-12871-1)

As the title suggests, the authors discuss right to privacy versus right to know issues using case studies to support the various views.

5.46.   Wishard, Laurie & Wishard, William. (1979). *Adoption: The grafted tree.* San Francisco: Cragmont Publications. 197 pp. (ISBN: 0-896-66006-0)

This adopted daughter and her father co-authored this book in an attempt to answer commonly asked questions concerning the adoption experience in a factual way.

Nonfiction References Dealing with Adopted and Foster Families

Journal Articles

Brodzinsky, D.M. & Brodzinsky, A.B. (1992). The impact of family structure on the adjustment of adopted children. *Child Welfare, 71,* (1), p. 69 ff.

Hodgkinson, H. (1991, September). Reform versus Reality. *Phi Delta Kappan, 73* (1), p. 9 ff.

Pardeck, J.T. & Pardeck, J.A. (1987, May-June). Bibliotherapy for children in foster care and adoption. *Child Welfare, 66* (3), p. 269 ff.

Sachdev, P. (1992). Adoption reunion and after: A story of the search process and experience of adoptees. *Child Welfare, 71* (1), p. 53 ff.

Ward, M. & Lewko, J.H. (1987, November-December). Adolescents in families adopting older children: Implications for service. *Child Welfare, 66* (6), p. 539 ff.

Warren, S.B. (1992, May). Lower threshold for referral for psychiatric treatment for adopted adolescents. *Journal of American Academy of Child Adolescent Psychiatry, 31* (3), p. 512 ff.

Books

Cline, R.K.J. (1990). *Focus on families.* Santa Barbara, CA: ABC-CLIO.
    233 pp. (ISBN: 0-87436-508-2)

CHAPTER 6

Abuse

In the Eighties, child abuse emerged as an important social issue and has escalated ever since. There are three basic types of child abuse: emotional, physical, and sexual. Emotional abuse refers to the belittling, rejecting, and neglectful treatment of a child, physical abuse is the nonaccidental physical injury of a child, and sexual abuse is any sex act intentionally imposed on a child. It has often been said that a society is judged by how it treats its weakest members. If that is true, then historians will judge our American society harshly for our treatment of children.

STARTLING INFORMATION ABOUT CHILD ABUSE

- Over 1,700,000 cases of abuse and neglect were reported in the United States during 1984, which was an increase of 158% over the number reported in 1976. (American Humane Association, 1986)

- In 1989, 1,849 children were abused in America daily. (Edelman, 1989)

- There are over two million cases of child abuse each year in the United States. (The Child Abuse Council, 1993)

- Seventy-eight percent of emotional, physical, and sexual abuse are performed by a member of the victim's immediate family. (Gil, 1988)

- Eight out of ten criminals in prison were abused when they were children. (Child Abuse Council, 1993)

Physical Abuse

• Fourteen percent of children between the ages of 3 and 17 experience family violence. (Craig, 1992)

• Between 16% and 30% of all physical abuse occur in adolescent males and females between the ages of 13 to 17 years of age. (Blum, 1987)

• In 1988, the reported cases of child maltreatment increased 66% over the previous 1980 incidence study. Approximately 1.5 million children experienced abuse or neglect, 10% were classified as serious, and about 1,100 cases were fatal. (United States Department of Health and Human Services)

• In 1978, 3.8% of deaths among children between the ages of 1 and 14 were attributed to homicide. (United States Department of Health and Human Services)

• Three child abuse deaths are believed to go undetected each day because no one bothers to perform an autopsy. (Lundstrom & Sharpe, 1991)

Sexual Abuse

• Among adolescents, about 70% of the reported cases of child abuse are sexual in nature. (Tower, 1987)

• In 1976, the American Humane Association published the first official estimate on the incidence of child sexual abuse, reporting 6,000 cases nationwide. By 1986, the national number hit 300,000, by 1991, 400,000, and since then it has climbed steadily.

• Approximately 27% of girls and 16% of boys are sexually abused before 18 years of age. (Krueger, 1993)

• Child sexual abuse has been reported up to 80,000 times a year, but the number of unreported instances is far greater. (The American Academy of Child & Adolescent Psychiatry, *Facts for Families*, 1992)

• Experts believe that almost 25% of children will be sexually abused before they become adults, and most of them will be abused by someone they know--not a stranger. (Child Abuse Council, 1993)

• Seven percent of Americans aged 18 to 22 have experienced at least one episode of nonvoluntary sexual intercourse; just under half of these experiences for women occurred before the age of fourteen. (National Survey of Children, 1987)

WARNING SIGNS OF AN ADOLESCENT WHO IS BEING ABUSED

- Negative self concept, low self esteem, feelings of worthlessness, depression, helplessness.

- Substance abusers.

- Anorectic behavior.

- Self-destructive comments, self-destructive behavior, accident prone, suicidal.

- Delinquency, truancy, running away.

- Psychosomatic complaints.

- Sleep problems, nightmares, anxiety.

- Depression or withdrawal from family or friends.

- Refusal to go to school, delinquency.

- Secretiveness.

- Unusual aggressiveness or passivity.

- Severe behavior changes.

Physically Abused

- Complains of soreness, moves awkwardly.

- Wears clothing that covers body that is inappropriate for weather.

- Cannot tolerate physical contact or touch.

- Frequent injuries, burns, or bald spots and doesn't want to explain how acquired.

- Afraid to receive medical help.

Sexually Abused

- Interpersonal difficulties and abnormal perspective on sexuality.

- Unusual interest in or avoidance of all things sexual in nature.

- Seductiveness, sexual acting out, promiscuity.

- Statements that their bodies are dirty or damaged, or fear that there is something wrong with them in the genital area.

- Receives unexplained gifts or money.

- Aspects of sexual molestation in drawings, games, fantasies.

- Early pregnancies.

- Prostitution, revictimization.

WHAT TO DO AND WHERE TO GO FOR HELP

- Understand that victims are often extremely fearful in telling, so encourage them to talk freely by not making judgmental comments and by listening attentively.

- A supportive, caring response is essential to helping the victim reestablish his or her trust in people.

- Never blame the victim and offer assurance that he or she did the right thing by telling.

- Professional evaluation and treatment as soon as possible is the best way to overcome the development of serious problems for that person as an adult.

- Report any suspicion of abuse and get professional help: Call the local Child Protection Agency, the local Department of Health and Rehabilitative Services, crisis intervention centers, mental health clinics, hospitals, a family physician, a clergy, a guidance counselor, or a teacher. If you want to report a suspected case of child abuse or neglect, call the Abuse Registry at 1-800-342-9152, HRS at 1-800-962-2873, or the Child Abuse Hotline at 1-800-422-4453. For more information, write to the National Committee to Prevent Child Abuse, 332 S. Michigan Avenue, Suite #1600, Chicago, Illinois, 60604; the C. Henry

Kempe National Center for the Prevention and Treatment of Child Abuse and Neglect, 1205 Oneida Street, Denver, Colorado, 80220; or the Abuse Registry, 2729 Fort Knox Boulevard, Tallahassee, Florida, 32308.

Annotated Young Adult Novels Dealing with Abuse

6.01.   Branscum, Robbie. (1986). *The girl*. New York: Harper & Row. 113 pp. (ISBN: 0-060-20702-7)

An 11-year-old girl and her four brothers and sisters are abandoned by their mother after their father dies. Their grandparents, who are sharecroppers, take in the children but only do so for the welfare checks they receive. An emotionally abusive grandmother and a sexually abusive uncle make life unbearable for "the girl" as she struggles just to survive one day at a time. This poignant book presents a realistic glimpse of life that, hopefully, is much different than our own.

6.02.   Davis, Terry. (1992). *If rock and roll were a machine*. New York: Delacorte Press. 209 pp. (ISBN: 0-385-30762-X)

Abuse takes many forms, and it's not until Bert Bowden is a junior in high school that he figures out his problem. Up until his 5th grade year, he was a boy who enjoyed doing well in school and sports. He had many friends and had the power and drive to attempt almost anything. That was until Mr. Lawler, his 5th grade teacher, decided he was a know-it-all who needed to be put in his place. Mr. Lawler encouraged the class to mock and taunt Bert whenever he made a mistake which devastated Bert and his self-esteem. In response to his junior teacher's composition assignment, "The Worst Thing that Ever Happened to Me," Bert gets a handle on his negative attitude. Ironically, it takes another teacher to help Bert undo the damage done by his abusive 5th grade teacher.

6.03.   Diggs, Lucy. (1988). *Moon in the water*. New York: Atheneum. 240 pp. (ISBN: 0-689-31337-3) (Out of Stock)

The cliché "you can pick your friends, but you can't pick your family" rings true for 15-year-old JoBob Draper. His father is an abusive bigot, and his mother only has enough energy to protect herself from her husband and is incapable of giving JoBob the nurturing that he needs. It would be better if his parents would just leave him alone, but his father forces him to participate in illegal cockfight gambling deals. JoBob is repulsed by the "sport" but participates out of fear of his father. JoBob finds happiness in his work at a local stable where his efforts pay off in his acquiring a horse as a gift.

Unfortunately, his father ruins that by underhandedly selling his horse to get money to pay off some creditors. Fortunately, JoBob's Japanese friend, Mariko, helps him to find the inner strength necessary to survive and make good choices for his own life.

6.04.   Hall, Lynn. (1987). *Flyaway*. New York: Charles Scribner's Sons. 128 pp. (ISBN: 0-684-18888-0) (Out of Stock)

To everyone on the outside, Ariel Brecht has it made. Her father bestows lavish gifts on her, and she has practically everything money can buy. Only Ariel, her sister, and her mother know the truth about this seemingly generous man who psychologically abuses the women in his life.

6.05.   Holman, Felice. (1986). *Slake's limbo*. New York: Aladdin. 128 pp. (ISBN: 0-689-71066-6)

Aremis Slake, 13, is unloved at home and is frequently abused by kids in the streets. He runs away and hides in the subway for 121 days, surviving that long by his ingenuity and scavenging. Slake's accomplishments help him rebuild his self-esteem. Although the novel realistically paints a rather grim portrait of failure on the part of guardians, schools, and social agencies, it also emphasizes the importance of self-reliance and self-esteem. (an American Library Association Best of the Best Books for Young Adults)

6.06.   Howker, Janni. (1986). *Isaac Campion*. 83 pp.

See Death and Dying

6.07.   Hunt, Irene. (1976). *The lottery rose*. New York: Charles Scribner's Sons. 185 pp. (ISBN: 0-684-14573-1)

A young boy victimized by child abuse from his mother and her boyfriend hasn't had a lot in his favor. After winning a rosebush in the lottery, 7-year-old Georgie learns to overcome his mistrust of the world.

6.08.   Major, Kevin. (1980). *Hold fast*. 170 pp.

See Death and Dying

6.09.   Martin, Katherine. (1989). *Night riding*. New York: Random House. 197 pp. (ISBN: 0-679-80064-6)

When Elizabeth Campbell's father is admitted to the hospital at the beginning of summer, she just knows she will have a boring summer. Elizabeth's summer is anything but boring, especially when Mary Faith

Hammond moves in next door. Mary Faith is 15, pregnant, and lives alone with her abusive father. Her mother is deceased, and it is suspected that her father is also the father of her child. Elizabeth knows that Mr. Hammond beats Mary Faith and believes it is his fault when she miscarries. Elizabeth fears for herself and her mother when Mr. Hammond seems to be ever present.

6.10.   Mazer, Harry. (1990). *The war on Villa Street*. New York: Dell Laurel-Leaf. 192 pp. (ISBN: 0-440-99062-9)

Not only is Willis Pierce a loner, he finds himself running away from all of his problems. In an attempt to escape the pain of his drunken, abusive father, he runs into Rabbit Slavin's gang on Villa Street. Willis teaches a retarded child to compete in sports and gets unbelievable ridicule for his kindness. Finally, through the confidence and self-respect gained from teaching the retarded boy, Willis learns that he must stop running from his problems and face them directly. He returns home and refuses to be bullied by his father again. (an American Library Association Best Book for Young Adults)

6.11.   Moeri, Louise. (1979). *The girl who lived on the Ferris wheel*. New York: E.P. Dutton. 117 pp. (ISBN: 0-525-30659-5)

Set during World War II, this novel is about Clotilde and her difficult relationship with her mother. Til's mother is divorced, abusive, and deranged. Til's one day of relief is the day her father comes to take her for an outing, away from her abusive mother's antics. Every Saturday they go to Playland to ride the Ferris Wheel, her father's favorite ride. Although Til doesn't particularly care for the ride, she does care for her father and cherishes the day they spend together.

6.12.   Newton, Suzanne. (1983). *I will call it Georgie's blues*. New York: Viking Press.. 197 pp. (ISBN: 0-670-39131-X)

Neal Sloan, a 9th grader, tells the story about his family's breakdown. Neal is a troubled teenager because his father, the preacher, expects his family to be perfect. Neal conceals his jazz piano playing from his father because he does not want his father to place more demands on him. His younger 7-year-old brother, Georgie, tries to cope by creating an imaginary world for himself where his parents are creatures from outer space. When Georgie runs away, the family is forced to admit there are problems and they seek family counseling.

6.13.   Piowaty, Kim Kennelly. (1983). *Don't look in her eyes*. New York: Macmillan/McElderry Books. 186 pp. (ISBN: 0-689-50273-7)

Jason's mother is abusive, and he finds it necessary to stay home and protect his younger brother from her tirades even though that means missing most of his 6th grade year. He's overjoyed when his mother abandons them but then has a whole new set of challenges to contend with. Finding food and a place to live become real issues, and he is afraid to ask for help for fear that he and his brother will be separated and sent to an institution.

6.14.   Roberts, Nadine. (1990). *With love from Sam and me*. 135 pp.

See Adopted and Foster Families

6.15.   Silsbee, Peter. (1987). *The big way out*. New York: Dell. 180 pp. (ISBN: 0-440-90499-4)

Fourteen-year-old Paul McNamara tells what it's like to be controlled by a manic-depressive father. He constantly lives in fear of his father's abusive threats and violence. His brother doesn't seem to think it's as bad as everyone else, and his mother insists that they keep their father's problem a secret. She tells people that he's on business trips when, in fact, he's having shock treatments at a nearby mental health facility. Unable to keep the trauma inside any longer, Paul tells his cousin but feels betrayed when she tells someone else.

Physical Abuse

6.16.   Armstrong, Louise. (1980). *Saving the big-deal baby*. New York: E.P. Dutton. 42 pp. (ISBN: 0-525-45050-5) (Out of Print)

Robbie, a 19-year-old, is married to another teen, Janine, who takes out all of her life's frustrations on their 14-month-old son. As a result, Robbie responds violently to her violence toward the baby. It isn't until they attend a parents' help group that they gain insights into their behaviors and attempt to change them.

6.17.   Asher, Sandy. (1987). *Everything is not enough*. New York: Dell. 155 pp. (ISBN: 0-440-20002-4)

While at his parents' summer home, Michael gets a job at the Jolly Mackerel where he befriends two co-workers, Linda and Tricia. He just wants to be friends, but Tricia has an overly possessive and insanely jealous boyfriend who misconstrues his friendliness. Under normal circumstances, he would just back off, but he finds that difficult when he learns that Tricia's boyfriend beats her.

6.18.   Byars, Betsy. (1985). *Cracker Jackson*. New York: Viking Kestrel. 147 pp. (ISBN: 0-670-80546-7)

Cracker cannot help but notice the bruises on Alma, his babysitter. Even though Cracker is only 11 years old, he is instrumental in getting Alma to get away from Billy Ray, her husband, who beats her and their baby. Billy Ray eventually turns his anger towards Cracker and his friends for getting involved.

6.19.   Conrad, Pam. (1987). *Holding me here*. New York: 147 pp.

See Divorced and Single Parents

6.20.   Cormier, Robert. (1990). *Other bells for us to ring*. New York: Delacorte Press. 136 pp. (ISBN: 0-385-30245-2)

Eleven-year-old Darcy Webster and her family move to Frenchtown, Massachusetts, where she meets Kathleen Mary O'Hara. Set in the Depression, Darcy's father joins the army but Kathleen Mary's father does not. Darcy soon learns that Kathleen Mary's father has a bad leg which prevents him from being able to serve. She also learns that Mr. O'Hara drinks too much and has a violent temper. After a tragic accident, Darcy loses the best friend she ever had.

6.21.   Cormier, Robert. (1992). *Tunes for bears to dance to*. 101 pp.

See Death and Dying

6.22.   Crutcher, Chris. (1990). *Stotan!* New York: Dell Laurel-Leaf. 192 pp. (ISBN: 0-440-97570-0)

Walter Dupree and his friends are on the varsity swim team. When they volunteer for Stotan Week, they know they are in for some tough workouts. "A Stotan is a cross between a Stoic and a Spartan. He's tough and he shows no pain." After some grueling physical workouts, the boys endure some emotional workouts as well. (an American Library Association Best of the Best Books for Young Adults)

6.23.   Culin, Charlotte. (1979). *Cages of glass, flowers of time*. New York: Bradbury Press. 316 pp. (ISBN: 0-87888-157-3).

The different aspects of abuse--physical, mental, and the abused child's feelings of obligation to take care of the abuser--are explored in this novel. The story centers around Claire, a 14-year-old girl who was abandoned by her father and put into the custody of an abusive, alcoholic mother. Claire is an aspiring artist, but her mother physically threatens her and forbids her to draw. As so many abused children do, Claire tries to protect her mother until she is almost killed by the woman. Claire wants to lead a normal life but is afraid to open up or get close to anyone. Finally, she meets an old black man, Mr. Beasley, who helps her feel that there are people that she can trust. She also meets and eventually falls in love with a boy from school, Clyde, who helps her develop inner strength. With the help of these two characters, Claire makes some wonderful discoveries and develops a conviction to be strong and survive.

6.24.   Davis, Jenny. (1988). *Sex education*. New York: Orchard Books. 150 pp. (ISBN: 0-531-05756-9)

Olivia and David meet in Mrs. Fulton's biology class, a class which has a profound effect on both of their lives. Disturbed by the growing number of teenage pregnancies, Mrs. Fulton decides to alter her teaching methods and make the assignments more real for the students. Olivia and David team up for the caring project, a project where they must learn how to care for someone other than themselves in a nonsexual way. When Mr. and Mrs. Parker move into their neighborhood, the pair decides that Mrs. Parker will be the recipient of their care--after all, she's pregnant.

6.25.   DeClements, Barthe. (1986). *I never asked you to understand me*. 138 pp.

See Death and Dying

6.26.   Geller, Mark. (1988). *Raymond*. New York: Harper & Row. 89 pp. (ISBN: 0-06-022207-7)

Raymond and his mother are regularly beaten by his abusive father. One day Raymond can't take it any longer and strikes back, hitting his father over the head with a porcelain statue. He runs away from home and then returns to convince his mother to join him in living with his sister.

6.27.   Roberts, Willo Davis. (1978). *Don't hurt Laurie!* New York: Atheneum. 166 pp. (ISBN: 0-689-30571-0)

At 11, Laurie knows about abuse "fist-hand" from her mother. Because she's scared to tell anyone, Laurie takes the abuse until her mother goes too far. After being beaten so badly by a poker that she is knocked out, Laurie finally tells someone what is going on. Her mother is hospitalized for mental illness and confesses that she, herself, had been an abused child.

6.28.   Sweeney, Joyce. (1984). *Center line*. New York: Delacorte Press. 246 pp. (ISBN: 0-385-29320-8)

Five brothers, aged 14 to 18, decide to run away from their physically abusive father. They steal their father's car and use the eldest brother's college savings to finance their escape from Ohio to Florida. Determined not to let their decision become a mistake, the brothers try to cooperate as much as their individual personalities will allow. Along the way, each boy experiences his own lessons of maturity, loyalty, and responsibility. One brother is left in Indiana to marry his new-found love, and another brother leaves for Chicago to find his own freedom. The other three brothers remain together in Florida, suffering from their past yet enjoying the success of their decision. (First Delacorte Press Prize for an Outstanding First Young Adult Novel and an American Library Association Best Book for Young Adults)

6.29.   Sweeney, Joyce. (1992). *Piano man.* New York: Delacorte Press. 227 pp. (ISBN: 0-385-30534-6)

Although this novel is primarily about the relationship between 14-year-old Diedre and her infatuation with a 26-year-old piano player, it also deals with the abusive relationship of Diedre's cousin and her violent boyfriend. Another subplot involves Diedre's mother who finally begins to date after the death of Diedre's father.

6.30.   Woolverton, Linda. (1987). *Running before the wind.* Boston: Houghton Mifflin. 152 pp. (ISBN: 0-395-42116-0)

The most important thing in Kelly's life at 13 is running. It used to be the same for her father until he developed Polio and is unable to run anymore. His handicap makes him abusive, and he goes crazy anytime the word "running" is even mentioned. Kelly's mother and sister do everything to placate her father, so Kelly is often the one to receive the brunt of his wrath. Eventually, Kelly is released from her father's anger but a new trap is in store for her; she, too, has a violent temper. (a 1989 Young Adults' Choice)

Sexual Abuse

6.31.   Asher, Sandy. (1983). *Things are seldom what they seem.* New York: Delacorte Press. 134 pp. (ISBN: 0-440-08932-8)

Mr. Carraway, the handsome drama coach, has all of the high school girls wanting to be in the school play. All of the girls, including Debbie's older sister, Maggie, and best friend, Karen, are crazy about him. Fourteen-year-old Debbie is not so sure. When Karen suddenly quits the play and Mr. Carraway resigns shortly thereafter, Debbie learns the horrible truth. Mr. Carraway has molested Karen as well as Maggie. When Mr. Carraway takes a job at another school, the girls are faced with an awful dilemma: Should they expose what he did to them and suffer the humiliation or allow him to continue molesting girls at this other school?

6.32.   Borich, Michael. (1987). *A different kind of love*. New York: Signet Books. 160 pp. (ISBN: 0451-14718-9) (Out of Print)

Fourteen-year-old Elizabeth, better known as Weeble, lives with her mother on the West Coast, far away from the rest of their family in Indiana. When Uncle Nicky, her mother's 25-year-old brother comes to visit, she turns to him for the love and support that seem to be missing from her life; she just loves her rock-and-roll-playing uncle. She sees Uncle Nicky as a father figure, but he sees her differently. When Uncle Nicky makes sexual advances, Weeble grapples with the problem of incest and confides in a trusted teacher who convinces Weeble to tell her mother.

6.33.   Crutcher, Chris. (1991). *Chinese handcuffs*. 220 pp.

See Stress and Suicide

6.34.   Dizenzo, Patricia. (1987). *Why me? The story of Jenny*. New York: Avon Flare. 144 pp. (ISBN: 0-380-00563-8)

Jenny accepted a ride home from what appeared to be nice boy. At first Jenny thought he missed her road by accident, but his intentions became perfectly clear when he pulled into a deserted factory road and threatened her with his knife. After the rape, Jenny is too ashamed, embarrassed, and afraid to tell anyone. Alone, she worries about the possibility of being pregnant and counts the days until her next period. She wonders about the possibility of disease and is traumatized each time she sees the rapist's face on almost any man. Finally, she tells her parents and the police but finds that her waiting to tell has made the situation even more complicated.

6.35.   Futcher, Jane. (1991). *Promise not to tell*. New York: Avon Books. 192 pp. (ISBN: 0-380-76037-1)

Without sounding preachy, this novel explores a teenage girl's dealing with her sexual abuse.

6.36.   Hamilton, Morse. (1990). *Effie's house*. New York: Greenwillow Books. 224 pp. (ISBN: 0-688-09307-8).

Bizzy Brooke, an already troubled teenager, runs away from home after getting pregnant by her fourth stepfather. While away, she records her thoughts about her mother and biological father, a man who was killed in Vietnam prior to her birth. She shares her views about her other stepfathers and her decision to keep the baby. The title reflects Bizzy's dream of wanting to provide her unborn baby with a stable home and family life, something Bizzy has never had.

6.37. Hermes, Patricia. (1985). *A solitary secret*. San Diego: Harcourt, Brace, & Jovanovich. 135 pp. (ISBN: 0-152-77190-5)

A 14-year-old girl describes the breakdown of her family, a breakdown which occurs because she has been frequently sexually abused by her father. The novel portrays her difficulty in trying to function outwardly and her struggle to cope emotionally.

6.38. Howard, Ellen. (1986). *Gillyflower*. New York: Atheneum. 106 pp. (ISBN: 0-689-31274-1)

Gilly's father is sexually abusing her when her mother is at work in the afternoons and evenings. Gilly feels terrible and wishes she were somebody else. She is additionally bothered with thoughts that her father is also molesting her younger sister, Honey.

6.39. Irwin, Hadley. (1985). *Abby, my love*. New York: Atheneum. 146 pp. (ISBN: 0-689-50323-7)

While Chip sits through Abby's high school graduation, he reminisces about their friendship of the past four years. Whenever they started getting too close by Abby's standards, Abby would suddenly become distant. Her discomfort with intimacy becomes apparent when Abby finally confides in him that her father, a man no one would suspect in a million years, has been sexually abusing her. With the help of Chip and Chip's mother, Abby exposes her father. Initially Abby's mother denies the accusations but is eventually convinced and seeks help for all concerned. (an American Library Association Best of the Best Books for Young Adults, a Notable Children's Trade Book in the Field of Social Studies, and an IRA/CBC Children's Choice)

6.40. Levy, Marilyn. (1989). *Putting Heather together again*. New York: Ballantine (Fawcett Juniper). 144 pp. (ISBN: 0-449-70312-6)

Seventeen-year-old Heather has dated Joe a few times, but one night he forces her to have sex with him. Because she feels unsure about her own role in regards to the rape, she has a difficult time letting her parents and friends know about it. Eventually she gets help, and the reader shares in Heather's feelings in coming to terms with what happened.

6.41. Maclean, John. (1989). *Mac*. New York: Avon Books. 192 pp. (ISBN: 0-380-70700-4).

Mac, an outgoing, vibrant 15-year-old, is a good student and a valued player on the school's soccer team. All of a sudden, for no apparent reason, Mac's personality completely changes: Mac's grades plummet, he starts fighting, quits the soccer team, and becomes very withdrawn and defiant. One of Mac's teachers notices the change in him and is instrumental in his talking to a guidance counselor but to no avail. A second counselor tries to help, and after many sessions, Mac finally reveals that he has been sexually abused. The terror and anxiety Mac has been living with over the last several months become evident. The remainder of the book deals with Mac making peace with himself, his family, and his girlfriend.

6.42.   Mazer, Norma Fox. (1989). *Silver*. New York: Avon Books. 208 pp. (ISBN: 0-380-75026-0)

Sarabeth Silver never thought of herself as poor until she transfers to a school "where all the rich kids go." She is the only person who lives in a trailer with a mother who cleans houses for a living. Sarabeth decides she wants to befriend Grant, a popular girl who is in tight with a bunch of really neat girls. In Sarabeth's eyes, these girls have ideal lives: They have nice friends, nice clothes, nice families, and live in nice houses. After Sarabeth is accepted into this group, she learns that they have their own problems--one girl has been sexually abused by her uncle.

6.43.   Miklowitz, Gloria D. (1989). *Secrets not meant to be kept*. New York: Dell Laurel-Leaf. 144 pp. (ISBN: 0-440-20334-1)

Adrienne is a 16-year-old girl who is having difficulty being close with Ryan, a boy she loves. She does not know why, but she has strange flashbacks of her early childhood which she does not understand. Becky, Adri's 3-year-old sister, begins to do things that indicate that unnatural things are going on at Treehouse the same preschool Adri attended when she was little. Memories and investigation lead Adri to uncover that the children at the preschool are being sexually abused by the staff. The novel deals with the denial and guilt that the parents feel when they find out about these horrors and provides a hopeful message for abused children.

6.44.   Nathanson, Laura. (1987). *The trouble with Wednesdays*. New York: Bantam Books. 176 pp. (ISBN: 0-553-26337-4)

It becomes very important for Becky to get her fang-like teeth fixed when she is in the 6th grade. At first she is overjoyed when her father's cousin, a dentist, agrees to fit her with braces and make the frequently needed adjustments. Unfortunately, her dream to feel pretty turns into a nightmare when he begins to touch her in inappropriate ways.

6.45.   Peck, Richard. (1990). *Are you in the house alone?* New York: Dell Laurel-Leaf. 176 pp. (ISBN: 0-440-90227-4)

Harassed by obscene notes and phone calls that go dead as soon as she answers, Gail Osburne is finally confronted by the tormentor and is raped. This novel is about Gail's problems--physical, emotional, and judicial--that she faces after her trauma. (an American Library Association Best of the Best Books for Young Adults, the Edgar Allan Poe Mystery Award, and a *School Library Journal* Best Book of the Year)

6.46.   Scoppettone, Sandra. (1991). *Happy endings are all alike.* 202 pp.

See Homosexuality

6.47.   Southerland, Ellease. (1989). *Let the lion eat straw.* New York: New American Library. 165 pp. (ISBN: 0-8124-2527-8)

Abeba Williams experiences many changes in just a short time. First, her mother moves her from the rural South to New York City to live with her new stepfather. Second, Arthur Lavoisier is completely different than expected; he is kind, loving and generous. When Arthur unexpectedly dies, she and her mother move into the ghetto because of the financial stress. Then her uncle forces himself on her in spite of her being only twelve. She eventually finds love from a minister and solace in her music.

6.48.   Tapp, Kathy Kennedy. (1989). *The sacred circle of the hula hoop.* New York: Margaret K. McElderry. 208 pp. (ISBN: 0-689-50461-6)

Robin tells the story of the effects of her sister's mental illness and suicide attempt on their family's lives. Robin gives Jen a hula hoop as a gift, and it symbolically represents how things can come full circle when it is revealed how Jen is a victim of sexual, child abuse.

6.49.   White, Ruth. (1992). *Weeping willow.* New York: Farrar, Straus, & Giroux. 246 pp. (ISBN: 0-374-38255-7)

Set in the Fifties when counseling was not an option, Tiny Lambert has had to deal with the sexual abuse by her stepfather--alone. She uses fantasy to escape her pain but chooses to tell her mother when the threat of her stepfather becomes a harsh reality for her younger half sister.

Annotated Young Adult Nonfiction Dealing with Abuse

6.50. Broadhurst, Diane D. (1984). *The educator's role in the prevention and treatment of child abuse and neglect.* Washington, D.C.: National Center on Child Abuse and Neglect. 53 pp. (serial reprint)

Educators are the people who see children on a daily basis. It is important for school personnel to be aware of and know what to do in cases of child abuse. Various topics are covered: recognizing the signs of neglect and/or abuse, reporting such cases--before and after, and preventing child abuse.

6.51. D'Ambrosio, Richard. (1990). *No language but a cry.* New York: Dell Laurel-Leaf. 320 pp. (ISBN: 0-440-36457-4)

This is the true story about a little girl who suffered from such emotional and physical abuse that she became mute. Through professional help, she is eventually freed from her terrifying memories.

6.52. Garbarino, James & Gilliam, Gwen. (1984). *Understanding abusive families.* New York: Free Press. 288 pp. (ISBN: 0-669-09782-9)

A discussion about why abuse exists in families and what to do about it is provided.

6.53. Kempe, C. Henry & Helfer, Ray E. (1980). *The battered child, 3rd edition.* Chicago, Illinois: University of Chicago Press. 440 pp. (ISBN: 0-226-43038-3)

The authors provide a historical overview of abuse, a look at other cultures, the relationship of alcohol and drugs to abuse, and the consequences of abuse and neglect.

6.54. Lynch, Margaret A. & Roberts, Jacqueline. (1982). *Consequences of child abuse.* London: Academic Press. 226 pp. (ISBN: 0-124-60570-2)

The authors did a follow-up study on 41 children out of an original sample of 42 and found that all but nine children had emotional problems they had to live with. As a result, the authors conclude that emphasis should be placed on the prevention of abuse rather than on more and better treatment.

6.55. O'Brien, Shirley. (1980). *Child abuse: A crying shame.* Provo, UT: Brigham Young University Press. 198 pp. (ISBN: 0-8425-1829-0)

Useful information is provided for anyone concerned about child abuse in this country. Parents, educators, day care personnel, students, or anyone who's concerned about kids will find it helpful. Useful statistics are also included.

Physical Abuse

6.56. Prendergast, Alan. (1986). *The poison tree: A true story of family violence and revenge.* New York: G.P. Putnam's Sons. 350 pp. (ISBN: 0-399-13138-8)

This is a truc story about the Jahnke family. Richard C. Jahnke married Maria and had two children, Deborah and Richard. Richard Senior was violently abusive to his wife and son and sexually abusive to his daughter. In 1982, young Richard couldn't take it anymore and murdered his father. This book, which reads like a novel, should only be read under the supervision of an adult. Many adolescents in abusive situations will see similar patterns in their own lives. It is imperative that teenagers are helped to find ways to solve their problems in constructive, acceptable, and non-violent ways.

Sexual Abuse

6.57. Bode, Janet. (1992). *The voices of rape: Healing the hurt.* New York: Dell. 143 pp. (ISBN: 0-440-21301-0)

In a very sensitive way, the author provides the victims with information to hclp ease their pain.

6.58. Hyde, Margaret O. (1987). *Sexual abuse: Let's talk about it.* Philadelphia: Westminster Press. 107 pp. (ISBN: 0-664-32725-7)

The author includes the stories of young adults who have been sexually abused and tells how children can protect themselves if they are victims. Addresses of places to go to for help and more information are also provided.

6.59. Kempe, Ruth S. & Kempe, C. Henry. (1984). *The common secret: Sexual abuse of children and adolescents.* New York: W.H. Freeman. 284 pp. (ISBN: 0-716-71625-9)

Using their 25 years of experience with child abuse studies as a base, the authors provide useful information regarding the nature of sexual abuse; the legal aspects of it; and how to detect, treat, and prevent such abuse. Technical terms are absent.

6.60.   Kosof, Anna. (1985). *Incest: Families in crisis.* New York: Franklin Watts. 101 pp. (ISBN: 0-531-10071-5)

The author explores the family situations where incest occurs and the importance of telling the secret. Children who have been the victims of incest and child abuse often grow up as troubled adults who repeat these abuses on their own children. The book includes a list of places a person can call or write to for additional information and help.

6.61.   Ledray, Linda E. (1986). *Recovering from rape.* New York: Henry Holt & Company. 258 pp. (ISBN: 0-030-64001-6) (Out of Stock)

Rape is a traumatic experience for even the most together and mature women. For adolescents, with their limited life experiences and generally protected environments, the long-term effects may seem impossible to overcome. Ledray offers some suggestions for victims and their families and friends on how to help the recovery process. Information is also included on how to report the crime, how to deal with child sexual abuse, profiles of rapists, and how to prevent such an attack. The author also provides a list of Rape Crisis Centers, a decent bibliography, and an excellent index.

6.62.   Mrazek, Patricia Beezley & Kempe, C. Henry. Eds. (1987). *Sexually abused children and their families.* New York: Permagon Press. 271 pp. (ISBN: 0-080-30194-0)

A comprehensive view of sexually abused children and their families is provided. Topics include the history of sexual abuse, its effects on families, treatment, being a parent at different ages--adolescence, early twenties, and mid-life--and the legal system in the U.S. and Europe as it pertains to abuse.

Nonfiction References Dealing with Abuse

Journal Articles

Adams-Tucker, C. (1985, January-February). Defense mechanisms used by sexually abused children. *Children Today, 14* (1), p. 8 ff.

Bear, T., Schenk, S., & Buckner, L. (1992-1993, December-January). Supporting victims of child abuse. *Educational Leadership, 50* (4), p. 42 ff.

Beck, M. (1984, August 20). An epidemic of child abuse. *Newsweek, 104* (8),p. 44 ff.

Brenner, A. (1985, May). Wednesday's child. *Psychology Today, 19* (5), p. 46 ff.

Craig, S.E. (1992, September). The educational needs of children living with violence. *Phi Delta Kappan, 74* (1), p. 67 ff.

Distad, L. (1987, June). A personal legacy. *Phi Delta Kappan, 68* (10), p. 744 ff.

Edelman, M.W. (1989, May). Defending America's children. *Educational Leadership, 46* (8), p. 77 ff.

Emans, R.L. (1987, June). Abuse in the name of protecting children. *Phi Delta Kappan, 68* (10), p. 740 ff.

Finkelhor, D. (1984, July-August). How widespread is child sexual abuse? *Children Today, 13* (4), p. 18 ff.

Fontana, V.J. (1984, July-August). When systems fail: Protecting the victim of child sexual abuse. *Children Today, 13* (4), p. 14 ff.

Harrison, R. (1986, September). The unspeakable problem of sexual abuse and what you can do about it. *Learning, 15* (2), p. 71 ff.

Harrison, R. (1985, August). How you can help the abused child. *Learning, 14* (1), p. 74 ff.

Henry, M.J. (1985, Spring). Family violence. *Early Childhood Education, 18* (1), p. 15 ff.

Herman, P. (1985, January-February). Educating children about sexual abuse: The teacher's responsibility. *Childhood Education, 61* (3), p. 169 ff.

Hittleman, M. (1985, January). Sexual abuse: Teaching about touching. *School Library Journal, 31* (5), p. 34 ff.

Hurwitz, B.D. (1985, April). Suspicion: Child abuse. *Instructor, 94* (8), p. 76 ff.

Karstaedt, J. (1985, Spring). A discussion on incest. *Early Childhood Education, 18* (1), p. 21 ff.

Krueger, M.M. (1993, March). Everyone is an exception: Assumptions to avoid in the sex education classroom. *Phi Delta Kappan, 74* (7), p. 569 ff.

Leo, J. (1984, April 23). Someday I'll cry my eyes out. *Time, 123* (17), p. 72 ff.

Lundstrom, M. & Sharpe, R. (1991). Getting away with murder. *Public Welfare, 49* (3), p. 18 ff.

Moore, K.A., Nord, C.W., & Peterson, J.L. (1989). Nonvoluntary sexual activity among adolescents. *Family Planning Perspectives, 21* (3), p. 110 ff.

Roscoe, B. (1984, Fall). Sexual abuse: The educator's role in identification and interaction with abuse victims. *Education, 105* (1), p. 82 ff.

Tanner, C. (1985, Summer). Helping abused children: Can we? How? *Education, 105* (4), p. 354.

Wilson, J., Thomas, D., & Schuette, L. (1983, Fall). The silent screams: Recognizing abused children. *Education, 104* (1), p. 100 ff.

Zigler, E. & Rubin, N. (1985, November). Why child abuse occurs. *Parents, 60* (11), p. 102 ff.

Books

Cline, R.K.J. (1990). *Focus on families.* Santa Barbara, CA: ABC-CLIO. 233 pp. (ISBN: 0-87436-508-2)

Garbarino, J., Guttman, E., & Seeley, J.W. (1986). *The psychologically battered child.* San Francisco: Jossey-Bass. 286 pp. (ISBN: 1-555-42002-8)

Gil, E. (1988). *Treatment of adult.* CA: Launch Press. 301 pp. (ISBN: 0-961-32056-7)

Mufson, S. & Kranz, R. (1993). *Straight talk about child abuse.* New York: Dell. (ISBN: 0-440-21349-5)

Tower, C.C. (1987). *How schools can help combat child abuse and neglect, 2nd Ed.* Washington, D.C.: National Education Association. 224 pp. (ISBN: 0-810-63295-0)

Walker, E., Bonner, B., & Kaufman, K. (1988). *The physically and sexually abused child.* New York: Permagon Press. 218 pp. (ISBN: 0-080-32768-0)

CHAPTER 7

Eating Disorders: Anorexia Nervosa and Bulimia

Poor nutritional habits, eating junk foods, and overeating because of tension or boredom are relatively common eating problems for adolescents. Anorexia nervosa and bulimia, on the other hand, are two very serious psychiatric eating disorders that are on the increase among teenage girls and young women. Although these disorders are predominantly found in adolescent girls, boys involved in sports requiring specific weights often engage in unhealthy eating behaviors. Adolescents with anorexia nervosa are starving themselves in a relentless pursuit to be thin. This behavior often reaches the point of serious damage to the body, and in some instances results in death. A bulimic teenager who is regularly bingeing and purging often suffers from dehydration, hormonal imbalance, the depletion of important minerals, and damage to vital organs. Our cultural obsession with weight and appearance has had its negative effect on our youth. Recent attention to the media's preoccupation with thin, attractive people might produce a more normal array of talent portrayed in advertising but don't count on it.

STARTLING INFORMATION ABOUT EATING DISORDERS

- One-third of high school girls perceive themselves as overweight, and those who think that their weight is okay are trying to lose weight anyway. (National Centers for Disease Control, 1991)

- Teenagers are very successful in hiding these disorders from their families and have been known to do so for months and years at a time. (American Academy of Child & Adolescent Psychiatry, *Facts for Families*, 1992)

- Approximately 2 out of 10 school-aged youth are affected by anorexia nervosa and bulimia. (Phelps & Bajorek, 1991)

Anorexia Nervosa

- Ninety-five percent of people with anorexia nervosa are female. (American Psychiatric Association, 1987)

- Anorexia nervosa usually affects girls between the ages of 13 and 19. (Field, 1987)

- The majority of teens who develop anorexia nervosa are either at normal weight or about 10% over; obese teens developing this disorder are the exception, not the rule. (Akeroy-Guillory, 1988)

- Between 5% and 10% of those who become anorectic will die because of medical problems associated with malnutrition. (Gilbert & DeBlassie, 1984)

Bulimia

- Eighty percent of all high school girls have intentionally exercised in order to lose weight, 21% have taken diet pills, and 14% have intentionally vomited to lose weight. (National Centers for Disease Control, 1991)

- Among high school girls who perceive themselves to be fat, 95% had tried to lose weight through exercise, 34% used diet pills, and 23% had vomited to lose weight. (National Centers for Disease Control, 1991)

- Bulimic teens can eat up to 20,000 calories of easily ingested, highly caloric food within a two-hour time frame before purging. (Phelps & Bajorek, 1991)

WARNING SIGNS OF ADOLESCENTS WITH EATING DISORDERS

Anorexia Nervosa

- Extreme weight loss.

- Perfectionists and high achievers at school who suffer from low self-esteem.

- Desperately need a feeling of control over their lives.

- Irrationally believe that they are fat regardless of how thin they really are, have an intense fear of gaining any weight, engage in frequent conversations about weight loss.

- Eat slowly in little bits, often rearrange food on plate to give the appearance that more was eaten than really was, avoid eating at the dinner table, adamantly refuse to eat, deny hunger and often "ate somewhere else".

- Skin looks dry, pale, or gray, then dark and scaly.

- Lanugo or baby-like hair on the body, thinning of hair on head, menstruation stops, brittle nails.

- Almost always cold due to lack of insulation from insufficient body fat, lethargic, suffer from insomnia.

Bulimia

- Binge on huge quantities of high-caloric food and then purge the body of dreaded calories by self-induced vomiting or by using laxatives.

- Binges may alternate with severe diets resulting in dramatic weight fluctuations.

- Adolescents often try to hide the signs of vomiting by running water while spending long periods of time in the bathroom.

- Overactivity and obsessive exercising.

- Digestive problems, nausea, and stomach cramps.

- Difficulty swallowing and retaining food.

- Bursting blood vessels in the eyes, excessive tooth decay and loss of tooth enamel.

WHAT TO DO AND WHERE TO GO FOR HELP

- Both anorexia nervosa and bulimia are serious disorders that cannot be taken lightly.

- Report any suspicious symptoms to a trained professional as soon as possible since success of recovery is related to early detection.

- Get professional help: Call crisis intervention centers, mental health clinics, hospitals, a family physician, a clergy, a guidance counselor, or a teacher. If you need immediate help, call the Rader Institute at 1-800-255-1818. For more information, write to the National Association of Anorexia Nervosa and Associated Disorders (ANAD), P.O. Box 7, Highland Park, Illinois, 60035; or The American Anorexia Nervosa Association (AANA), 133 Cedar Lane, Teaneck, New Jersey, 07666.

Annotated Young Adult Novels Dealing with Eating Disorders

7.01.   Hautzig, Deborah. (1989). *Second star to the right*. New York: Alfred A. Knopf. 151 pp. (ISBN: 0-394-82028-2) (Out of Stock)

Fourteen-year-old Leslie Hiller tries to remember details which may have contributed to her acquiring anorexia nervosa; she honestly doesn't know the cause. After all, she has wealthy, loving parents who think she is wonderful. Her story begins at a point of normalcy and moves to the reality of a hospital ward where she is among eating disorder patients. Solutions and answers are not given, and no miracle cure changes Leslie's life. The book simply attempts to help the reader understand the confusion and helplessness that an anorectic experiences.

7.02.   Holland, Isabelle. (1973). *Heads you win, tails I lose*. Philadelphia: J.B. Lippincott. 159 pp. (ISBN: 0-397-31380-2)

Melissa is a troubled 15-year-old with verbally abusive parents. Her parents constantly fight and use her as a weapon to hurt each other. Melissa is overweight and extremely self-conscious about it. If she were just thin, Melissa believes her world would be better because she would be popular and loved. She finds a bottle of diet pills in her mother's dresser and becomes addicted to them. She is unaware of her self-destructive behavior and doesn't realize that she is upsetting those who care about her. She finally admits that she has a problem and gets the medical attention that she needs.

7.03.   Josephs, Rebecca. (1980). *Early disorder*. New York: Farrar, Straus, & Giroux. 185 pp. (ISBN: 0-374-14579-2)

Written in first person, this is the story of Willa Rahv and her struggle with feelings of inadequacy. Her mother is a "supermom," a woman who left her career in order to raise her family. Willa's mother does everything right-- too right. In vivid description, Willa tells about her need to drop half of her body weight in order to be happy because "Calories are the one thing [she] can control. The only thing."

7.04.   Levenkron, Steven. (1991). *The best little girl in the world.* New York: Warner Books. 253 pp. (ISBN: 0-446-35865-7)

Francesca, whose alias is Kessa, is a 15-year-old girl who almost entirely stops eating. Kessa think she's grotesquely overweight even though she is only five-foot-four and 98 pounds. She saves pictures of the thinnest models from fashion magazines and chants, "Soon I'll be thinner than all you. The thinner is the winner." The story is her journey into a fantasy world and back to healthy reality. The novel accurately details what a person goes through who suffers from anorexia nervosa and is a good read for anyone with a penchant for dieting too much. (an American Library Association Best Book)

7.05.   Levenkron, Steven. (1986). *Kessa.* New York: Warner Books. 247 pp. (ISBN: 0-445-20175-4)

A sequel to *The Best Little Girl in the World,* tells the story of Kessa's struggle not to succumb to the fatal disease of anorexia nervosa again. Kessa reveals her true feelings about the world and herself during her therapy sessions. Additionally, Kessa finds herself on the other side of the situation as she watches a close friend suffer from the disease and feels powerless to help.

7.06.   Madison, Winifred. (1979). *A portrait of myself.* New York: Random House. 239 pp. (ISBN: 0-394-84021)

Catherine D'Amato enjoys dancing and is hoping to make the dance team at her school. When she doesn't make the tryouts, she becomes depressed and obsessed with becoming just like her tall and slender gym teacher Miss Alcott. Miss Alcott is unaware of Catherine's unhealthy eating habits and overreacts negatively when Catherine visits her at her home. Miss Alcott's rejection puts Catherine over the edge and Catherine makes a suicide attempt which ultimately leads to help.

7.07.   Oppenheimer, Joan L. (1987). *Toughing it out.* New York: Simon & Schuster Trade. (ISBN: 0-373-98003-5)

A teenage girl develops a very poor self image and feels insignificant and unwanted due to her home environment. Her father is a hard driving executive who doesn't want to get involved with mere family problems, and her mother is constantly driving her daughter to do better in everything. When she begins dieting to lose a few extra pounds, she suddenly finds an aspect of her life that she controls and takes it to unfortunate extremes. She is initially successful at hiding her bizarre eating habits, fainting spells, and nausea, but eventually her behavior is noticed by her mother who reacts poorly to the possibility of her daughter's being anorectic. A caring and understanding doctor takes a personal interest in the girl's case when she is hospitalized, and he manages to help her rebuild her self esteem. In the process, he lets her parents know that they must alter their lifestyles to prevent a reoccurrence.

7.08. Snyder, Anne. (1988). *Goodbye, paper doll*. New York: Signet Books. 155 pp. (ISBN: 0-451-15943-8)

Although Rosemary is bright and beautiful, she gets caught up in anorexia nervosa. This novel explores the question as to why a 17-year-old girl who has everything going for her decides to starve herself to death.

7.09. Stren, Patti. (1986). *I was a 15-year-old blimp*. New York: Signet Books. 160 pp. (ISBN: 0-451-14577-1)

Fifteen-year-old Gabby thinks she is too fat to attract the attention of a particular boy she likes. Because she wants instant results, she resorts to taking laxatives and purging (throwing up) her meals. Things get out of hand and Gabby's parents end up having to send her to a special camp for people with eating disorders. Without sounding preachy, Stren sends the message that there is help available for bulimic individuals.

7.10. Terry, Susan. (1988). *Nell's quilt*. New York: Scholastic. 177 pp. (ISBN: 0-590-41914-5)

Nell feels like she is living in the dark ages even though it is 1899. She has aspirations of getting an education and making something of herself, but her parents are trying to coerce her into marrying her cousin. She decides to fight this insanity by making herself undesirable and escaping into the creation of a new quilt. As the quilt gets heavier, Nell gets lighter while she slowly starves herself.

Annotated Young Adult Nonfiction Dealing with Eating Disorders

7.11. Bruch, Hilde. (1979). *The golden cage: The enigma of anorexia Nervosa*. New York: Vintage Trade Books. 159 pp. (ISBN: 0-394-72688-X)

In this book, Dr. Bruch presents detailed case studies of anorectic individuals in order to give a vivid picture of the disease's possible causes, effects, and treatment.

7.12.   Eagles, Douglas A. (1987). *Nutritional diseases*. New York: Franklin Watts/First Books. 96 pp. (ISBN: 0-531-10391-9)

Diseases that are related to nutritional disorders are examined in this book. Included is information about anorexia nervosa and bulimia, osteoporosis, arteriosclerosis, phenylketonuria, and diabetes. The development, symptoms, treatment, and possible prevention of these disorders are also included.

7.13.   Ikeda, Joanne. (1987). *Winning weight loss for teens*. Menlo Park, CA: Bull Publishing Company. 103 pp. (ISBN: 0-915-95084-7)

The author presents a program for teenagers to alter their eating habits in order to lose weight. She encourages the participant to obtain familial support and to keep a food diary. Nutritional needs, exercise, and reasonable goals are stressed.

7.14.   Kolodny, Nancy J. (1992). *When food's a foe: How to confront and conquer eating disorders*. Boston: Little, Brown, & Company. 198 pp. (ISBN: 0-316-50181-6)

The causes and effects of bulimia and anorexia nervosa are discussed as well as ways these eating disorders can be prevented. This book is presented in a hands-on fashion. The reader is asked to engage in responding to checklists, questionnaires, and exercises in order to find solutions to personal problems.

7.15.   Miller, Caroline Adams. (1988). *My name is Caroline*. New York: Doubleday. 278 pp. (ISBN: 0-385-24208-5)

The author was 15 when she started bingeing and purging her food in order to stay thin for the swim team. Food became an obsession and a way for Caroline to feel in control of her life. After years of eating abuse, the bulimia got out of control and Caroline had to get help from professionals. A bulimia self test is included as well as information where one can get help and additional information.

7.16.   O'Neill, Cherry Boone. (1988). *Starving for attention*. New York: Dell. 240 pp. (ISBN: 0-440-17620-4)

This is the true story about Pat Boone's daughter, Cherry. Cherry's problem with anorexia nervosa began when she and her sisters started performing with their famous father. After awhile her eating disorder became so acute that it became a struggle between life and death. Cherry survived through her own courage and the undying support of her husband.

Nonfiction References Dealing with Eating Disorders

Journal Articles

Akeroyd-Guillory, D. (1988, September). A developmental view of anorexia nervosa. *The School Counselor, 36* (1), p. 24 ff.

Gilbert, E.H. & DeBlassie, R.R. (1984, Winter). Anorexia nervosa: Adolescent starvation by choice. *Adolescence, 19* (76), p. 839 ff.

Goode, E.E. (1988). Eating disorders hit both sexes and all incomes. *U.S. News and World Report,* p. 74 ff.

Goodman, N. (1992, August). My sister's illness and me. *Seventeen Magazine, 51* (8), p. 126 ff.

Lehrman, K. (1987, September). Anorexia and bulimia: Causes and cures. *Consumer Research,* p. 29 ff.

Marquardt, D. (1987, May). A thinly disguised message. *MS,* p. 33 ff.

Nassar, C.M., Hodges, P., & Ollendick, T. (1992, May). *The School Counselor, 39* (5), p. 338 ff.

Oldis, K. (1986, January). Anorexia nervosa: The more it grows, the more it starves. *English Journal, 75* (1), p. 84 ff.

Pantanizopoulos, J. (1990, Fall). 'I'll be happy when I'm thin enough:' The treatment of anorexia nervosa in adolescent literature. *The ALAN Review, 17* (1), p. 9 ff.

Phelps, L. & Bajorek, E. (1991). Eating disorders of the adolescent: Current issues in etiology, assessment, and treatment. *School Psychology Review, 20* (1), p. 9 ff.

Schwartz, D.M. & Thompson, M.G. (1981, March). Do anorectics get well? Current research and future needs. *American Journal of Psychiatry, 138* (3), p.319 ff.

Turvey, J.S. (1986, January). Anorexia nervosa: The more it grows, the more it starves. *English Journal, 75* (1), p. 84 ff.

Books

Arnold, C. (1984). *Too fat? Too thin? Do you have a choice?* New York: William Morrow. 100 pp. (ISBN: 0-688-02779-2)

Brumberg, J.J. (1989). *Fasting girls: The surprising history of anorexia nervosa.* New York: New American Library. 370 pp. (ISBN: 0-452-26327-1)

Field, H.L. & Domangue, B.B. (1987). *Eating disorders throughout the life span.* New York: Praeger. 157 pp. (ISBN: 0-275-92212-X)

Fitcher, M. (1990). *Bulimia nervosa: Basic research, diagnosis & therapy.* Chichester: John Wiley & Sons. 364 pp. (ISBN: 0-471-92405-9)

Landau, E. (1983). *Why are they starving themselves?* New York: Julian Messner. 110 pp. (ISBN: 0-671-45582-6)

Maloney, M. & Kranz, R. (1991). *Straight talk about eating disorders.* New York: Facts on File. 122 pp. (ISBN: 0-816-02414-6)

O'Neill, C.B. (1982). *Starving for attention.* New York: Continuum Publishing Company. 187 pp. (ISBN: 0-826-40209-7)

Oppenheimer, Joan L. (1987). *Toughing it out.* New York: Simon & Schuster Trade. (ISBN: 0-373-98003-5)

Palmer, R.L. (1980). *Anorexia nervosa: A guide for sufferers and their families.* New York: Penguin Books. 156 pp. (ISBN: 0-14-022065-8)

Ruckman, Ivy. (1983). *Hunger scream.* New York: Walker. 188 pp. (ISBN: 0-802-76514-9)

Willey, Margaret. (1983). *The bigger book of Lydia.* New York: Harper & Row. 215 pp. (ISBN: 0-060-26486-1)

CHAPTER 8

Alcohol and Drugs

The rapid growth of alcohol and drug use and abuse involving teenagers is one of the most pressing problems facing American society. School-age children are particularly susceptible to drug experimentation because of peer pressure and availability. Additionally, the national message of "Just Say No" is mixed up in the 100,000 beer commercials youth will see before their 18th birthdays, competing against countless slogans like, "Why ask why? Try Bud Dry." Unfortunately, the adolescent who learns to rely on substances to escape from daily stress will not learn much about healthier ways of coping with life. These teens will rely on chemicals instead of their brains to get through tough times and will pass that coping mechanism onto their own children. It has been said, "what we don't give back, we pass on." Through education, it is possible to break this growing cycle of substance abusers.

STARTLING INFORMATION ABOUT ALCOHOL AND DRUGS

- Between 11% and 18% of all babies born in the United States have been exposed prenatally to alcohol and/or drugs. (National Institute on Drug Abuse, 1992)

- By the year 2000, as many as four million drug exposed children will be attending school. (March of Dimes)

- Children growing up in substance abusing families learn not to trust, learn to be totally in control or totally out of it, learn to act out inappropriately, and learn how to deny their feelings. (Gress, 1992)

- Adolescents who begin to smoke or drink during their early teens are at particularly high risk for developing drug dependencies. (American Academy of Child & Adolescent Psychiatry, *Facts for Families*, 1992)

- By the time students become high school seniors, 90% have experimented with alcohol use and nearly two-thirds have used drugs. (National Institute on Drug Abuse, 1992)

Alcohol

- Alcohol-related accidents are the leading cause of deaths among teenagers. (National Association of State Boards of Education and the American Medical Association, 1990)

- Ten percent of any high school class in the U.S. (or two students per classroom) are beginning to exhibit some distracting symptoms of chemical dependency. (Dean, 1985)

- In 1986, about half of 13-year-old girls had been drunk at least once and 17% had been very drunk; for 17-year-old boys, the figures are 80% and 50% respectively. (Special Committee of the Royal College of Psychiatrists)

- Seventy-five percent of students report that they have used alcohol by the 8th grade. (Nowinski, 1990)

- According to the last several Gallup Polls of the Public Attitude Towards the Public Schools, dating back to 1986, drug use among students has consistently been identified as the number one problem faced by our public schools.

- Children of alcoholic parents have a 50-50 chance of becoming alcoholics themselves. (Ostrower, 1987)

- Approximately 350,000 newborns each year have been exposed prenatally to alcohol. (Stevens & Price, 1992)

- Between one-fourth and one-third of the entire school age population are living in a family with one or more alcoholics. (Gress, 1988)

- At least seven million children living in the United States have alcoholic parents. (American Academy of Child & Adolescent Psychiatry, *Facts for Families*, 1992)

Drugs

- Approximately 400,000 newborns each year have been exposed prenatally to crack or cocaine. (Waller & Scheckler, 1993)

- Inner-city teens facing unwanted pregnancies commonly use cocaine as a way to abort their babies. (Gregorchik, 1992)

- In 1974, the average age American high school students tried marijuana was 16; in 1984, the average age reported was 12. (Nowinski, 1990)

- In 1987, 1 in 15 teenagers admitted to trying cocaine, and 1 in 10 had smoked marijuana. By the senior year, 40% had used dangerous drugs, and 60% had used marijuana. (National Adolescent Student Health Survey)

WARNING SIGNS OF AN ADOLESCENT INVOLVED WITH ALCOHOL AND DRUGS

- Lasting fatigue, repeated health complaints, red and dull eyes, dilated pupils, steady cough.

- Personality change, sudden mood swings, irresponsible behavior, low self-esteem, depression, generally apathetic, decreased attention span, increased need for immediate gratification.

- Argumentative, breaks rules, withdraws from friends and family.

- Failure in school, sleeping in school, truancy, discipline problems, drop in grades.

- New friends who are less interested in standard home and school activities, problems with the law, wears less conventional styles in clothing, listens to heavy metal music.

- Indefinable fears, paranoia.

WHAT TO DO AND WHERE TO GO FOR HELP

- An effective way for concerned adults to help adolescents is to honestly discuss with them the use and abuse of alcohol and drugs.

- All adults can help adolescents by setting an example by living a drug-free life and not treating drug or alcohol use as glamorous or funny.

- Adolescents from substance abusing homes need to know that they are not the cause of the problem and that things can get better for them even if their parent or parents don't change.

- Get professional help: Call Alcoholics Anonymous, Al-Anon, Ala Teen, Adult Children of Alcoholics (ACOA), crisis intervention centers, mental health clinics, hospitals, a family physician, a clergy, a guidance counselor, or a teacher. If you need immediate help, call the 24-hour Drug and Alcohol Response Team at 1-800-868-8789. For more information, write to the American Academy of Child and Adolescent Psychiatry, 3615 Wisconsin Avenue, NW, Washington, D.C., 20016-3007; or to the Center for Alcohol and Substance Abuse Research and Prevention (CASARP), University of South Florida, Tampa, Florida, 33620-5650.

Annotated Young Adult Novels Dealing with Alcohol and Drugs

8.01. Adler, C.S. (1980). *In our house, Scott is my brother*. New York: Macmillan. 139 pp. (ISBN: 0-027-00140-7)

Jodi, a 13-year-old girl, has been living alone with her father since her mother's death three years ago. When her father marries Donna who brings her son, Scott, into the family, her life is completely disrupted. Scott ridicules Jodi, her friends, and her school, and constantly gets her in trouble for things that he does wrong. Jodi later learns that her new stepmother has a drinking problem and has relied on Scott for many years. Jodi develops new respect for Scott but their relationship is short-lived when Donna decides that she wants to leave.

8.02. Anonymous. (1972). *Go ask Alice*. New York: Avon Books. 189 pp. (ISBN: 0-380-00523-9)

This supposedly nonfiction book recounts a two year struggle of a middle-class, 15-year-old girl's growing up in the late 1960's while battling a drug addiction. Written in the form of a diary, which she calls "my only friend," the language and feeling have a sincerity that more than compensates for the occasional dated references to Haight-Ashbury, rolling hair on orange juice cans, and white pantsuits. From confusion about sex, love, and peer approval, Alice tries escaping from the confusion of growing up to the helpless horror of drug addiction which hits home the "Just Say No" message to teenagers. This book is powerful enough to shock some current and would-be drug users into reconsideration. (a Christopher Award Winner and an ALA Best Book for Young Adults)

8.03.   Arrick, Fran. (1984). *Nice girl from a good home*. New York: Bradbury Press. 199 pp. (ISBN: 0-027-05840-9)

Dory, a 16-year-old, has a lot of family problems. On the top of her list is her father who has developed a drinking problem since he has lost his job. Her mother compounds problems because she is a compulsive shopper and cannot stop it while her husband is unemployed. Dory's brother, Jeremy, is disappointed that he cannot go to a prestigious college because his family can't afford it anymore. Dory is upset that everything concerning her family life is out of control.

8.04.   Bell, William. (1987). *Crabbe's journey*. Boston: Little, Brown, & Company. (ISBN: 0-316-08837-4) (out of Print)

Franklin follows in his parents footsteps and becomes an alcoholic. His wealthy father practices law and his mother tends to the house, but neither tends to Franklin's needs. They send him to a psychiatric hospital where he escapes but realizes he's ill-equipped to survive on his own. Franklin has an accident and is helped by a woman who is also on the run; she committed a "mercy killing." Together they learn about survival and inner strength, and Franklin learns about the dangers of alcohol when they are confronted by drunken hunters.

8.05.   Bennet, Jay. (1982). *The executioner*. 176 pp.

See Death and Dying

8.06.   Bennet, Jay. (1987). *The haunted one*. 176 pp.

See Death and Dying

8.07.   Bridgers, Sue Ellen. (1987). *Permanent connections*. New York: Harper & Row. 264 pp. (ISBN: 0-06-020711-6)

This is the story of a young, middle-class, 17-year-old boy who lives with his family in Montclair, New Jersey. Because he is unable to deal with the strong criticism of his father and is unable to communicate openly with his family, Rob floats through school staying high most of the time to avoid conflicts and confrontations. After an uncle breaks a hip and is unable to maintain his farm in North Carolina, Rob is brought in to help his relatives. Rob hates living on the farm and can't relate to this new family either. Things change when he falls in love with Ellery Collier, a responsible "misfit" who helps him begin his ascent from apathy. Rob learns that what he does affects others, and their actions affect him also.

8.08.   Brooks, Bruce. (1989). *No kidding*. New York: Harper & Row. 207 pp. (ISBN: 0-06-020723-X)

Set in the 21st century, this futuristic novel looks at the possibility of alcoholism reaching epidemic proportions in the United States. The story centers around 14-year-old Sam whose mother is in a rehabilitation center. Sam's younger brother, Ollie, is in a foster home and is getting involved in a religious cult, and Sam is denying himself the childhood he needs as he tries to be the responsible one in his family.

8.09.   Bunting, Eve. (1990). *A sudden silence*. New York: Fawcett/Juniper Books. 105 pp. (ISBN: 0-449-70362-2)

Life for Jesse has always been tough since his little brother, Bryan, is deaf. Things get a whole lot tougher when Bryan is killed in a hit-and-run accident by a drunk driver. Jesse heard the car and barely jumped to safety; Bryan did not. Jesse and Chloe, Bryan's girlfriend, decide to find this person so that justice may be served. During their pursuit, they learn about alcoholism, grief, guilt, and our legal system.

8.10.   Butterworth, William Edmund. (1979). *Under the influence*. New York: Four Winds Press. 247 pp. (ISBN: 0-590-07465-2)

Keith Stevens and Allan Correli, two high school seniors, meet and befriend each other at football practice. Both of their parents lost their spouses through death and strike up their own relationship. Mrs. Stevens solicits the help from Mr. Correli, a police chief, to help her with her son's drinking problem. Keith's drinking unfortunately leads to tragedy for himself and others.

8.11.   Carter, Alden R. (1991). *Up country*. New York: Scholastic Books. 256 pp. (ISBN: 0-590-43638-4)

Sixteen-year-old Carl Staggers is doing his best to make something of himself in spite of his alcoholic mother and his involvement with stolen car stereos. He studies hard, hoping to be valedictorian of his class, so he can earn a college scholarship which will take him out of his miserable home life. Unfortunately, his mother messes that up when she is arrested for DWI, and he is placed in the care of an aunt and uncle who live nowhere near his school district.

8.12.   Childress, Alice. (1982). *A hero ain't nothing but a sandwich*. New York: Avon Books. 128 pp. (ISBN: 0-380-00132-2)

This novel centers around a 13-year-old drug addict from a New York ghetto. Each chapter is a first person account by various friends, family members, teachers, and pushers who know Benjie Johnson. Although it is written in black dialect and includes a lot of profanity, it is easy to understand and has a powerful message. (an American Library Association Best of the Best Books for Young Adults)

8.13.   Cole, Barbara S. (1989). *Alex the great*. New York: Rosen. 72 pp. (ISBN: 0-8239-0941-7)

Alex and Deonna are best friends, and their friendship is an example of proof that opposites attract. Deonna is a tennis star who tries hard in all that she attempts, even school. Alex, on the other hand, is a "druggie" who skips school and steals and deals to support her drug habit. Both girls have some difficult decisions to make, and each shares a different point of view.

8.14.   Colman, Hila. (1989) *Suddenly*. 128 pp.

See Death and Dying

8.15.   Corcoran, Barbara. (1984). *The woman in your life*. New York: Atheneum. 159 pp. (ISBN: 0-689-31044-7) (Out of Print)

Monty Montgomery has been rejected by her mother and her father is dead. She's searching for love during her 18th year and finds it, she thinks, in Aaron Helding. Aaron gets her to transport drugs for him across the Mexican border, and she gets caught and sent to a federal prison. This book alternates between Monty's diary entries and her descriptions of her prison stay. Although it is definitely a hard way to learn, Monty learns a lot about life, living, and loving.

8.16.   Cormier, Robert. (1991). *We all fall down*. New York: Delacorte Press. 193 pp. (ISBN: 0-385-30501-X)

Buddy has problems, and he takes his problems and forces them on other people; Buddy is an alcoholic teenager. He and three other teenagers vandalize a house and attack a 14-year-old girl. Her older sister wants justice, but "The Avenger" wants revenge.

8.17.   Daly, Jay. (1980). *Walls*. New York: Harper & Row. 214 pp. (ISBN: 0-060-21392-2)

Frankie O'Day, better known as "The Shadow," is overwhelmed by his problems: He has an alcoholic father, questionable friends, and a new romance he's unsure about. He "deals" with his inner conflicts by writing graffiti on walls.

8.18.   Deaver, Julie Reece. (1989). *Say goodnight, Gracie*. 224 pp.

See Death and Dying

8.19.   Due, Linnea A. (1988). *High and outside*. San Francisco: Spinsters unt Lute. 195 pp. (ISBN: 0-933-21658-0)

Niki Etchen has everything going for her during her junior year of high school: She is an honor student, editor of the school newspaper, and an awesome pitcher for the girls' softball team. This novel explores how such a girl could become involved with alcohol and how alcoholism can destroy a life.

8.20.   Ellis, Bret Easton. (1985). *Less than zero*. New York: Simon & Schuster. 208 pp. (ISBN: 0-671-54329-6)

Returning home from a break from college, Clay finds the same old crowd doing the same old things. Clay is different: He begins to look around at life and searches for its meaning. Still apart from life in the fast lane, he walks somewhat slower and sees what drugs are doing to his friends. Explicit, graphic language is used, but the novel poignantly displays some realistic conflicts facing young people in trouble. There is a movie available by the same name.

8.21.   Fosburgh, Liza. (1990). *The wrong way home*. New York: Bantam Starfire. 192 pp. (ISBN: 0-553-05883-5)

See Death and Dying

8.22.   Fosburgh, Liza. (1990). *Cruise control*. New York: Bantam Books. 224 pp. (ISBN: 0-553-28441-X)

Gussie Smith can no longer deal with his family problems, particularly his mother's alcoholism. When things get too harried for this 16-year-old, he gets in his mom's car and "cruises" until he feels more in control. On one outing, Gussie meets Flame who is a runaway. They pick up Gussie's younger brother to have some fun and adventure, until Gussie finds out his mother has had a breakdown. He learns that the family must face their problems together if they are to survive. This novel addresses the problems of children who are raised by alcoholics and how they can cope and adjust to their situation.

8.23.   Fox, Paula. (1990). *The moonlight man*. New York: Dell. 192 pp. (ISBN: 0-440-20079-2)

Fifteen-year-old Catherine Ames becomes confused during a visit with her father, a man she has never really known or understood since her parents' divorce. Soon she discovers that alcohol is directing his life and messing things up. During the day, he is a sensitive, fun, caring father, but at night, he is a drunken, delirious stranger. During an awkward confrontation, her father promises to quit drinking but Catherine is skeptical. (an American Library Association Notable Book)

8.24.   Gilmore, H.B. (1985). *Ask me if I care*. New York: Ballantine Books. 180 pp. (ISBN: 0-449-70201-4)

Fourteen-year-old Jenny is having difficulty getting along with her mother and stepfather. Since things are just not working out, they send Jenny to live with her father and stepmother. Although Jenny hasn't seen her father in six years, she hopes that things will be better. Unfortunately, his forgetting to pick her up at the airport sends a message Jenny doesn't want to hear. Jenny meets a neighbor, Pete, who introduces her to a life of drugs, and Jenny is receptive to this kind of escape. Things get out of hand and a friend overdoses leaving Jenny to do some soul-searching about where her life is heading.

8.25.   Glasgow, Jack. (1985). *The big deal*. New York: Bantam Books. 167 pp. (ISBN: 0-553-24990-8)

Alex is from a broken home, and his mother has too many problems of her own to worry about his. Perhaps that is why Alex chooses to socialize with the biggest drug dealer at school and become a dealer himself. Alex ends up owing thousands of dollars to a gang that doesn't care about him, and he has to figure out how to placate them by himself.

8.26.   Greene, Sheppard M. (1988). *The boy who drank too much*. New York: Dell Laurel-Leaf. 144 pp. (ISBN: 0-440-90493-5)

This novel is narrated by a ninth grade boy whose name is never mentioned in the story. The narrator befriends Buff Saunders, a new kid at school, and the two boys play on the school's hockey team. Buff's story is a realistic and dramatic portrayal of a young man torn by alcoholism and the conflicting demands of his alcoholic, abusive father, hockey, and his own values. Buff compounds already existing problems by resorting to alcohol himself. The narrator talks about how he must help Buff, but he also experiences a lot of difficulties as he tries to help his friend.

8.27.   Halvorson, Marilyn. (1986). *Cowboys don't cry.* 176 pp.

          See Death and Dying

8.28.   Halvorson, Marilyn. (1988). *Let it go.* New York: Dell Laurel-Leaf.
          235 pp. (ISBN: 0-440-20053-9)

When Red Cantrell's brother overdoses on drugs and becomes permanently hospitalized due to brain damage, his father decides to relocate his family from the temptations of the big city life in favor of Alderton, a ranching community. At first, Red is a real tough guy but eventually softens and befriends Lance, a country boy with his own problems.

8.29.   Hamilton, Dorothy. (1984). *Joel's other mother.* Scottsdale, PA:
          Herald Press. 120 pp. (ISBN: 0-8361-3355-2)

Joel used to be proud of his mother, but all of that has changed since she has become an alcoholic. She used to be pretty and fun, but now all that she does is sleep all day or staggers about the house. Most days, she doesn't even bother to get dressed. Joel is so ashamed of her that he no longer lets anyone come over to his house, not even his best friend, Chris. Finally, Joel unknowingly does something that helps his mother see herself as others see her.

8.30.   Hamilton, Virginia. (1987). *A white romance.* New York: Philomel
          Books. 191 pp. (ISBN: 0-399-21213-2)

Talley attends an all-black high school that has been recently integrated. Talley meets and befriends Didi, a white girl, who shares in her love of running. Unfortunately, Didi introduces Talley to drugs, heavy metal music, and romance with the high school's new, white drug dealer.

8.31.   Hinton, S.E. (1989). *Rumble fish.* 122 pp.

          See Dropouts and Delinquency

8.32.   Hinton, S.E. (1989). *That was then, this is now.* New York: Dell.
          224 pp. (ISBN: 0-440-98652-4)

Bryon and Mark have been best friends since childhood and have loved each other as brothers. As teenagers, they begin to develop separate identities and each is painfully aware that they are growing apart. Life on the wrong side of town dished them both unfair servings of violence and poverty. Bryon doesn't want to fight anymore, especially after meeting Cathy, but Mark still thinks that paybacks are a part of life. When Bryon discovers that Mark is selling drugs to make money, he realizes the oneness they experienced was a thing of the past--that was then. Now, the climax of the book, involves a decision Bryon must make which will determine Mark's future. (an American Library Association Notable Children's Book and Best of the Best Books for Young Adults)

8.33.   Holland, Isabelle. (1979). *Heads you win, tails I lose*. New York: Dell Laurel-Leaf. 159 pp. (ISBN: 0-397-31380-2)

Things are going badly for Melissa: She's just been rejected by the boy next door who she's crazy about, her parents are constantly fighting with her feeling in the middle, and she has low self-esteem due to her weight problem. When she begins to get involved in a school play, she begins to take diet pills and sleeping pills. Before long, things get worse as she finds she needs the pills just to make it through the day.

8.34.   Holland, Isabelle. (1985). *Jenny kiss'd me*. New York: Fawcett Juniper. 201 pp. (ISBN: 0-449-70065-8)

It has been particularly rough for Jill Hamilton since her mother died. Her father resorts to Scotch for his answers and takes his emotional pain out on her by cutting her down all of the time. Convinced that no one will ever want to date her, Jill is easy prey for Nathan and his sexual desires. Jill has a lot of issues to face and overcome, and she eventually begins to take charge of her life.

8.35.   Horwitz, Joshua. (1985). *Only birds and angels fly*. New York: Harper Collins. 192 pp. (ISBN: 0-06-022599-8) (Out of Print)

This novel deals with the effects of drug abuse on the lives of two young friends, Chris and Danny, as they progress from adolescence to early adulthood. Written from the point of view of Danny, this story explores just how devastating Chris's use of drugs can have on a friendship. The question is raised as to whether or not a friendship can be strong enough to endure such pressures. Although the story is set in the sixties, the problems presented are really the same kind of problems encountered by today's adolescents.

8.36.   Howe, Fanny. (1987). *Taking care*. New York: Avon Flare. 160 pp. (ISBN: 0-380-89864-0)

Sixteen-year-old Pamela has decided that "if you can't beat them, you might as well join 'em." Pamela, like her alcoholic parents, has a drinking problem of her own. Through a chance encounter, Pamela learns that the choices she makes, she makes for herself.

8.37.   Irwin, Hadley. (1990). *Can't hear you listening.* New York: Macmillan. 208 pp. (ISBN: 0-689-50513-2)

Troubled by her parents' recent separation, Tracy and her friends begin experimenting with alcohol and drugs. When Stanley, her long-time friend, begins to act weird, Tracy must confront the situation and decide what to do. Her inner struggle with her conscience helps her to clarify her values and decide what she wants to do with her life.

8.38.   Kehret, Peg. (1991). *Cages.* New York: Dutton Children's Books. 160 pp. (ISBN: 0-525-65062-8)

Being raised by an alcoholic stepfather has its negative effects on Kit. After being caught shoplifting, Kit is ordered to perform community service as part of her sentence. Kit helps in an animal shelter where she learns some things that only animals can teach a person.

8.39.   Levy, Marilyn. (1986). *Summer snow.* 171 pp.

See Divorced and Single Parents

8.40.   Levy, Marilyn. (1988). *Touching.* New York: Fawcett. 165 pp. (ISBN: 0-449-70267-7)

Eve Morrison's father is an alcoholic, and her mother deserted the family to become a "porno queen." Her father is generally okay when he is sober, but life gets pretty intolerable when he's drunk. Eve keeps a duffel bag packed so she can go and stay at a friend's house during particularly rough times. On one occasion Eve breaks her arm and vows never to return, but her father's pleas and promises of sobriety always manage to get her to come back. Things get really volatile when Eve gets cast in the school play, a previous interest of her mother that infuriates her father. The night her father, in a drunken stupor, mistakes her for her mother and approaches her is the night that Eve decides she must leave for good.

8.41.   Luger, Harriett. (1983). *The un-dudding of Roger Judd.* 137 pp.

See Divorced and Single Parents

8.42.   Major, Kevin. (1990). *Far from shore.* New York: Dell Laurel-Leaf. 224 pp. (ISBN: 0-440-92585-1)

Chris's family is falling apart, and he is ready to drop out of school. At first he finds some relief by drinking but then things get worse, much worse, as he finds himself being arrested for a crime he doesn't remember committing.

This story focuses on Christopher's struggle to make a life for himself in the midst of a family torn apart by unemployment, alcoholism, and his own rebellious needs. (a *School Library Journal* Best Book of the Year and a Canadian Young Adult Book Award)

8.43.   Mathis, Sharon Bell. (1972). *Teacup full of roses*. 125 pp.

        See Poverty

8.44.   Mathis, Sharon Bell. (1990). *Listen for the fig tree*. 175 pp.

        See Youth with Disabilities

8.45.   Mazer, Harry. (1990). *The war on Villa Street*. 192 pp.

        See Abuse

8.46.   Mazer, Norma Fox. (1991). *When we first met*. 199 pp.

        See Death and Dying

8.47.   McAfee, Carol. (1992). *Who's the kid around here, anyway?* New York: Ballantine Books. 153 pp. (ISBN: 0-449-70411-4)

        Maddie Winchirch, at 16 years of age, has become an enabler to her mother's alcoholism. She has assumed the roles of mother to her brothers, maid of the house, and caretaker of her father. When Maddie wins the award of her dreams and there is no family support for her, she takes a nose dive and starts dating the hood of the school. She begins to do those things she despises: She smokes, drinks, and does some drugs. With the help of a savvy guidance counselor and a disaster which motivates her mother to seek help, Maddie overcomes her enabling behavior and starts assuming responsibility for her own actions.

8.48.   Meyer, Carolyn. (1991). *The two faces of Adam*. New York: Bantam Starfire. 166 pp. (ISBN: 0-553-28859-8)

        Adam is Adam at high school but becomes Ninja outside of school. Ninja frequently calls "Ears," the school's Hotline for troubled teens. Ninja's problem is that he has a brother who is dealing drugs and doesn't know what to do about it. Ninja repeatedly talks with Lan Nguyen, a Vietnamese refugee, who has a very anti-drug stance. Things get complicated when Lan befriends Adam and then learns that Adam really is Ninja.

8.49.   Miklowitz, Gloria. (1990). *Anything to win*. New York: Dell. 160
         pp. (ISBN: 0-440-20732-0)

An intelligent, talented varsity quarterback begins taking steroids and
suffers because of his decision. In spite of his coach's dictum to "win at any
cost," Cam Potter learns that there are some prices one shouldn't have to pay to
win. This novel convincingly shows how a good, level-headed kid can get
caught up in the lure of steroids and shows that habits can be broken by the
right arguments.

8.50.   Myers, Walter Dean. (1984). *Motown and Didi*. New York: Viking
         Kestrel. 174 pp. (ISBN: 0-670-49062-8)

Didi is a black teenager who lives in Harlem with her mother and
younger brother. Although their father abandoned them when they were little,
Didi is a good student who dreams of getting a scholarship so she can go to
college. Plans go awry when Didi's mother suffers a stroke and her brother
starts shooting heroin. After Didi tells the police the identity of the pusher,
Touchy has her beaten up. Motown, a 17-year-old living on his own, saves her.
Motown works hard, reads books that "the professor" gives him, and wants to
lead a decent life. Didi and Motown find themselves falling in love, but Didi
does not want to be 18, pregnant, and doomed to live in a one bedroom
apartment in Harlem for the rest of her life. Didi leaves but returns to Harlem
when Tony overdoses on drugs.

8.51.   Myers, Walter Dean. (1988). *Scorpions*. 216 pp.

See Dropouts and Delinquency

8.52.   O'Dell, Scott. (1978). *Kathleen, please come home*. Boston:
         Houghton Mifflin. 196 pp. (ISBN: 0-395-26453-7)

Kathleen gets mixed up with the wrong crowd and becomes addicted
to drugs. When her mother accidentally causes the death of her illegal alien
boyfriend, Kathleen runs away to Mexico. In Mexico, she learns she is
pregnant and must fight her drug habit for the sake of the child. This book is
written in an unusual manner: Half of the book is Kathleen's diary, the other
half is her mother's.

8.53.   Orgel, Doris. (1989). *Crack in the heart*. New York: Fawcett
         Juniper. (ISBN: 0-449-70204-9)

Loneliness leads Diana, a teenage girl, to drugs. This "easy way out"
turns out to be the hardest mistake of her life.

8.54.   Paulsen, Gary. (1983). *Dancing Carl*. New York: Bradbury Press. 105 pp. (ISBN: 0-02-770210-3).

Carl, a worn-out veteran of World War II, returns to McKinley, Minnesota with a drinking problem. He gets a job tending the town's skating rink that two particular twelve-year-olds, Willy and Marsh, frequent. The boys observe Carl's drinking behavior and the effects his drinking has on others. Finally, with the help of Miss Helen, Carl slowly regains his self-worth and self-esteem.

8.55.   Peck, Richard. (1987). *Princess Ashley*. New York: Delacorte Press. 208 pp. (ISBN: 0-385-29561-8)

Chelsea Olinger is not too thrilled about going to a new high school, nor is she pleased that her mother has taken a job as the school's guidance counselor but under her maiden name. Things look up for Chelsea when Ashley Packard, the most in-girl at school, decides to take Chelsea under her wing. Despite her mother's strong objections to their friendship, Chelsea continues to socialize with that crowd until she experiences a rude awakening.

8.56.   Peck, Richard. (1991). *Unfinished portrait of Jessica*. 162 pp.

See Divorced and Single Parents

8.57.   Roos, Stephen. (1989). *You'll miss me when I'm gone*. New York: Dell. 208 pp. (ISBN: 0-440-20485-2) (Out of Print)

Sixteen-year-old Marcus is the son of a wealthy parents, but their recent divorce has left the family situation very tense. Marcus begins drinking to escape from his problems, just like his mother. Marcus thinks he can quit at any time but then realizes he has lost control when he accidentally attempts suicide. The book does not offer any easy solutions for Marcus' problems, but it does bring him to the realization that he is an alcoholic who needs help.

8.58.   Scoppettone, Sandra, (1980). *The late great me*. New York: Bantam Books. 256 pp. (ISBN: 0-553-25910-5)

Geri Peters, an insecure 17-year-old, tries to solve her problems of being nobody by becoming an alcoholic. In the story, Geri describes her eventual journey to alcoholism and some of the pressures that prompted her to take that route. (California Young Readers Medal)

8.59.   Snyder, Anne. (1986). *My name is Davy, I'm an alcoholic*. New York: Signet Books. 144 pp. (ISBN: 0-451-16181-5)

Davy Kimble is a lonely, 15-year-old boy with a drinking problem. Davy tries to come to grips with his problem on his own, but his success is limited and ends miserably when his girlfriend dies. After finally hitting bottom, his guilt drives him to AA for the help he so desperately needs. This story has a strong and open message for teenagers about the damage of alcoholism. There are parts of the book that need to be considered with discretion.

8.60.   Snyder, Zilpha Keatley. (1988). *The birds of summer*. New York: Dell Laurel-Leaf. 192 pp. (ISBN: 0-440-20154-3) (Out of Print)

While most 16-year-olds are concerned about boyfriends, Summer is concerned about holding her family together. She cares for her little sister and tries to save her mother, an irresponsible woman who got stuck in the Sixties, from drug dealers.

8.61.   Stoehr, Shelley. (1991). *Crosses*. New York: Delacorte Press. 153 pp. (ISBN: 0-385-30451-X)

Nancy is having an horrific ninth grade year: The emotional pain inflicted upon her by her alcoholic parents causes her to participate in many self-destructive behaviors. Besides smoking, stealing, lying, and taking drugs, she often cuts herself with glass because the physical pain is much easier to deal with than the emotional pain. She befriends Katie, another dysfunctional teenager, whose life ends in tragedy. Nancy's parents eventually join Alcoholics Anonymous, and Nancy is influenced by her friend's death to do some work on her own behavior. (an honor book in the Eighth Annual Delacorte Prize for a First Young Adult Novel Contest)

8.62.   Stolz, Mary. (1974). *The edge of next year*. 195 pp.

See Death and Dying

8.63.   Strasser, Todd. (1979). *Angel dust blues*. 204 pp.

See Dropouts and Delinquency

8.64.   Strasser, Todd. (1990). *The accident*. 192 pp.

See Death and Dying

8.65.   Talbert, Marc. (1985). *Dead birds singing*. 170 pp.

See Death and Dying

8.66.   Talbert, Marc. (1991). *Pillow of clouds*. 204 pp.

        See Divorced and Single Parents

8.67.   Thompson, Thomas. (1989). *Richie*. 308 pp.

        See Dropouts and Delinquency

8.68.   Voigt, Cynthia. (1987). *Izzy, willy-nilly*. 262 pp.

        See Youth with Disabilities

8.69.   Wagner, Robin S. (1975). *Portrait of a teenage alcoholic*. New
        York: Ballantine Books. 120 pp. (ISBN: 0-345-31165-5)

        Sarah Hodges is 15 years old and an alcoholic. She has been drinking
for two years because of difficulties resulting from her parents' divorce. She
resents her stepfather and drinks to feel better about things, especially since she
sees him and her own mother drinking practically every night. Over time she
begins to do things which are destructive to herself and people around her.
Noone, especially Sarah, wants to admit that she has a drinking problem until
she is hospitalized after a bash. Help is available but is effective only if she and
her parents are willing to acknowledge the problem which Sarah eventually
does.

8.70.   Winthrop, Elizabeth. (1978). *Knock, knock, who's there?* 192 pp.

        See Death and Dying

8.71.   Woodson, Jacqueline. (1991). *The dear one*. 145 pp.

        See Teenage Pregnancy

8.72.   Zindel, Paul. (1983). *Pardon me, you're stepping on my eyeball!* 199
        pp.

        See Growing Up: Alienation and Identity

Annotated Young Adult Nonfiction Dealing with Alcohol and Drugs

8.73.   Berger, Gilda. (1987) *Crack: The new drug epidemic*. New York:
        Franklin Watts/Impact Books. 128 pp. (includes black & white photo
        inserts) (ISBN: 0-531-10410-9)

This book opens with the story of Len Bias, a rising basketball star who died from a drug overdose. Other chapters include information about users, the dangers of drug use, the manufacture and sales of drugs, the care and treatment of the abuser, and what is being done to stop the crack trade. A useful glossary and a list of places to go for additional help and information are also included.

8.74.   Chomet, Julian. (1987). *Cocaine and crack*. New York: Franklin Watts/Impact Books. 62 pp. (ISBN: 0-531-10435-4)

Cocaine used to be the drug used by rich people, but now it and crack are widely available for anybody. These highly addictive drugs have negative repercussions for the user. This book examines where crack and cocaine come from and the effects of taking these drugs on the human body.

8.75.   Coffey, Wayne. (1988). *Straight talk about drinking: Teenagers speak out about alcohol*. New York: New American Library. 164 pp. (ISBN: 0-452-26061-2)

In eight chapters, teenagers share their experiences with alcohol. They tell about peer pressure, driving under the influence, and their false confidence that they could stop at any time. Additionally, Coffey includes a useful appendix which has a test developed by the National Council on Alcoholism for determining if a problem exists. Addresses and phone numbers of agencies where teenagers can get help are also included.

8.76.   Cohen, Daniel and Cohen, Susan. (1992). *A six-pack and a fake I.D.: Teens look at the drinking question*. New York: Dell. (ISBN: 0-440-21297-9)

The authors present a straightforward discussion of personal experiences, legal information, and scientific facts about teenage drinking. Although adults would prefer that teenagers didn't drink, the fact of the matter is that teenagers are finding it more and more difficult to say no when their parents and friends drink. Taking the stance that the decision to drink is a personal rather than a moral decision, the authors provide useful information to help the reader make an informed decision. Using true stories told by teenagers, the authors present the reasons why teenagers drink, the role of alcohol in a teen's life, and its effects on a teenager's body. Information about groups that can help an alcoholic teenager is also provided.

8.77.   Cole, Lewis. (1989). *Never too young to die: The death of Len Bias*. New York: Pantheon Books. 252 pp. (ISBN: 0-394-56440-5)

Len Bias had a great future in store for him, especially after being named the first-round draft pick of the Boston Celtics. Before he ever had a chance in the big leagues, he lost everything--including his life--because of a cocaine overdose. This book explores the infamous night in 1986 when Len Bias died and the circumstances surrounding his death.

8.78.   Dolan, Edward F., Jr. (1986). *Drugs in sports*. New York: Franklin Watts. 122 pp. (ISBN: 0-531-10157-6)

The public has become more aware of the drug problem in sports, especially after the deaths of Boston Celtic draft choice Len Bias and Cleveland Brown's Don Rogers. Written for parents, coaches, athletes, and teachers, this book examines the problems of drugs from junior high athletic competitions to the pro's.

8.79.   Felsted, Carla Martindell. (Ed.). (1986). *Youth and alcohol abuse: Readings and resources*. Phoenix: Oryx. 219 pp. (ISBN: 0-89774-251-6)

This reference text is divided into four major sections. Section one is an overview with statistics from the National Council on Alcoholism and the Gallup Youth Survey. Section two focuses on the detection, prevention, and treatment of an alcohol problem. Section three discusses important issues relative to children of adult alcoholics and drunk driving. Section four provides an annotated list of good nonfiction and fiction books for young people.

8.80.   Johnson, Vernon. (1986). *Intervention: How to help someone who doesn't want help*. Minneapolis: Johnson Institute Books. 116 pp. (ISBN: 0-9359-0831-5)

Johnson, of the Johnson Institute in Minneapolis, addresses the problems of "chemical dependency," a disease commonly referred to as alcoholism or drug addiction. Written for people who are wanting to take action, this book is divided into two main parts: Part One describes the disease; and Part Two explains, in detail, how to proceed with treatment. Johnson lists 30 questions that you can ask in order to determine if you or a friend or relative is ready for help. The book is written in nontechnical language and provides a thorough explanation with examples on how to conduct each step.

8.81.   Lightner, Candy & Hathaway, Nancy. (1990). *Giving sorrow words: How to cope with grief and get on with your life*. 243 pp.

See Death and Dying

8.82.   Meyer, Caroline. (1979). *The center: From a troubled past to a new life*. New York: Atheneum. 193 pp. (ISBN: 0-6895-0143-9)

This is a deeply touching story for anyone who has ever been confused by adolescent pressures or cared about someone who has. The novel centers around the life of David Peterson, a young teen, and his experiences during a two year stay at the Vitam Center in Norwalk, Connecticut. David was sent to this rehabilitation center because of his drug use that led him to skip school and shoplift. David participates in self analysis and learns about his secrets, his fears, and his negative feelings which have kept him from happiness for so long. Emotions are intense, but the center offers long lasting effects for his active participation. Finally, David experiences joy and peace when he finds the true reality of his life without drugs or alcohol. Strong language is used, and there are several references to homosexuality. (an ALA Best Book for Young Adults and a Notable Children's Trade Book in the Field of Social Studies)

8.83.   Porterfield, Kay Marie. (1985). *Coping with an alcoholic parent*. New York: Rosen Publishing Group. 134 pp. (ISBN: 0-8239-0662-0)

This book, written for a teenage audience, addresses the problems of being raised by an alcoholic parent. Teenagers who have an alcoholic mother or father often feel trapped, guilty, and angry. This book provides the reader with helpful information on how to understand and deal with the numerous problems in such a family.

8.84.   Pownall, Mark. (1987). *Inhalants*. New York: Franklin Watts. 62 pp. (ISBN: 0-531-10434-6)

The use of inhalants is on the rise largely due to their easy availability. Many glues, aerosols, and paints give off vapors that, if inhaled into the lungs in a concentrated form, can give the user the sensation of being high. The negative side effects of using inhalants are a change in behavior, impaired health, and sometimes death. This book includes valuable information about inhalants and ways to get help if a problem is suspected.

8.85.   Ryan, Elizabeth A. (1992). *Straight talk about drugs and alcohol*. New York: Dell. 144 pp. (ISBN: 0-440-21392-4)

Ryan answers some commonly asked questions by teenagers about drugs and alcohol without sounding judgmental. The appendix includes a list, by state, of where teenagers can go for help if they or someone they know has a drug or alcohol problem.

8.86.   Scales, Cynthia. (1990). *Potato chips for breakfast: The true story of growing up in an alcoholic family.* New York: Bantam Books. 192 pp. (ISBN: 0-553-28166-6)

Scales tells what it was like surviving in a family where both parents were alcoholics. The message is clear: Children do not have to wait for their parents to stop drinking before they can help themselves to a better life.

8.87.   Waller, Mary Bellis. (1993). *Crack-affected children.* Newbury Park, CA: Corwin Press. 96 pp. (ISBN: D2901-6051-4)

Sixty-three teachers share their trial and error experiences of working with children who have drug problems. Together, they arrive at strategies that help students control their behavior so they can learn.

8.88.   Woods, Geraldine. (1986). *Drug use and drug abuse, 2nd edition.* New York: Franklin Watts. 64 pp. (ISBN: 0-531-10114-2)

Written for middle school students, this book offers an objective presentation of current research and theories related to the development of a drug problem. Particularly helpful is a section called "If You Need Help" which lists organizations with hotlines or drop-in facilities.

Nonfiction References Dealing with Alcohol and Drugs

Journal Articles

Bangle, E. (1985, June). Is teenage alcohol abuse a tradition? *Thrust, 14* (7), p. 23 ff.

Barone, D. (1993, February). Wednesday's child: Literacy development of children prenatally exposed to crack or cocaine. *Research in the Teaching of English, 27* (1), p. 7 ff.

Burgess, D.M. & Streissguth, A.P. (1992, September). Fetal alcohol syndrome and fetal alcohol effects: Principles for educators. *Phi Delta Kappan, 74* (1), p. 24 ff.

Dean, O. (1989). Facing chemical dependency in the classroom. *Florida Health Communications.*

Divoky, D. (1989, April). Ritalin: Education's fix-it drug? *Phi Delta Kappan, 70* (8), p. 599 ff.

Eitzen, D.S. (1992, April). Problem students: The sociocultural roots. *Phi Delta Kappan, 73* (8), p. 584 ff.

Gregorchik, L.A. (1992, May). The cocaine-exposed children are here. *Phi Delta Kappan, 73* (9), p. 709 ff.

Gress, J.R. (1992, Fall). Family substance abuse and teacher education. *Action in Teacher Education, 14* (3), p. 20 ff.

Gress, J.R. (1988, March). Alcoholism's hidden curriculum. *Educational Leadership, 45* (6), p. 18 ff.

Harper, T.W. (1991, Spring). Education vs. drug abuse: Strategies for the '90s. *Florida ASCD Journal, 7*, p. 46 ff.

Hawley, R.A. (1991, September). Legalizing the intolerable is a bad idea. *Phi Delta Kappan, 73* (1), p. 62 ff.

Hawley, R.A. (1987, May). Kappan special report--School children and drugs: The fancy that has not passed. *Phi Delta Kappan, 68* (9), p. K1 ff.

Mann, P. (1985, September 24). Drugs? Not my child. *Family Circle*, p. 18 ff.

McClellan, M.C. (1990, June). Practical applications of research: The problem of teenage drinking. *Phi Delta Kappan, 71* (10), p. 810 ff.

Ostrower, E.G. (1987, January). A counseling approach to alcohol education in the middle schools. *The School Counselor, 34* (3), p. 209 ff.

Reagan, N. (1984, October). The drug abuse epidemic. *American Education, 20* (8), p. 2 ff.

Roberts, T.B. (1991, September). When the drug war hits the fan. *Phi Delta Kappan, 73* (1), p. 58 ff.

Sautter, R.C. (1992, November). KAPPAN Special Report--Crack: Healing the children. *Phi Delta Kappan, 74* (3), p. K1 ff.

Shannon, J. (1986, September). In the classroom stoned. *Phi Delta Kappan, 68* (1), p. 60 ff.

Shannon, D.M., Jones, F.R., & Gansneder, B.M. (1993). The identification of adolescent substance misuse using school-reported factors. *High School Journal, 76* (2), p. 118 ff.

Stevens, L.J. & Price, M. (1992). Meeting the challenge of educating children at risk. *Phi Delta Kappan, 74* (1), p. 18 ff.

Tyler, R. (1992, May). Prenatal drug exposure: An overview of associated problems and intervention strategies. *Phi Delta Kappan, 73* (9), p. 705 ff.

Waller, M.B. & Scheckler, P. (1992-1993, December-January). Helping crack-affected children succeed. *Educational Leadership, 50* (4), p. 57 ff.

Wells, S. (1984, Spring). Adolescent alcohol and substance abuse. *Voices, 20* (1), p. 52 ff.

Journal Themes

Helping Youngsters Cope with Life. (1988, March). *Educational Leadership, 45* (6).

Books

DuPont, R.L. Jr. (1985). *Getting tough on gateway drugs: A guide for the family.* Rockville, MD: America Council for Drug Addiction. 352 pp. (ISBN: 0-88048-035-1)

Fraser, C. & Sullivan, D. (1990). *Burnt: A teenage addict's road to recovery.* New York: Signet Books. 272 pp. (ISBN: 0-451-16856-9)

Gold, M. (1984). *800 cocaine.* New York: Bantam Books. 98 pp. (ISBN: 0-553-34094-8)

Hyde, M.O. (1990). *Drug wars.* New York: Walker. 112 pp. (ISBN: 0-8027-6900-4)

Hyde, M.O. (1986). *Mind drugs, 5th edition.* New York: Dodd-Mead. 191 pp. (ISBN: 0-3960-88139)

Johnston, L. (Ed.). (1986). *Drug use among American high school students, college students, and other young adults: National trends through 1985.* Washington, D.C.: National Institute on Drug Abuse. 237 pp. (Monthly Catalogue: GP86015531)

Mann, P. (1985). *Marijuana alert.* New York: McGraw-Hill. 526 pp. (ISBN: 0-07-039906-9)

Nowinski, J. (1990). *Substance abuse in adolescents and young adults.* New York: Norton. 246 pp. (ISBN: 0-393-70097-6)

Polson, B. & Newton, M. (1985). *Not my kid: A parent's guide to kids and drugs.* New York: Avon Books. 260 pp. (ISBN: 0-380-69997-4)

CHAPTER 9

Poverty

There is an increasing gap between the haves and the have-nots. Nowadays, the have-nots are largely found in single-parent homes which is an increasing percentage of our society. Until our children's basic needs are met-- food, shelter, and clothing--we cannot expect that they will learn much in our nation's schools. When students drop out of school, it increases the likelihood that they will stay poor or resort to lives of crime. According to projections made by the Children's Defense Fund, each dollar spent to improve pre-school education saves about $5.00 later on which would have to be spent for special education, crime, and welfare costs. Our children are our best investment.

STARTLING INFORMATION ABOUT POVERTY

- In 1987, teen parents made up a significant number of homeless families seeking shelter, and many of these teens were products of the child welfare system. (Ziefert & Brown, 1991)

- Since 1987, one-fourth of all pre-school children in the United States have been in poverty. (Hodgkinson, 1991)

- In 1988, 40% of shelter users were families with children, and between 50,000 and 200,000 children have no home. (Hodgkinson, 1991)

- The poverty rate for children in young families doubled from 20% in 1973 to 40% in 1990. (Johnson, Summ, & Weill, 1992)

- About 40% of our nation's poor are children. (Howe, 1991)

- In 1991, 15 million children were being raised by single mothers whose family income averaged about $11,400 in 1988 dollars (within $1,000 of the poverty line). (Hodgkinson, 1991)

- Estimates of the number of children in America who are homeless on any given night range from 68,000 to half a million. (Linehan, 1992)

- The U.S. Department of Education estimates that there are 322,000 homeless school-age children. (Crosby, 1993)

- In 1992, 50% of families headed by single women lived in poverty, compared to 11.4% of two-parent families. (Kirst, 1993)

- Twenty percent of American children live in poverty and more than one-third will live in a single parent household headed by a woman at some time in their lives. (National Commission on Children, 1991)

- One child in seven grew up in poverty in 1970, one child in six in 1980, one child in five in 1990, and it is probable that one child in four will live in poverty by the year 2000. (Howe, 1991)

- Children in homeless families often experience developmental delays, severe depression, anxiety, and learning disorders. (Bassuk & Rubin, 1987)

- Every day in America, 1,375 teenagers drop out of school. (Edelman, 1989)

- High school dropouts between the ages of 18 to 24 earn an average of $6,000 per year, and those dropping out of school now have only one chance of three in finding a full-time job. (Hayes, 1992)

WHAT TO DO AND WHERE TO GO FOR HELP

- Encourage all teenagers especially pregnant ones to stay in school.

- Get professional help: Call the Salvation Army, HRS, crisis intervention centers, mental health clinics, hospitals, a family physician, a clergy, a guidance counselor, or a teacher. If you know of a pregnant teenager who needs immediate help, call the Pregnancy Hotline at 1-800-238-4269. For more information, write to the American Academy of Child and Adolescent Psychiatry, 3615 Wisconsin Avenue, NW, Washington, D.C., 20016-3007.

Annotated Young Adult Novels Dealing with Poverty

9.01. Anderson, Mary. (1991). *The unsinkable Molly Malone*. New York: Harcourt, Brace, & Jovanovich. 202 pp. (ISBN: 0-15-213801-3)

Molly Malone is regarded by her high school friends as a "Sixties throwback" because she is an artist who is concerned about the urban homeless. Although Molly is just 16 years old, she spends time with children living in a welfare home in New York. It is through this experience that Molly discovers her own identity and finds ways that all can participate in helping those who are less fortunate.

9.02. Betancourt, Jeanne. (1990). *Not just party girls*. New York: Bantam Books. 176 pp. (ISBN: 0-553-28514-9)

Anne, Kate, and Jane are the original party animals. At 16, all they can think and talk about are boys, clothes, vacations, and parties. Things change when Anne does an internship for her social studies class at a missionary camp for migrant workers.

9.03. Bridgers, Sue Ellen. (1988). *Home before dark*. New York: Alfred A. Knopf. 150 pps. (ISBN: 0-394-93299-4).

Fourteen-year-old Stella Mae Willis is the oldest child in a family of migrant workers. She has spent most of her life moving from one harvest to another, living out of an old, beaten-up station wagon with her parents and her younger brothers and sister. Stella's father decides to bring his family to settle on a tobacco farm in North Carolina where he was raised. In an old sharecropper's cabin, the Willis family develops roots for the first time, and Stella develops a meaningful friendship with a boy who works on the same farm. After her mother dies from a fatal accident and her father finds another woman to marry, Stella refuses to leave the cabin--her only real home--to move with the family into her stepmother's larger house in town. Eventually Stella learns that belonging doesn't come from living in one particular place but from the giving and sharing between people. (a *New York Times* Outstanding Book of the Year, an American Library Association Notable Children's Book and Best Book for Young Adults)

9.04. Brooks, Bruce. (1984). *The moves make the man*. New York: Harper & Row. 280 pp. (ISBN: 0-06-020679-9)

Jerome Foxworthy, an 11-year-old black boy growing up on the edge of poverty, has dreams of a different life. Jerome is not only an awesome basketball player, but he is excellent academically as well. He become the first and only black student to integrate the largest white school in Wilmington,

North Carolina. Jerome meets Bix Rivers, a student who can't stand anything fake including moves in basketball which are what makes Jerome so talented. Bix vows to have nothing false in his life but then pulls the biggest move of all. (1984 ALA Notable Children's Book, 1985 Newbery Honor Book, & 1985 Best Book for Young Adults)

9.05.   Childress, Alice. (1982). *A hero ain't nothing but a sandwich.* New York: Avon Books. 128 pp. (ISBN: 0-380-00132-2)

See Alcohol and Drugs

9.06.   Collier, James Lincoln. (1987) *Outside looking in.* New York: Macmillan. 179 pp. (ISBN: 0-02-723100-3)

Fourteen-year-old Fergy is tired of living in a van with his parents and his younger sister, Ooma. Fergy becomes even more disgruntled and frightened when his father tries to make things better by stealing a fancy recreational vehicle. He and Ooma decide to run away from their conditions and end up at their grandparents'. With their help, Fergy comes to terms with his family situation and his own expectations.

9.07.   Collier, James Lincoln. (1989). *When the stars begin to fall.* New York: Dell Laurel-Leaf. 176 pp. (ISBN: 0-440-20411-9)

Harry White is determined to overcome the "trash" label placed upon his family. When he learns that a local factory is polluting the river, he comes up with a bold plan to stop the destruction. Hopefully, then, the town will respect him. (an American Library Association Best Book for Young Adults)

9.08.   Colman, Hila. (1988). *The double life of Angela Jones.* New York: William Morrow. 160 pp. (ISBN: 0-688-06781-6)

Angela Jones grew up in a poor neighborhood in New York. Her life changes dramatically when she receives a scholarship to an exclusive school in New Hampshire where she meets Andy, a wealthy boy. Angela is confronted with a difficult decision: Should she lead Andy on into thinking that she comes from wealth, or should she maintain her self-respect and risk losing him by revealing her real background?

9.09.   Harris, Mark J. (1989). *Come the morning.* New York: Bradbury Press. 176 pp. (ISBN: 0-027-42750-1)

Things go from bad to worse when Ben's father deserts the family. Although Ben is just 13 years old, he willingly cares for his younger brother and sister and offers words of encouragement to his mother who's trying her best to provide for the family. The family becomes destitute and eventually joins the homeless. A wino helps Ben realize that his father is probably gone forever, and a director at a shelter gives him the encouragement he needs to pull the family together.

9.10.   Hassler, Jon. (1980). *Jemmy*. New York: Margaret K. McElderry. 180 pp. (ISBN: 0-689-50130-7) (Out of Stock)

After her mother dies, Jemmy Scott has to quit school in order to keep house for her father and take care of her younger brother and sister. Not only does she try to keep her family together, but she also struggles against poverty, ignorance and prejudice; Jemmy is half-Indian. (a Notable Children's Trade Book in the Field of Social Studies and a Children's Book of the Year)

9.11.   Herzig, Alison Cragin & Mali, Jane Lawrence. (1990). *Sam and the moon queen*. New York: Clarion Books. 176 pp. (ISBN: 0-395-53342-2)

Sam and his mother move into a new apartment which seems too small. Needing some space, Sam tries to find comfort in the basement but finds a homeless girl and her injured dog instead.

9.12.   Hinton, S.E. (1979). *Tex*. New York: Delacorte Press. 194 pp. (ISBN: 0-440-08641-8).

Tex is a 15-year-old, country boy whose father is away more than home; his mother died when he was little. Tex believes that his dad is working hard at the rodeo and doesn't really mean to stay away so long without sending money home. But Mace, Tex's older brother who is raising Tex, knows better. Tex begins to hate Mace for always putting down their father and for selling Tex's horse in order to pay the bills. Although he tries his best, Mace is unable to protect Tex from the headaches and heartaches of growing up. The hardest lesson for Tex is learning his father's secret. At this point, Tex begins to mature and appreciate Mace's love and concern. (an American Library Association Best of the Best Books for Young Adults, a *School Library Journal* Best Book of the Year, and *Booklist* Reviewers' Choice)

9.13.   Hinton, S.E. (1989). *The outsiders*. 156 pp.

See Dropouts and Delinquency

9.14.   Hinton, S.E. (1989). *That was then, this is now*. 224 pp.

See Alcohol and Drugs

9.15.   Hunt, Irene. (1987). *No promises in the wind*. New York: Berkley.
        100 pp. (ISBN: 0-425-09969-5)

Josh is a 15-year-old boy who is angry with his father for losing his job
and resents the fact that there are no jobs to be found. Because of the pressure
of the Depression, Josh and his best friend, Howie, leave home so there will be
more food for the other family members. Joey, Josh's little brother, begs to be
included. Josh protests, but Howie points out the advantage of a "cute little
guy" being included for begging purposes so they can eat. They have no food,
money, or knowledge of where they are going or how they will survive. Josh
abandons his dream of a musical career and his education for this trek through
a cold, hostile world. He eventually matures with the realization that life is
what you make it, and people are a summation of their experiences.

9.16.   Jones, Adrienne. (1987). *Street family*. New York: Harper & Row.
        274 pp. (ISBN: 0-06-023049-5)

Chancy is 15 years old and Joshua is 14 years old when they decide to
run away from their present situations: Chancy is running away from a school
for troubled girls in Texas, and Joshua is running away from his abusive
stepmother and her boyfriend. Both end up homeless and on the streets where
they befriend Doc, a Vietnam veteran who's an alcoholic; Nellie Brect, a
grumpy bag lady; and Dundee and Hector, two mental misfits. They join
together for survival and live underneath a Los Angeles freeway. Chancy is
determined to mold this unlikely group into the family she's always wanted.

9.17.   King, Buzz. (1990). *Silicon songs*. 160 pp.

See Death and Dying

9.18.   Lipsyte, Robert. (1987). *The contender*. New York: Harper & Row.
        167 pp. (ISBN: 0-694-05602-2)

It would be easier for Alfred Brooks to join a gang and steal, mug, and
take drugs, but Alfred doesn't want that for himself. Realizing that it will take
guts and determination to be different from what his environment cultivates, he
resorts to boxing. He soon realizes that he hasn't the killer instinct necessary to
be a champion, but he gains something intrinsically more valuable. Alfred
finds self-respect and the courage to contend with the cold, cruel realities of life
in the ghetto where dying is a big part of living.

9.19.   Lyon, George. (1990). *Borrowed children*. New York: Bantam
        Books. 176 pp. (ISBN: 0-553-28380-4)

Set in Kentucky during the Depression, this is the story about 12-year-old Amanda and her dreams in contrast to poverty. Amanda has to quit school and take care of her family while her mother recuperates from a difficult birth. Amanda longs to be someplace glamorous but things seem futile for her in Kentucky. Finally, she gets to go to Memphis to visit her grandparents. During that trip, Amanda discovers the common thread that holds her family together.

9.20.   Mathis, Sharon Bell. (1972). *Teacup full of roses.* New York: Avon Books. 125 pp. (ISBN: 0-380-00780-0)

The story involves three days before Joe Brooks' high school graduation. He and his two brothers live in the ghetto in Washington, D.C. Paul, the oldest, is a talented artist who is addicted to drugs much to the dismay of the younger two. David, the youngest, tries to escape his surroundings through school and athletics but doesn't get the praise and encouragement from his mother that he needs. His mother focuses her energies on Paul and his drug problem. The protagonist, Joe, is a very loving brother who makes personal sacrifices to help his family.

9.21.   Mazer, Norma Fox. (1989). *Silver.* 208 pp.

See Abuse

9.22.   Meriwether, Louise. (1986). *Daddy was a number runner.* New York: The Feminist Press. 237 pp. (ISBN: 0-935312-57-9)

Fran Coffin, a 12-year-old beautiful girl, is faced with the harsh realities that a black girl must face growing up in Harlem. Not only is she molested, but she soon discovers that there are not as many opportunities available for her in her pursuit of the American Dream.

9.23.   Myers, Walter Dean. (1984). *Motown and Didi.* 174 pp.

See Alcohol and Drugs

9.24.   Myers, Walter Dean. (1988). *Scorpions.* 216 pp.

See Dropouts and Delinquency

9.25.   Myers, Walter Dean. (1990). *Hoops.* New York: Dell Laurel-Leaf. 192 pp. (ISBN: 0-440-93884-8)

Seventeen-year-old Lonnie Jackson has had problems with his mother ever since his father left. Lonnie finds shooting hoops at a nearby basketball court a good way to forget about everything and hopes that it will be his ticket out of the ghetto. One day, Lonnie finds a wino sleeping on the court and asks him to move so he can play. The wino eventually leaves but not until he's given a good word-bashing to Lonnie. When a new team forms to participate in a local basketball tournament, Lonnie is recruited. He quits when he recognizes the coach of the new team, the wino from the courts. After Lonnie watches the team practice and sees that Coach Cal knows what he is doing, he decides to rejoin the team. He and Cal become friends, and Lonnie learns that Cal used to be a professional basketball player. Lonnie learns more about life when their friendship ends in a tragic way. (an American Library Association Best of the Best Books for Young Adults)

9.26.   Myers, Walter Dean. (1987). *The outside shot*. New York: Dell Laurel-Leaf. 192 pp. (ISBN: 0-440-96784-8)

In this involving sequel to *Hoops*, Lonnie has earned a basketball scholarship to a midwestern college but finds himself unprepared for the pressures of classes, love, college sports and corruption. (an American Library Association Best Book)

9.27.   Naylor, Phyllis R. (1990). *Send no blessings*. New York: Atheneum. 231 pp. (ISBN: 0-689-31582-1)

Beth, a 10th grader, is the oldest of many children. She is embarrassed by her poor and uneducated family and hates the dilapidated trailer they call home. Drawn to the illusion of possible escape when a 22-year-old asks her to marry him, Beth snaps out of it and decides she does not want to repeat the mistakes of her own parents.

9.28.   Paterson, Katherine. (1991). *Lyddie*. New York: Lodestar Books. 182 pp. (ISBN: 0-525-67338-5)

Lyddie Worthen is forced to alter her plans when her mother makes her go to work to help pay for the family's debts. The story, set in mid-19th century Vermont, traces three years of Lyddie's life as a worker in a tavern and then in a factory.

9.29.   Paulsen, Gary. (1990). *The crossing*. New York: Dell Laurel-Leaf. 128 pp. (ISBN: 0-440-20582-4)

Manny Bustos, a 14-year-old orphan, is struggling just to stay alive in the midst of unbelievable poverty on the streets of Juarez, Mexico. Across the border he sees two things: a dream of a better life in America and Sergeant Robert S. Locke, a Vietnam veteran with a drinking problem and an attitude.

Manny finally gets the courage to cross the Rio Grande to get into America, but he has no idea of the courage it will take to face Sergeant Locke. (Literary Merit)

9.30.   Petersen, P.J. (1990). *The boll weevil express.* 192 pp.

See Dropouts and Delinquency

9.31.   Santiago, Danny. (1984). *Famous all over town.* 240 pp.

See Dropouts and Delinquency

9.32.   Southerland, Ellease. (1989). *Let the lion eat straw.* 165 pp.

See Abuse

9.33.   Strang, Celia. (1981). *This child is mine.* New York: Beaufort. 156 pp. (ISBN: 0-825-30049-5)

A 14-year-old lives in a family with numerous problems. When her sister has an illegitimate child, the protagonist decides that she will be this baby's "mother."

9.34.   Wilkinson, Brenda. (1980). *Ludell.* New York: Bantam Books. 168 pp. (ISBN: 0-553-12894-9)

Ludell Wilson, a young black girl growing up in the rural South, knows first-hand what it means to do without. Her family is poor--real poor--but Ludell finds life's treasure in the simple things.

Annotated Young Adult Nonfiction Dealing with Poverty

9.35.   Berck, Judith. (1992). *No place to be: Voices of homeless children.* Houghton Mifflin. 137 pp. (ISBN: 0-395-53350-3)

This is a compilation of 30 interviews Ms. Berck conducted with youth living in poverty. These children, ranging in age from 9 to 17, openly share what it is like for them growing up in welfare hotels or shelters for the homeless in New York City. Some poetry is included.

9.36.   Brown, Claude. (1990). *Manchild in the promised land.* New York: Macmillan. 416 pp. (ISBN: 0-025-17325-1)

The author tells a chilling account of what it was like for him growing up in Harlem.

9.37.   Lyons, Mary E. (1990). *Sorrow's kitchen.* New York: Charles Scribner's Sons. 144 pp. (ISBN: 0-684-19198-9)

This biography is about Zora Neale Hurston, a black writer born in Florida at the turn of the century. Through hard work and determination, Zora acquired an education and eventually became the only Southern woman to be part of the Harlem Renaissance, a Black Arts Movement in the 1920's. Best known for *Their Eyes Were Watching God,* Zora died the same way she entered this world--in poverty.

9.38.   Meltzer, Milton. (1986). *Poverty in America.* New York: William Morrow. 122 pp. (ISBN: 0-688-05911-2)

This readable book presents the economic history of our country and suggests possible solutions for eliminating poverty in America. When facts are included, they are done in meaningful ways to make readers examine their own attitudes about the poor.

Nonfiction References Dealing with Poverty

Journal Articles

Bassuk, E.L. & Rubin, L. (1987, April). Homeless children: A neglected population. *American Journal of Orthopsychiatry, 57* (2), p. 279 ff.

Carey-Webb, A. (1991, November). Homelessness and language arts: Contexts and connections. *English Journal, 80* (7), p. 22 ff.

Crosby, E.A. (1993, April). The at-risk decade. *Phi Delta Kappan, 74* (8), p. 598 ff.

Duran, B.J. & Weffer, R.E. (1992, Spring). Immigrants' aspirations, high school process, and academic outcomes. *American Educational Research Journal, 29* (1), p. 163 ff.

Edelman, M.W. (1989, May). Defending America's children. *Educational Leadership, 46* (8), p. 77 ff.

Gonzalez, M.L. (1991, September). School-community partnerships and the homeless. *Educational Leadership, 49* (1), p. 23 ff.

Haberman, M. (1991, December). The pedagogy of poverty versus good teaching. *Phi Delta Kappan, 73* (4), p. 290 ff.

Hayes, L. (1992, January). Building schools for tomorrow. *Phi Delta Kappan, 73* (5), p. 413 ff.

Hodgkinson, H. (1991, September). Reform versus reality. *Phi Delta Kappan, 73* (1), p. 9 ff.

Hofferth, S.L. (1987, February). Implications of family trends for children: A research perspective. *Educational Leadership, 44* (5), p. 78 ff.

Howe II, H. (1991, November). America 2000: A bumpy ride on four trains. *Phi Delta Kappan, 73* (3), p. 192 ff.

Hutchison, L. (1993, February). Homelessness and reader-response: Writing with a social consciousness. *English Journal, 82* (2), p. 66 ff.

Johnson, C.M., Summ, A.M., & Weill, J.D. (1992, September). America's young families face vanishing economic dreams. *Economic Digest, 58* (1), p. 4 ff.

Kirst, M.W. (1993, April). Strengths and weaknesses of American Education. *Phi Delta Kappan, 74* (8), p. 613 ff.

Knapp, M.S. & Shields, P.M. (1990, June). Reconceiving academic instruction for the children of poverty. *Phi Delta Kappan, 71* (10), p. 752 ff.

Knapp, M.S., Turnbull, B.J., & Shields, P.M. (1990, September). New directions for educating the children of poverty. *Educational Leadership, 48* (1), p. 4 ff.

Linehan, M.F. (1992). Children who are homeless: Educational strategies for school personnel. *Phi Delta Kappan, 74* (1), p. 61 ff.

Pallas, A.M., Natriello, G., & McDill, E.L. (1989, June-July). The changing nature of the disadvantaged population: Current dimensions and future trends. *Educational Researcher, 18* (5), p. 16 ff.

Richmond, G. (1990, November). The student incentive plan: Mitigating the legacy of poverty. *Phi Delta Kappan, 72* (3), p. 227 ff.

Stevens, L.J. & Price, M. (1992, September). Meeting the challenge of educating children at risk. *Phi Delta Kappan, 74* (1), p. 18 ff.

Ziefert, M. & Brown, K.S.   (1991, April).   Skill building for effective intervention with homeless families.   *Families in Society: The Journal of Contemporary Human Services*, p. 212 ff.

Journal Themes

Children of Poverty. (1990, June). *Phi Delta Kappan, 71* (10).

Books

Meltzer, Milton. (1986). *Poverty in America.* New York: William Morrow. 122 pp. (ISBN: 0-688-05911-2)

CHAPTER 10

Dropouts and Delinquency

Teenagers are having to cope in a society that constantly exposes them to violence, drugs, gangs, danger, and fear. Couple those things with an unstable family and economic deprivation and chances increase that delinquency will occur. In some schools, there are probably some days that more guns are brought to school than books. If we fail in our attempt to meet the needs of society's youth, the cost of that failure will be another generation of adolescents who will fail in school, hit the streets, join gangs, deal drugs, engage in violence, commit crimes, need welfare, and give birth to the next generation who will continue the trend. We either pay now, or we will surely pay later.

STARTLING INFORMATION ABOUT DROPOUTS AND DELINQUENCY

- In the 1985-1986 school year, more than 600,000 young people dropped out of public schools at a projected cost to society of $120 billion in lost productivity during their lifetimes. (Hamby, 1989)

- In 1988, the dropout rate among high school students was 28.9%. (Monroe, Borzi, & Burrell, 1992)

- Every day in America, 1,375 teenagers drop out of school. (Edelman, 1989)

- In 1986, the unemployment rate of high school dropouts between 20 and 24-years of age was double that of those who graduated. (Monroe, Borzi, & Burrell, 1992)

- High school dropouts between the ages of 18 to 24 earn an average of $6,000 per year, and those dropping out of school only have one chance of three in finding a full-time job. (Hayes, 1992)

- More than 80% of America's one million prisoners are high school dropouts, and we spend more than $20,000 per year per prisoner. (Hodgkinson, 1991)

- At least 2 million school-age children have no adult supervision at all after school. (Hodgkinson, 1991)

- Adolescents who repeatedly steal have difficulty trusting others and forming close relationships. (American Academy of Child & Adolescent Psychiatry, *Facts for Families*, 1992)

- Teenage arrests have tripled since 1950. (National Association of State Boards of Education and the American Medical Association, 1990)

- From 1980 through 1989, more than 11,000 people died in the United States as a result of homicide committed by teenagers using firearms, cutting instruments, or blunt objects. (Crosby, 1993)

- For those children growing up in poor, high crime neighborhoods, one in three has seen a homicide by the time they are adolescents. (Beck, 1992)

- Homicide is the leading cause of death among 15 to 19-year-old minority youth. (National Association of State Boards of Education and the American Medical Association, 1990)

- In 1987, approximately 400,000 teenagers carried handguns to school. (American Academy of Child & Adolescent Psychiatry, *Facts for Families*, 1992)

- Everyday in America, nine children die from gunshot wounds. (Edelman, 1989)

- Gunshot wounds to children ages 16 and under have increased 300% in major urban areas since 1986. (American Academy of Child & Adolescent Psychiatry, *Facts for Families*, 1992)

- At least 25 million American households keep handguns, and 50% of owners keep them loaded. (American Academy of Child & Adolescent Psychiatry, *Facts for Families*, 1992)

- There were 40,000 victims of school violence in 1990, and 15% of students said that their schools had gangs. (U.S. Justice Department)

- More high school students said that they would join in or silently support a racial confrontation than said they would condemn or try to stop one. (Harris Poll, 1990)

- Klanwatch, a project of the Southern Poverty Law Center, documented more than 270 incidents of hate crimes in schools and colleges during 1992; more than half of them were committed by teenagers. (O'Neil, 1993)

- Approximately 20% to 25% of students are victimized by racial or ethnic incidents in the course of a school year. (National Institute Against Prejudice and Violence, 1992)

WARNING SIGNS THAT MIGHT TRIGGER DELINQUENCY

- Being raised in a dysfunctional family where parents are alcoholics or drug abusers.

- Experiencing ongoing family violence that escalates when conditions worsen.

- Increasing vulnerability to increasingly stressful events in the home environment.

- Having easy access to alcohol and firearms.

WHAT TO DO AND WHERE TO GO FOR HELP

- Provide emotional stability, model flexibility and responsibility, and explain the importance of realistic goal setting.

- Foster warm and encouraging relationships.

- Provide alternative ways of solving problems without violence.

- Disapprove of violent TV episodes that children see, and stress the belief that such behavior is not the best way to solve problems.

- Store all firearms unloaded and uncocked in a securely locked container, and store the ammunition in a separate locked container; only a responsible adult should know where the containers are located.

- Get professional help: Call crisis intervention centers, mental health clinics, police departments, hospitals, a clergy, a guidance counselor, or a teacher. If you need immediate help, call the National Crisis Alert at 1-800-231-1295 or the National Runaway Hotline at 1-800-231-6946. For more information, write to the American Academy of Child and Adolescent Psychiatry, 3615 Wisconsin Avenue, NW, Washington, D.C., 20016-3007.

Annotated Young Adult Novels Dealing with Dropouts and Delinquency

10.01. Ames, Mildred. (1978). *What are friends for?* New York: Charles Scribner's Sons. 145 pp. (ISBN: 0-684-15991-0)

See Divorced and Single Parents

10.02. Arrick, Fran. (1983). *Chernowitz.* New York: New American Library. 192 pp. (ISBN: 0-451-15350-2)

Bobby Cherno is a 15-year-old high school freshman who has grown up in the same house and circulated among the same group of friends all of his life. Bobby has never been particularly aware of his Jewish heritage until Emmet Sundback moves into his neighborhood. Emmet is a bully. He tortures Bobby with intimidation and even manages to get Bobby's former friends to join in ostracizing him. Bobby decides to fight back when a swastika is painted on the family car and Emmet intentionally kills his cat. Bobby sets it up so that Emmet gets suspended from school. Afterwards, Emmet's father beats Emmet so badly that he must be hospitalized, and Bobby is left to reflect on his own behavior.

10.03. Arrick, Fran. (1988). *Steffie can't come out to play.* New York: Dell Laurel-Leaf. 160 pp. (ISBN: 0-440-97635-X)

Stephanie Rudd, a 14-year-old, runs away from her dismal home to glamorous New York City to become a model. Instead, she becomes one of Favor's string of prostitutes until a policeman, Calvin Yarbro, finds her. (an American Library Association Best Book for Young Adults)

10.04. Arrick, Fran. (1991). *Where'd you get the gun, Billy?* New York: Bantam Books. 104 pp. (ISBN: 0-553-07135-1)

In the opening pages, Billy, a high school senior, intentionally shoots his girlfriend and is apprehended before turning the gun on himself. David, a classmate who barely knows Billy, is not only disturbed by the tragedy but is troubled by the nagging question of how a teenager could acquire a Smith and Wesson .38 Chief Special in the first place? He goes to the police station for answers and meets Lieutenant Wisnewski who answers David's question by telling him the plausible story of a gun with six different owners.

10.05. Arter, Jim. (1991). *Gruel and unusual punishment*. New York: Delacorte Press. 103 pp. (ISBN: 0-385-30298-3)

Arnold is repeating the 7th grade largely because of his inappropriate behavior. His annoying behavior prompts his teacher "Apeface" to take a special interest in him. Meanwhile, an emotionally-disturbed student, Edward Straight, plans to murder Apeface, and Arnold has a chance to save his teacher and himself in the process.

10.06. Bernard, Ashley. (1975). *Terry on the fence*. New York: S.G. Phillips. 196 pp. (ISBN: 0-875-99222-6)

Terry Harmer, an 11-year-old boy, runs away from home after a fight with his mother and sister. He runs into a gang of hoodlums who force him into membership. Les, the ringleader, decides that the boys will break into Terry's school and steal the radios there. During the theft, they are seen by the janitor and Terry has a chance to make things right or get more involved. The British slang might make this a difficult read for some.

10.07. Bonham, Frank. (1972). *Durango street*. New York: Dell Laurcl-Leaf. 160 pp. (ISBN: 0-440-92183-X)

Rufus has recently been released from a detention center. Rufus is faced with a terrible dilemma: Should he rejoin his gang and risk violating parole or should he try to risk it alone?

10.08. Butterworth, William. (1980). *Leroy and the old man*. New York: Four Winds Press. 154 pp. (ISBN: 0-590-07638-8)

Eighteen-year-old Leroy is sent to live with his grandfather in the country after he witnesses a crime. Although he's there for his safety, Leroy hates country living. When Leroy's no-good father offers him a chance to be a numbers' runner in New York City, Leroy must decide between right and wrong.

10.09.   Calvert, Patricia. (1989). *When morning comes*. New York: Charles
          Scribner's Sons. 153 pp. (ISBN: 0-684-19105-9)

See Adopted and Foster Families

10.10.   Clymer, Eleanor. (1989). *My brother, Stevie*. New York: Holt,
          Rinehart, & Winston. 73 pp. (ISBN: 0-440-40125-9)

See Death and Dying

10.11.   Colman, Hila. (1985). *Claudia, where are you?* New York: Pocket
          Books. 168 pp. (ISBN: 0-671-42450-5)

          The mixture of new emotions, awkward physical growth, desired
independence but need for dependence, make the teenage years a difficult
period for both Claudia and her parents. Claudia is unhappy at home. Feeling
suffocated and inadequate, she runs away to New York in hopes of finding a
new life with meaning. By running away from home and her problems,
Claudia's search is not an easy one. On her journey, she finds terror,
loneliness, love, and no easy answers.

10.12.   Cormier, Robert. (1986). *The chocolate war*. New York: Dell. 192
          pp. (ISBN: 0-440-94459-7)

          Having recently lost his mother in death and feeling the overwhelming
effects of that loss upon both him and his father, Jerry Renault, a New England
high school student ponders the poster in his locker--"Do I dare disturb the
universe?" Being a freshman who is trying out for the varsity football team is
tough enough, but Jerry also has Archie Costello, the leader of the secret school
society--the Vigils--and master of intimidation, to contend with as well. Archie
himself is intimidated by an insecure teacher, Brother Leon, especially during
this year's annual chocolate sale. When Jerry refuses to be bullied into selling
the chocolates, the Vigils turn Jerry from hero to outcast of Trinity School by
utterly destroying him in front of the whole school. (an American Library
Association Notable Children's Book, a Best of the Best Book for Young
Adults, a *School Library Journal* Best Book of the Year, & a *New York Times*
Outstanding Book of the Year)

10.13.   Cormier, Robert. (1985). *Beyond the chocolate war*. New York:
          Dell. 288 pp. (ISBN: 0-440-90580-X)

          Beyond the Chocolate War is the sequel to *The Chocolate War*, but
this time the story shifts from Jerry Renault to the effects that Archie Costello
and the Vigils have on the school. Obie revolts against Archie and tries to hurt
him. Finally, Obie realizes that as bad as Archie has been, he never forced

anybody to do anything against his will. The book deals very well with the situation teens often face when they want to be part of a group and want to be independent at the same time. (an IRA/CBC Children' Choice)

10.14.   Cormier, Robert. (1991). *We all fall down*. New York: Delacorte Press. 193 pp. (ISBN: 0-385-30501-X)

Teenagers who have been raised in "normal families" participate in random violence. Besides exploring the motivating evil forces that drive these kids, the effects of their violence on innocent victims is also portrayed.

10.15.   Crawford, Charles P. (1977). *Letter perfect*. New York: E.P. Dutton. 167 pp. (ISBN: 0-525-33635-4) (Out of Print)

Three boys, Chad, Toad, and B.J., make it a practice to play practical jokes on people for kicks. They lose sight of what a practical joke means when they find a letter to Mr. Patterson, a despised English teacher. The boys think it will be funny to blackmail him, but their joke ends up having the resignation of their teacher. After Mr. Patterson resigns, Chad begins to question his friendship with Toad and B.J. and think about what he has done.

10.16.   Duncan, Lois. (1973). *I know what you did last summer*. Boston: Little, Brown & Company. 199 pp. (ISBN: 0-316-19546-4)

One morning, Julie James receives two letters. One is an acceptance letter to Smith College, and the other is an anonymous one with the following message: "I know what you did last summer." Julie painfully remembers how she and three of her friends concealed their responsibility for a hit and run accident. Written as a mystery, the story slowly unfolds as the four teenagers relive their nightmare.

10.17.   Duncan, Lois. (1978). *Killing Mr. Griffin*. Boston: Little, Brown, & Company. 243 pp. (ISBN: 0-316-19549-9)

Five teenagers, Mark, David, Jeff, Sue, and Betsy, are frustrated by Mr. Griffin's unfair grading procedures. They decide to kidnap and verbally abuse him in order to make him experience the same kind of anguish they all were feeling in his English class. Unfortunately, they are unaware of his heart condition (angina) and the negative effects a bad scare can have on him. What starts out as a practical joke ends up as a tragedy for these five impressionable teenagers to live with for the rest of their lives. This novel focuses on the subject of peer pressure and exposes some of the hidden reasons why some teenagers turn to lives of crime. (an American Library Association Best of the Best Books for Young Adults)

10.18. Duncan, Lois. (1987). *The twisted window*. New York: Delacorte Press. 183 pp. (ISBN: 0-385-29566-9)

Tracy wants to help Brad get his little sister, Mindy, back. Brad explained how his stepfather, Mr. Carver, just took her and the police wouldn't do anything to get her back. The two devise a plan to kidnap Mindy. Tracy arranges to babysit for the Carvers, Brad will come in and tie her up to make it look like she had no choice, and Brad will take his little sister home. While Tracy and Brad are packing Mindy's clothes, Mr. Carver unexpectedly comes home and Tracy discovers that things are not as they seem.

10.19. Forshay-Lunsford, Cin. (1986). *Walk through cold fire*. New York: Dell Laurel-Leaf. 205 pp. (ISBN: 0-440-99322-9)

Desiree has had to make a lot of adjustments since her mother's death. Her father remarries a woman who Desiree despises. While they are honeymooning in the Bermudas, they leave Desiree with her aunt and uncle. While there, she befriends a group of kids from the bad side of town. Desiree ignores the fact that these kids are delinquents who deal drugs but focuses on the fact that they are loyal to one another. Desiree is shocked into reality about the kind of crowd she is associating with when one of her friends dies.

10.20. Geller, Mark. (1988). *Raymond*. 89 pp.

See Abuse

10.21. Glasgow, Jack. (1985). *The big deal*. 167 pp.

See Alcohol and Drugs

10.22. Greene, Bette. (1991). *The drowning of Stephan Jones*. 217 pp.

See Homosexuality

10.23. Hall, Lynn. (1984). *Uphill all the way*. New York: Charles Scribner's Sons. 121 pp. (ISBN: 0-684-18066-9)

Callie's goal in life is to become the best farrier in Liberty, Oklahoma. She takes a summer job with the local veterinarian in order to save money for a truck. When Truman, the veterinarian's stepson, arrives on the scene, everyone's life is disrupted. Truman has just been released from a state correctional ranch and is still following a loser path. Callie sets out to straighten him out but finally gives up after he steals her father's truck to commit another robbery.

10.24.   Hinton, S.E. (1989). *The outsiders*. New York: Dell. 156 pp.
(ISBN: 0-440-96769-4)

This novel, written when the author was 17 years old, is about the violence between two gangs, the Socials (Socs) and the Jets (Greasers). The Socs are the rich kids who live on the West side of town, and the Greasers live on the East side of town and are often mistaken for hoods. Ponyboy Curtis, a 14-year-old Greaser, tells what life is like being an outsider. Since the death of his parents, his family has consisted of two older brothers and the gang of Greasers. Ponyboy has to witness three deaths before he begins to understand his brothers, his gang, himself, and the unique quality in each individual. Regardless of the facades worn by people or the social class one belongs to, people are fragile, mortal beings with common problems and feelings. Ponyboy ultimately discovers that life is rough all over, even for the Socs, and that he can choose what he wants out of life. (an American Library Association Best of the Best Books for Young Adults)

10.25.   Hinton, S.E. (1988). *Taming the star runner*. New York: Delacorte Press. 181 pp. (ISBN: 0-440-50058-3)

Travis Harris, a 16-year-old, assaulted his stepfather and nearly killed him. As an alternative to juvenile hall, Travis stays with his Uncle Ken on a ranch in Oklahoma where he is launched into a search to find himself. Travis has misgivings about his new home, especially since his uncle has just separated from his wife and son. Initially Travis is primarily interested in being cool, but then he makes a strange and wonderful alliance with the young woman who runs the riding school at the ranch. She has a beautiful and wild horse named Star Runner who is like Travis--"always on edge, about to explode." Travis realizes his own worth after falling in love, finding an adult who honestly cares about him, helping to train a horse, and publishing his first novel. Through determination, hard work, and an open mind, Travis learns how to appreciate his individuality and share the pleasure he finds in his writing. The novel extols the benefits of reaching for one's dreams, and not being daunted when things go awry. (an American Library Association Best Book for Young Adults and a YASD Recommended Book for Reluctant Readers)

10.26.   Hinton, S.E. (1989). *Rumble fish*. New York: Dell Laurel-Leaf. 122 pp. (ISBN: 0-440-97534-4)

Rusty James, a 14-year-old boy from the tough side of town, talks with his fists. Because he never knew his mother and his father is a drunk, the values of his life are centered around his love and emulation for his older brother, Motorcycle Boy. Rusty dreams of street gangs and one day becoming as calm and courageous as his brother is within the violent sub-culture. Rusty's quest for what can never be prevents him from obtaining an identity of his own and maintaining friendships. His youth is spent fighting back, both literally on the street and figuratively against what he is unable to face--reality. (an American Library Association Best Book for Young Adults, a *School Library Journal* Best Book of the Year, and a Kirkus Choice)

10.27. Hobbs, Will. (1991). *Downriver*. New York: Atheneum. 204 pp. (ISBN: 0-689-31690-9)

Eight troubled teenagers spend nine weeks together in Discovery Unlimited, a summer Outward Bound Program designed to teach them self-reliance, discipline, and survival skills. Dissatisfied by their adult white-water rafting guide, they steal the van and rafting equipment and decide to run the Colorado River by themselves. They quickly learn that self-reliance is one thing but cooperation is often better. Additionally, they learn that "you make decisions, you make choices, you live by the consequences."

10.28. Hoh, Diane. (1991). *The invitation*. New York: Scholastic. 169 pp. (ISBN: 0-590-44904-4)

Four predominantly unpopular girls are invited to attend Cassandra Rockham's annual fall gala which is considered "the party" of the year. The girls are suspicious of their invitations but cannot resist the temptation of being included in this wealthy girl's exclusive party. After they arrive, they find out that they are the entertainment for the night. Cass locks the four in separate areas of her mansion so the others can participate in a "People Hunt." Meanwhile, Lynn, an emotionally disturbed adolescent, is lurking on the grounds hoping to get revenge by turning the hunt into actual murders. Evidently, Lynn and Shane, one of the intended victims, were involved in a shoplifting crime. Shane's parents moved to a nearby town to escape the scandal, leaving Lynn alone to bear the brunt of the shame.

10.29. Holland, Isabelle. (1985). *Hitchhike*. New York: Dell Laurel-Leaf. 144 pp. (ISBN: 0-440-93663-2)

Sixteen-year-old Pat is furious with her father because he has broken his promise to pick her up at the end of her exclusive school's term in order to go camping. When her father wires her the money to buy a plane ticket, she decides to spend the money in a way that will shock and anger him--she will hitchhike home. Her first ride is with Mr. Elmendorf who shares his agony of having a teenage daughter who ran away from home three years ago. Her next ride is with four young men whose company she thinks she will enjoy more; she is almost dead wrong. They decide to kidnap her and hold her for ransom, knowing that her parents are likely to pay big bucks for her safe return. Pat spends the longest three hours of her life tied up in a loft above the room where these four derelicts argue about how much ransom to ask for, when to kill her, where to hide the body, and whether or not to gang rape her now or make plans later. Pat ultimately gets home a little stronger, wiser, and sadder having learned some valuable lessons in the much renowned "college of hard knocks."

10.30.   Jaspersohn, William. (1990). *Grounded*. New York: Bantam Books. 244 pp. (ISBN: 0-553-05450-3)

Joe Flower runs away from home after his father calls him "lazy and irresponsible" one too many times. He makes his way to Cape Cod where he hopes he'll find people there who will appreciate him. Instead, he meets 16-year-old Nan Wright who helps him face up to some unpleasant realities.

10.31.   Jones, Adrienne. (1987). *Street family*. 274 pp.

See Poverty

10.32.   Kehret, Peg. (1991). *Cages*. New York: 160 pp.

See Alcohol and Drugs

10.33.   Lasky, Kathryn. (1986). *Prank*. New York: Dell Laurel-Leaf. 176 pp. (ISBN: 0-440-97144-6)

Birdie Flynn's family is constantly fighting about something, and her sister is frequently beaten by her husband. After Birdie's 16-year-old brother, Timmy, vandalizes a synagogue and gets caught, Birdie finds herself confronting her own bigotry. Nothing ever comes easy for her, but Birdie is determined to create a better life and future for herself. The novel gives the reader a sense of growth and hope.

10.34.   Lowry, Lois. (1984). *Anastasia at your service*. New York: Dell-Yearling. 160 pp. (ISBN: 0-440-40290-5)

Anastasia, a gangly 12-year-old, is hired by Mrs. Bellingham, a rich old lady, to do light work. She is upset when that work includes kitchen detail and is further angered when Mrs. Bellingham intends to charge her for a silver spoon which she mangled in the garbage disposal. Mrs. Bellingham's granddaughter, Daphne, is an incipient punker who is also irritated by the old woman. The two girls become friends and decide to get their revenge by sabotaging Mrs. Bellingham's big benefit by inviting various local derelicts to attend. When the girls discover what the benefit is for, they try to undo their plans but wind up getting the short end of the stick all the way around.

10.35. MacKinnon, Bernie. (1984). *The meantime*. Boston: Houghton Mifflin. 181 pp. (ISBN: 0-395-35387-4)

During Luke's 17th year, his family moves out of the ghetto and into suburban Flower Heights. Luke and his younger sister, Rhonda, quickly learn that racial lines have been clearly drawn both in their new neighborhood and at school. Even though Luke wants no part of a black-white conflict, he finds himself right in the middle of one when he befriends a white girl and an exceptional teacher. (an American Library Association Best of the Best Books for Young Adults)

10.36. Major, Kevin. (1990). *Far from shore*. 224 pp.

See Alcohol and Drugs

10.37. Major, Kevin. (1990). *Hold fast*. New York: Dell Laurel-Leaf. 224 pp. (ISBN: 0-440-93756-6)

Michael and Curtis have two things in common: They are both cousins and runaways. Together, they struggle to survive without family, friends, or money as they wander through the harsh landscape of Newfoundland. (5th) (a *School Library Journal* Best Book of the Year, the Canada Council Children's Literature Award, an Association of Canadian Libraries Book of the Year, and Hans Christian Andersen Honor List)

10.38. Mazer, Harry. (1985). *When the phone rang*. 181 pp.

See Death and Dying

10.39. Morgenroth, Barbara. (1981). *Will the real Renie Lake please stand up*. 164 pp.

See Divorced and Single Parents

10.40. Murphy, Barbara Beasley. (1977). *No place to run*. New York: Bradbury Press. 176 pp. (ISBN: 0-878-88116-6)

Billy Jansen befriends Milo the Cougar and learns New York City's street life. Their favorite activity is writing graffiti on sidewalks and walls. Things go too far when they spray paint an old tramp who's sleeping on a bench and the man dies. Billy's reaction is to shut down and stop talking, even to his parents.

10.41.   Myers, Walter Dean. (1988). *Won't know till I get there*. 192 pp.

See Adopted and Foster Families

10.42.   Myers, Walter Dean. (1988). *Scorpions*. New York: Harper & Row. 216 pp. (ISBN: 0-06-024364-3)

Twelve-year-old Jamal Hicks has some tough decisions. As a black boy growing up on the streets of Harlem, opportunities are scarce but drugs are plentiful. His older 17-year-old brother, Randy, is in jail for a gang-related robbery where a delicatessen owner was killed. Jamal's family needs to raise $2,000.00 to appeal the case, but it will take forever to do that if he continues with his current job that pays $15.00 a week. Jamal is tempted by Randy's gang for a quick fix: If he and his best friend, Tito, join the gang and sell drugs he will get the money soon. Of course, if he joins the gang, he is liable to end up just as his brother--in jail.

10.43.   Nostlinger, Christine. (1976). *Girl missing*. New York: Franklin Watts, Inc. 139 pp. (ISBN: 0-531-00346-9)

Twelve-year-old Erika is the younger sister of a 14-year-old runaway. Erika desperately tries to find her sibling, and the reader is guided through the days and the events of this young girl's attempt to contact her sister. Through Erika's search, she acquires new perceptions of herself, her family, and others. Erika matures considerably through this difficult situation.

10.44.   Pascal, Francine. (1985). *Runaway*. New York: Bantam Books. 176 pp. (ISBN: 0-553-26682-9)

Jessica is jealous of her twin sister who, in Jessica's eyes, is more adored by the rest of the family. No one realizes that Jessica is feeling unwanted until she runs away with a boy from school. It is rumored that Nicky does drugs and socializes with the wrong crowd, but the two of them understand each other because they both feel unloved. Eventually, Jessica begins to realize that her family really does love her.

10.45.   Petersen, P.J. (1990). *The boll weevil express*. New York: Dell Laurel-Leaf. 192 pp. (ISBN: 0-440-91040-4)

Three teenagers--Lars, Doug, and Doug's little sister--run away from suburbia to San Francisco. Lars wants to get away from his stifling farm life, and Doug is a delinquent from a local youth home. After a series of mishaps, the three of them finally get to the city which is nothing it was cracked up to be. Almost immediately they find that they must beg and steal just to survive.

10.46. Petersen, P.J. (1990). *Would you settle for improbable?* New York: Dell Laurel-Leaf. 160 pp. (ISBN: 0-440-99733-X)

Arnold Norberry has made some big mistakes in his life. After he is released from Juvenile Hall and enrolls in Marshall Martin Junior High School, he finds that reforming is more difficult than he thought in spite of everyone's good intentions. (an American Library Association Best Book for Young Adults)

10.47. Pike, Christopher. (1988). *Last act.* New York: Pocket Books. 226 pp. (ISBN: 0-671-73683-3)

Melanie was feeling very left out at her new school until she was asked to audition for the school play. Things were turning around for her or so it seemed. She was making new friends and having a wonderful time until opening night. Apparently, her new friends had been keeping a horrible secret from her but had told the police that Melanie was the one they wanted.

10.48. Powers, Bill. (1978). *The weekend.* New York: Franklin Watts. 90 pp. (ISBN: 0-531-01467-3)

Jimmy Scott is falsely accused of beating up an old man's wife. The police pick him up and he spends the weekend in a juvenile detention center; it is a nightmarish experience.

10.49. Ruckman, Ivy. (1983). *In a class by herself.* San Diego: Harcourt, Brace, & Jovanovich. 208 pp. (ISBN: 0-152-38242-9) (Out of Print)

Since Dyna Suggs is a juvenile, she is given a second chance after she is caught for a robbery. Dyna tries to start over at a new school, Bonneville High, but her first day as a senior is one she lives to regret. Unable to pay some required fees, Dyna gets an old accomplice to break into and steal from a house. Dyna wrestles with her conscience afterwards, knowing she has broken a promise to Gram and herself. Later, Dyna becomes very interested in her creative writing class and a certain student, Parker. Dyna and Parker mature and learn more about each other while putting together a project for their class's news program. Weeks before graduation, Dyna is arrested and charged with the breaking and entering she committed at the beginning of the year. Her classmates, although surprised, remain supportive and attend her hearing. Although Dyna has changed considerably from the Dyna who committed the crime, she still must pay for her criminal actions.

10.50. Santiago, Danny. (1984). *Famous all over town.* New York: Plume. 240 pp. (ISBN: 0-452-25974-6)

Rudy Medina is a 14-year-old member of a Chicano street gang in Los Angeles. This coming of age novel insightfully depicts what it's like to grow up in a less than ideal circumstance.

10.51.   Sebestyen, Ouida. (1990). *Words by heart*. New York: Bantam Books. 144 pp. (ISBN: 0-553-27179-2)

Set in 1910, Lena learns what it is like to be an outsider. Her family is the only black family in a small, Southern town. At every turn it seems that Lena confronts fear and hatred, especially when 16-year-old Tater Hanley shoots Ben Sills, a black man, because he is perceived to be a threat to Tater's drunken father's job. (an American Library Association Best Book for Young Adults, *Booklist* Reviewers' Choice, a *School Library Journal* Best Book of the Year, an International Reading Association Children's Book Award, and the American Book Award.)

10.52.   Sebestyen, Ouida. (1990). *On fire*. New York: Bantam Books. 192 pp. (ISBN: 0-553-26862-7)

In this sequel to *Words by Heart*, 12-year-old Sammy Haney learns of the brutal murder his favorite brother, Tater, has committed. Meanwhile, Tater has run away to escape his crimes and find work. Hoping to prevent his older brother from further trouble, Sammy follows him to a mining town in Colorado where he convinces Tater to return home and face the consequences.

10.53.   Shyer, Marlene Fanta. (1980). *My brother, the thief.* 138 pp.

See Adopted and Foster Families

10.54.   Strasser, Todd. (1979). *Angel dust blues*. New York: Dell. 204 pp. (ISBN: 0-440-90952-X)

Alex Lazar is the handsome son of wealthy parents who finds that selling drugs is one way to escape from boredom. His senior year becomes a complicated time after being arrested for his drug deals. He is faced with the difficult decision of whether or not to turn in Michael, his equally-guilty friend. Alex emerges a different person after a jail term, but Michael is progressively destroyed by the drugs. Ellen, the new girl in his life, helps Alex through these trying times.

10.55.   Sweeney, Joyce. (1984). *Center line*. 246 pp.

See Abuse

10.56. Thompson, Thomas. (1989). *Richie*. New York: Signet Books. 308 pp. (ISBN: 0-451-16129-7) (Out of Print)

Richie Diener cannot relate to his father and makes matters worse when he develops a drug habit. Their final confrontation ends in tragedy and death.

10.57. Tolan, Stephanie S. (1991). *Plague year*. New York: Fawcett. 184 pp. (ISBN: 0-449-70403-3)

David's life was pretty normal until Bran and his father moved into town; Bran Slocum was different. Not only does his ponytail and earring set him apart from his classmates at Ridgewood High, but Bran's father's crime sets him apart from the community as well. When the small town learns that Bran is the son of a serial killer, the people react negatively and violently. Molly stands up to defend Bran, but David, her best friend, is torn between helping Bran or helping the cause.

10.58. Ure, Jean. (1990). The other side of the fence. New York: Delacorte Press. 176 ff. (ISBN: 0-385-29627-4)

After a huge fight with his father, Richard leaves home. While away, he meets a runaway named Bonny who helps him find some self-respect. Meanwhile, Richard helps Bonny to discover the good that's in herself.

10.59. Voigt, Cynthia. (1987). *The runner*. New York: Fawcett Juniper. 224 pp. (ISBN: 0-449-70294-4)

The first of the Tillerman novels, *The Runner* is the story of Samuel "Bullet" Tillerman, a high school senior and loner whose chief concern in life is running. Set in the turbulent era of the late Sixties, Bullet finds himself dealing with the integration of public schools and the Vietnam War. Bullet is a cross country runner; he chooses not to participate in team sports. Although Bullet is respected at school, he does not allow himself many friends. Trouble begins at his school when black students begin joining the athletic teams. While Bullet is not openly hostile to the black students, he insists that he does not mix with them. Only upon discovering that his friend and boss is part black does Bullet begin to question his own prejudices. (an American Library Association Best of the Best Books for Young Adults and a Notable Children's Trade Book in the Field of Social Studies)

10.60. Voigt, Cynthia. (1986). *Come a stranger*. New York: Atheneum. 190 pp. (ISBN: 0-689-31289-X)

This is the story of Wilhemina Smith's experiences from the 5th to the 10th grade. As a child, Mina wins a scholarship that enables her to attend an all-white ballet dance camp. Mina wants to be a dancer but is unaware of the problems she will encounter because she is black. As her family and Tamer Shipp, a minister, help her to deal with these problems, Mina realizes the value of being what God intended her to be. (a Children's Book of the Year)

10.61.   White, Ellen Emerson. (1987). *Life without friends.* 250 pp.

See Death and Dying

10.62.   Wilkinson, Brenda. (1987). *Not separate, not equal.* New York: Harper & Row. 152 pp. (ISBN: 0-06-026479-9)

Malene is one of six blacks to integrate a Georgia public high school during the Civil Rights Movement in the mid-Sixties. Malene experiences unbelievable hatred and racism.

10.63.   Wortis, Avi. (1983). *Sometimes I think I hear my name.* New York: New American Library. 144 pp. (ISBN: 0-451-14341-8)

Conrad Murray's personality suffers from his parents' divorce. He has a habit of lying which he does to compensate for the absence of a normal life with a mother and father. He cleverly escapes from his present guardians, an aunt and uncle, to go to New York to see his parents. His adventures there lead him into a special relationship with Nancy Sperling. She is able to help him face some bitter, but very present realities.

10.64.   Yep, Laurence. (1991). *The star fisher.* New York: William Morrow. 150 pp. (ISBN: 0-688-09365-5)

Fifteen-year-old Joan must act as an interpreter for her Chinese family. She directly hears the hurting prejudicial slurs which forces her to grow up faster than most.

10.65.   Zindel, Paul. (1990). *I never loved your mind.* New York: Bantam Books. 144 pp. (ISBN: 0-553-27323-X)

Two bright but lost high school students drop out of school in order to search for meaning to life in a world that they find unbearable. (a *New York Times* Outstanding Book of the Year)

10.66.   Zindel, Paul & Dragonwagon, Crescent. (1982). *To take a dare.* New York: Harper & Row. 249 pp. (ISBN: 0-060-26859-X)

Chrysta runs away from home at the age of 13 to be free of her parents. She hitchhikes around the country for two years until, tired of running, she settles down in a small town in Arkansas. Chrysta gets a job, falls in love, and has a drastic operation. Additionally, she meets and takes care of a young boy whose parents have deserted him. Through all of these changes and responsibilities, Chrysta realizes that freedom doesn't have to mean running. Freedom can mean a home where there is love and happiness. The reader should be forewarned that this novel contains harsh language and explicit sexual passages.

Annotated Young Adult Nonfiction Dealing with Dropouts and Delinquency

10.67. Bing, Leon. (1991). *Do or die.* New York: Harper Collins. 277 pp. (ISBN: 0-060-16326-7)

The author discusses the reasons why gangs have become such a strong force in America.

10.68. Brown, Waln K. (1983). *The other side of delinquency.* New Brunswick, NJ: Rutgers University Press. 188 pp. (ISBN: 0-813-50994-7)

The author reveals his tragic past as a juvenile delinquent and shares his struggles to escape from the violent lifestyle and institutions that possessed him.

10.69. Gardner, Sandra. (1983). *Street gangs.* New York: Franklin Watts. 86 pp. (includes photo inserts) (ISBN: 0-531-04666-4)

Nowadays, street gangs are a part of life in many cities. This book examines why young people join street gangs and describes what gang life is like. An entire chapter is devoted to the House of Umoja, a special Philadelphia-based group home that tries to reduce gang violence and to improve the job skills of its residents. The relationship that exists between adult criminal organizations and street gangs is also explored.

10.70. Heide, K.M. (1992). *Why kids kill parents: Child abuse and adolescent homicide.* Columbus: Ohio State University Press. 197 pp. (ISBN: 0-814-20573-9)

After presenting case studies of teenagers who murdered their parents, the author analyzes their reasons and proposes what needs to be done to prevent such tragedies from occurring. Heide is an internationally recognized consultant on adolescent homicide and family violence.

10.71. Hyde, Margaret O. & Hyde, Lawrence E. (1985). *Missing children.* New York: Franklin Watts. 104 pp. (ISBN: 0-531-10073-1) (Out of Print)

   This book examines why young people run away from their homes and what happens to them once they are on the streets. Over one million children leave their homes each year, half of them run away and the other half are abducted. Abductions by parents and strangers and the groups devoted to finding missing children are also discussed. The author also provides a resource section that includes hotlines, helpful agencies, and a bibliography.

10.72. McGeady, Sister Mary Rose. (1991). *God's lost children: The shocking story of America's homeless kids.* New York: Covenant House. 115 pp.

   Fourteen young people share the reasons they ran away from home and finally ended up at the Covenant House. The author provides tips for parents to get along with their teenagers better and also suggests other ways for parents to become more involved. This is book one in a series being published by the Covenant House Program of Public Awareness.

10.73. Meyer, Caroline. (1979). *The center: From a troubled past to a new life.* 193 pp.

   See Alcohol and Drugs

10.74. Prendergast, Alan. (1986). *The poison tree: A true story of family violence and revenge.* 350 pp.

   See Abuse

10.75. Ritter, Bruce. (1989). *Covenant House: Lifeline to the street.* New York: Doubleday Image Paperback. 264 pp. (ISBN: 0-385-26004-0)

   Father Bruce Ritter, a Franciscan priest, shares the letters he has written over a 20 year span. During those years, he spent his time trying to get street kids off of the street through the establishment of the Covenant House.

10.76. Wirths, Claudine G. & Bowman-Kruhm, Mary. (1987). *I hate school: How to hang in and when to drop out.* New York: Thomas Y. Crowell. 115 pp. (ISBN: 0-690-04556-5)

Using a question and answer format, these authors offer sound advice to troubled students. Besides providing information on the consequences of dropping out of school, the book offers suggestions on how to improve study skills and general tips on how to succeed in school.

Nonfiction References Dealing with Dropouts and Delinquency

Journal Articles

Alderman, M.K. (1990, September). Motivation for at-risk students. *Educational Leadership, 48* (1), p. 27 ff.

Beck, J. (1992, May 19). Inner-city kids beat the odds to survive. *The Tampa Tribune.*

Berg, I., Goodwin, A., Hullin, R., & McGuire, R. (1987, February). School attendance, visits by EWOs and appearance in juvenile court. *Educational Research, 29* (1), p. 19 ff.

Burke, J. (1991, September). Teenagers, clothes, and gang violence. *Educational Leadership, 49* (1), p. 11 ff.

Crosby, E.A. (1993, April). The at-risk decade. *Phi Delta Kappan, 74* (8), p. 598 ff.

Edelman, M.W. (1989, May). Defending America's children. *Educational Leadership, 46* (8), p. 77 ff.

Finn, J.D. (1989, summer). Withdrawing from school. *Review of Educational Research, 59* (2), p. 117 ff.

Finn, J.D. (1991, January/February). How to make the dropout problem go away. *Educational Researcher, 20* (1), p, 28 ff.

Gage, N.L. (1990, December). Dealing with the dropout problem. *Phi Delta Kappan, 72* (4), p. 280 ff.

Gillen, J.M. (1992, March). Accounts/A lesson from *Macbeth.* *English Journal, 81* (3), p. 64 ff.

Grannis, J.C. (1991, October). Dropout prevention in New York City: A second chance. *Phi Delta Kappan, 73* (2), p. 143 ff.

Guthrie, G.P. & Guthrie, L.F. (1991, September). Streamlining interagency collaboration for youth at risk. *Educational Leadership*, *49* (1), p. 17 ff.

Hamby, J.V. (1989, February). How to get an "A" on your dropout prevention report card. *Educational Leadership*, *46* (5), p. 21 ff.

Hill, D. (1991, December). Tasting failure: Thoughts of an at-risk learner. *Phi Delta Kappan*, *73* (4), p. 308 ff.

Hodgkinson, H. (1991, September). Reform versus Reality. *Phi Delta Kappan*, *73* (1), p. 9 ff.

Hurley, D. (1985, March). Arresting delinquency. *Psychology Today*, *19* (3), p. 62 ff.

Koff, R.H. & Ward, D. (1990, November). Philanthropy, the public schools, and the university: A model for at-risk youth. *Phi Delta Kappan*, *72* (3), p. 223 ff.

Mahle, B. (1992, September). Lenny wasn't difficult--he was impossible. *Learning*, *21* (2), p. 66 ff.

Marble, G. (1992-1993, December-January). Plea from a prisoner. *Educational Leadership*, *50* (4), p. 61 ff.

Monroe, C., Borzi, M.G., & Burrell, R.D. (1992, January). Communication apprehension among high school dropouts. *The School Counselor*, *39* (4), p. 273 ff.

O'Neil, J. (1993, May). A new generation confronts racism. *Educational Leadership*, *50* (8), p. 60 ff.

Perrin, J. (1990, October). The learning styles project for potential dropouts. *Educational Leadership*, *48* (2), p. 23 ff.

Roth, J. & Hendrickson, J.M. (1991, April). School and youth organizations: Empowering adolescents to confront high-risk behavior. *Phi Delta Kappan*, *72* (8), p. 619 ff.

Ryan, S.M. & Brewer, B. (1990, January). Changing the English curriculum for at-risk high school students. *Journal of Reading*, *33* (4), p. 270 ff.

Books

Sander, Daryl. (1991). *Focus on teens in trouble*. Santa Barbara, CA: ABC-CLIO. 182 pp. (ISBN: 0-874-36207-5)

CHAPTER 11

Teenage Pregnancy

While adults are debating about whether or not teenagers should be taught about safe sex, the fact remains that teenage pregnancy has become a huge problem for this society and is getting increasingly more problematic. More often than not, unmarried teenagers are engaging in sexual activity. More often than not, teenage mothers drop out of school and never return. More often than not, these mothers and their babies become part of the welfare system and have little chance of leaving it. It is time to reverse this trend so that unwanted pregnancies occur less often or not at all.

STARTLING INFORMATION ABOUT TEENAGE PREGNANCY

- In 1984, the annual teen birth rate in the United States was the highest among industrialized nations with one million births to girls between 15 to 19 years of age or a rate of 233 pregnancies per 1,000 girls. (Blum, 1987)

- In 1987, approximately 500,000 babies were delivered to women 19 years of age or younger (Moore, 1989), between 20% to 25% of the fathers were adolescents (National Center for Health Statistics, 1987), and 125,000 of those babies were delivered to junior high school girls. (Cahill, 1987)

- In 1988, the Children's Defense Fund estimated that 488 babies were born every day to girls younger than 18 years of age. (Rogers & Hughes Lee, 1992)

- Approximately three-fourths of the mothers who gave birth between the ages of 15 to 17 are on welfare. (Simkins, 1984)

- Half of all first teen pregnancies occur within the first six months of the first sexual experience. (Kennedy, 1987)

- Half of teenage mothers will have a second pregnancy within 36 months. (Simkins, 1984)

- By the age of 15, a fourth of the girls and a third of the boys are sexually active. (Gibbs, 1993)

- Sixty-two percent of males and 43% of females believe that sexual intercourse with someone they have dated for a long time is acceptable; the average age of first intercourse is 16. (National Adolescent Student Health Survey, 1988)

- More than half of high school students have had intercourse at least once, and many participate in intercourse on a regular basis. (Krueger, 1993)

- Three out of four teenagers have had sexual intercourse by their senior years. (Males, 1993)

- Twenty-seven percent of sexually active teenagers never use contraceptives, and 39% said they preferred not to use any method. (Harris Planned Parenthood Poll, 1986)

- According to the TIME/CNN Poll, 60% of parents tell their daughters to wait until marriage for sex but less than 50% tell their sons the same thing. (Gibbs, 1993)

- In a 1988 poll, two-thirds of 18 to 44-year-olds admitted that they engaged in premarital sex and few said they regretted it. (Males, 1993)

- Teenagers average five hours of television viewing a day which exposes them to roughly 14,000 sexual encounters per year. (Center for Population Options, 1993)

WHAT TO DO AND WHERE TO GO FOR HELP

- It is imperative that the teenager have a source of support during and after the pregnancy.

- Be adamant about medical attention, especially during a teen mother's first trimester.

- If someone you know is pregnant, discuss the problem openly and frankly while showing genuine, nonjudgmental concern.

- Encourage pregnant teenagers to finish school.

- Get professional help: Call a local ALPHA House, crisis intervention center, mental health clinic, hospital, a family physician, a clergy, a guidance counselor, or a teacher. If you know of a pregnant teenager who needs immediate help, call the Pregnancy Hotline at 1-800-238-4269. For more information, write to the American Academy of Child and Adolescent Psychiatry, 3615 Wisconsin Avenue, NW, Washington, D.C., 20016-3007.

Annotated Young Adult Novels Dealing with Teenage Pregnancy

11.01. Angelou, Maya. (1990). *Gather together in my name.* New York: Bantam Books. 192 pp. (ISBN: 0-553-26066-9)

Rita Johnson, a 17-year-old black girl, takes responsibility for her own life after the birth of her illegitimate son. By traveling around the country and working odd jobs, Rita is able to support her son and herself. This somewhat autobiographical novel is Ms. Angelou's account of how difficult it is to raise a son when mom is just a teenager herself. (an American Library Association Best Book for Young Adults)

11.02. Armstrong, Louise. (1980). *Saving the big-deal baby.* 42 pp.

See Abuse

11.03. Baldwin, James. (1988). *If Beale Street could talk.* New York: Dell. 213 pp. (ISBN: 0-440-34060-8)

Tish and Fonny are a black couple doing their best trying to make it in New York. Fonny is always at odds with his family and is sent to jail for a crime he didn't commit. Meanwhile, Tish is pregnant which is the last thing they need as teenagers right now. Fortunately, Tish's family offers support, and the young couple find comfort in the love they have for each other.

11.04. Betancourt, Jeanne. (1991). *Sweet sixteen and never . . .* New York: Bantam Books. 144 pp. (ISBN: 0-553-25534-7)

Julie supports a friend in her decision to terminate her pregnancy and then learns, by reading an old diary, that her own mother had been pregnant at sixteen. (an IRA/CBC Children's Choice)

11.05. Blume, Judy. (1975). *Forever*. New York: Bradbury Press. 199 pp. (ISBN: 0-027-11030-3)

Although the protagonist doesn't get pregnant, this novel tackles the sensitive topics of falling in love and losing one's virginity. Katherine meets, falls in love with, and has her first sexual experience with Michael, her forever love. Her parents don't want her to make any decisions she will later regret, her grandmother preaches to her about the importance of safe sex, and her little sister wants to be just like her. Michael's feelings are also explored, particularly when Katherine's feelings begin to diminish for him. (an American Library Association Best of the Best Books for Young Adults)

11.06. Calvert, Patricia. (1988). *Stranger, you and I*. New York: Avon Flare. 160 pp. (ISBN: 0-380-70600-8)

During Hugh McBride's 17th year, he finds himself playing counselor to his best friend, his parents, and his little brother during a time when he dreams of a writing career. Hugh tells the story about his friendship with Zee and what she goes through during her junior year in high school. Zee gets pregnant after a one night rendezvous with Jordie, a senior boy she's crazy about. Zee doesn't want to tell Jordie about his being the father and relies on Hugh for emotional support. Hugh offers to marry her, but he ends up just helping her decide what to do. His parents, meanwhile, decide to separate and his little brother intentionally tries to prevent him from going away after graduation. One by one all of the problems are resolved but not without some struggles.

11.07. Childress, Alice. (1982). *Rainbow Jordan*. New York: Avon Books. 128 pp. (ISBN: 0-380-58974-5)

Rainbow Jordan got that name because her mother told her that people usually find gold at the end of rainbows which makes them happy; Rainbow prefers to be called Rainey. Because Rainey's mother, Kathie, had her at 15 and married Rainey's 16-year-old father, she never had time to do the things teenagers normally did. Kathie neglects Rainey and often leaves her at home without supervision. Even though Rainey is 14 years old now, it still hurts when she has to go back to Josephine Lamont's house for care. When Rainey's mother is supposed to show up for a parent conference at school and doesn't show, Rainey finally realizes that she has been only fooling herself about her mother's love. (a *School Library Journal* Best Book of the Year & an American Library Association Best Book)

11.08. Eyerly, Jeanette. (1977). *He's my baby now*. Philadelphia: J.B. Lippincott. 156 pp. (ISBN: 0-397-31744-1)

This is the story of a 16-year-old boy who learns that the baby he thought he paid to have aborted has just been born. His curiosity overwhelms him, and he visits the hospital to see his son. Being in the presence of this fragile creature of his own making has a profound impact on him, and he finds himself searching for ways to prevent the adoption proceedings from happening. The story is one of sudden maturity as this unwed father musters the strength and courage to consent to what is best for all concerned.

11.09. Eyerly, Jeanette. (1987). *Someone to love me*. Philadelphia: J B. Lippincott. 168 pp. (ISBN: 0-397-32205-4.

Because Patrice's parents are involved with their own lives rather than hers, she seeks the love from a boy who is also very self-centered. He is always too busy to go anywhere but is ever-present when there is a possibility for sexual intimacy. Patrice feels guilty about their sexual encounters and rejects contraceptives because it would appear that she was planning for sex--this way it just happens. When the inevitable happens, Patrice is forced to make the biggest decision of her life.

11.10. Ferris, Jean. (1989). *Looking for home*. New York: Farrar, Straus, & Giroux. 167 pp. (ISBN: 0-374-34649-6)

Daphne has never had it easy, and things get a lot tougher for her after she becomes pregnant. She decides not to tell the baby's father and is too scared to tell her father, so she drops out of school and runs away. She finds a waitressing job and a circle of people who offer her the support she needs.

11.11. Hamilton, Morse. (1990). *Effie's house*. 224 pp.

See Abuse

11.12. Head, Ann. (1968). *Mr. and Mrs. Bo Jo Jones*. New York: Signet. 192 pp. (ISBN: 0-451-16319-2)

July Greher and her boyfriend, Bo Jo, are typical high school students with a lot going for them. When July becomes pregnant (after their first time), their dreams are shattered and their lives are necessarily rerouted. Bo Jo and July decide to marry, and they encounter many of the pressures and hardships a young couple can face: parental disapproval, interrupted educations, alienation from peers, and responsibilities associated with early marriage and impending parenthood. (an American Library Association Best of the Best Books for Young Adults)

11.13. Holland, Isabelle. (1992). *The long search*. New York: Fawcett. (ISBN: 0-449-22009-5)

Claudia Ransom, now 17, is driven to find out what happened to the baby she put up for adoption. Claudia wonders where her baby is, who's taking care of it, and if she or he is all right. The big question for Claudia is whether or not she can put the past to rest and get on with her life.

11.14.   Klein, Norma. (1987). *It's not what you'd expect*. New York: Avon Books. 128 pp. (ISBN: 0-380-00011-3)

Carla and Oliver Simon are two very talented and enterprising, 14-year-old twins. Their summer project is to open a little gourmet French restaurant called "Chez Simon." In the midst of their hard work and success, Carla has to face the reality of her parents' separation. Additionally, she cannot understand how her older brother, Ralph, could have been so stupid to have gotten his girlfriend pregnant even though they have been dating virtually since childhood. Life just doesn't seem anything like what Carla expected. Lucky for her, she has a very intelligent and understanding twin who takes the time to help Carla better understand herself and the world around her.

11.15.   Klein, Norma. (1989). *No more Saturday nights*. New York: Fawcett Juniper. 272 pp. (ISBN: 0-449-70304-5)

After dating for awhile, Tim and Cheryl discover that she is pregnant. They discuss abortion, but Cheryl is not happy with the idea. Cheryl comes from a poor family and decides to offer the baby to an infertile couple in a nearby town. When Tim learns of her plans, he decides to take her to court for custody of the child. This 17-year-old wins the battle and prepares for his new son's arrival. Because Tim is about to enter a pre-med program at a prestigious college in New York City, everyone tells him that he will never be able to raise a baby and go to school at the same time. Tim is determined to prove them wrong, especially his father who is one of his harshest critics. The baby not only changes Tim's life but also positively affects his relationship with his father. This book explores the ups and downs of raising a newborn: juggling college life, dealing with the social stigma surrounding the "Mr. Mom" image, and healing family relationships.

11.16.   Lee, Benjamin. (1979). *It can't be helped*. 155 pp.

See Death and Dying

11.17.   Martin, Katherine. (1989). *Night riding*. 197 pp.

See Abuse

11.18.   McDermott, Alice. (1988). *That night*. New York: Plume. 192 pp. (ISBN: 0-06-097141-X)

When Sheryl gets pregnant at 15 years of age, her mother decides that she will take Sheryl out of school, send her away to have the baby, give it up for adoption, and then bring her back to resume her life as much as possible. The father of the baby, Rick, was never consulted, and Sheryl's mother underestimated his love for her daughter. Because of her inconsideration, there is a violent scene when Rick finds Sheryl and forcefully tries to remove her from her house.

11.19.   O'Dell, Scott. (1978). *Kathleen, please come home.* 196 pp.

See Alcohol and Drugs

11.20.   Peck, Richard. (1992). *Don't look and it won't hurt.* New York: Dell. 173 pp. (ISBN: 0-440-21213-8)

When Ellen becomes pregnant at 17 years of age, her parents make her leave home to have the baby. This novel is about her struggle to make the decision of whether or not to keep the baby or give it up for adoption. Her sister, Carol, shows up and tries to help her through this difficult time.

11.21.   Prince, Alison. (1980). *The turkey's nest.* New York: William Morrow. 223 pp. (ISBN: 0-688-22224-2)

Although Kate's mother is sympathetic when she learns of Kate's pregnancy, her boyfriend is intolerant of the situation. She decides to go live with a widowed aunt out in the country but has a hard time adjusting to the rural life among other things.

11.22.   Rodowsky, Colby. (1992). *Lucy Peale.* New York: Farrar, Straus, & Giroux. 167 pp. (ISBN: 0-374-36381-1)

Lucy Peale is the 17-year-old daughter of a fundamentalist preacher who's in a big mess--she's pregnant and she doesn't even love the boy who's halfway responsible. When her father demands that she repent for her sin in front of the entire congregation, Lucy decides that it is time to leave her family and start her life on her own. Lucy finds that she misses the comforts of home but is encouraged by a new friend who offers his help to her.

11.23.   Rylant, Cynthia. (1990). *A kindness.* New York: Dell Laurel-Leaf. 128 pp. (ISBN: 0-440-20579-4)

Chip Becker is very close to his mother, a single parent he calls Anne. When Anne becomes pregnant and will not disclose the identity of the father, their relationship is destroyed. (an American Library Association Best Book for Young Adults, an *American Bookseller* Pick of the Lists, a *School Library Journal* Best Book of the Year)

11.24. Strang, Celia. (1981). *This child is mine.* 156 pp.

See Poverty

11.25. Truss, Jan. (1980). *Bird at the window.* New York: Harper & Row. 215 pp. (ISBN: 0-060-26137-4)

Angela Moynahan doesn't want to talk with anyone about her pregnancy, not even with her understanding mother. In order to escape from small town gossip, Angela decides to go and stay with her grandparents in England. There she struggles with the decision to keep the baby or have an abortion.

11.26. Willey, Margaret. (1988). *If not for you.* New York: Harper Collins. 160 pp. (ISBN: 0-06-026499-3)

Although Linda drops out of school in order to marry Ray and have his baby, this is really Bonnie's story. Linda is Bonnie's best friend's sister, and Bonnie is caught up in the romance of it all. Reality about the hardships faced by teenage parents begins to set in when Bonnie does some babysitting for the couple and Linda shares some of her feelings. Contrasted by Bonnie's beginning relationship with Robert, this novel also exposes the confusion often associated with a first romance.

11.27. Woodson, Jacqueline. (1991). *The dear one.* New York: Dell. 145 pp. (ISBN: 0-440-21420-3)

Afeni has a lot to deal with for a 12-year-old girl: Her grandmother has recently died, her parents have recently divorced, and her mother is a recovering alcoholic. Feni's mother complicates things even more when she agrees to let a college friend's daughter, Rebecca, live with them for awhile. Feni is not happy about sharing her bedroom with someone, especially a 15-year-old pregnant girl in the latter stages of her pregnancy. Rebecca, too, is unhappy with the arrangement. Not only is she having to deal with all of the decisions associated with teenage pregnancy, but she cannot stand Afeni and her mother is gay. Eventually, Rebecca learns about acceptance and the two girls start sharing their feelings with one another and become close.

11.28. Zindel, Paul. (1984). *My darling, my hamburger.* New York: Bantam Books. 128 pp. (ISBN: 0-553-27324-8)

This story probes the thoughts of two teenage couples, Liz and Sean and Maggie and Dennis, and the lessons they learn about love and sex in their final year before graduation. The girls are best friends with normal teenage anxieties about growing up, relationships, and sex. After Liz is unjustly called a tramp by her stepfather, she gives in to Sean's pressure for sex but gets pregnant. Sean offers to marry her until his father instigates their break up. Liz opts for an illegal abortion but experiences complications as a result. Maggie tries to help, but her decisions cost her a friend.

Annotated Young Adult Nonfiction Dealing with Teenage Pregnancy

11.29. Bowe-Gutman, Sonia. (1987). *Teen pregnancy.* Minneapolis: Lerner. 71 pp. (ISBN: 0-8225-0039-6)

Students with middle school reading levels could understand this factual book dealing with several aspects associated with teenage pregnancy: health risks for teenage mothers and their babies, financial demands for raising a baby, birth control, family planning and adoption, and organizations that are available for assistance. Besides some easy-to-understand research data, the author includes five case studies of pregnant teens.

11.30. Ewy, Donna & Ewy, Rodger. (1985). *Teen pregnancy: The challenges we faced, the choices we made.* New York: New American Library/Signet Books. 285 pp. (ISBN: 0-451-13915-1)

This book, written by teens who have been there, explores the confusing and often contradictory emotions that a teenager faces when pregnant. This book explains every aspect of pregnancy, from conception through various methods of childbirth. This is a very readable book, void of difficult technical jargon.

11.31. Gravelle, Karen & Peterson, Leslie. (1992). *Teenage fathers.* New York: Julian Messner. 102 pp. (ISBN: 0-671-72850-4)

Thirteen male teenagers share their experiences of becoming first-time fathers between the ages of 12 and 19. Their degrees of involvement range from one teen who offered absolutely no emotional or financial support to another who has legally fought for visitation rights. A list of further readings and agencies who help teenage fathers are included.

11.32. Kuklin, Susan. (1991). *What do I do now? Talking about teenage pregnancy.* New York: G.P. Putnam's Sons. 179 pp. (ISBN: 0-399-21843-2)

Teen mothers, their mothers, and caregivers share their experiences regarding this issue. The teenagers talk frankly about the decisions they faced concerning abortion, keeping their babies, or giving them up for adoption. A section is included about available facilities and programs, and a glossary follows the text.

11.33. Miner, Jane Claypool. (1985). *Young parents.* New York: Julian Messner. 159 pp. (ISBN: 0-671-49848-7)

Miner discusses the choices available to pregnant teenagers and the consequences of each choice. Topics include the following: the relationship with the baby's father, how to deal with parents, rejection from peers, bonding with the baby, and financial concerns.

11.34. Richards, Arlene & Willis, Irene. (1983). *What to do if you or someone you know is under 18 and pregnant.* New York: Lothrop, Lee & Shepard. 256 pp. (ISBN: 0-688-01044-X)

The authors provide a lot of advice and information for young mothers on various topics: sex, birth control, pregnancy, abortion, adoption, childbirth, single parenting, marriage, and infant care. (an American Library Association Best of the Best Books for Young Adults)

11.35. Westheimer, Ruth. (1993). *Dr. Ruth talks to kids.* New York: Macmillan. (ISBN: 0-027-92532-3)

This book, geared for kids between the ages of 8 and 14, is based on her belief that kids should be taught everything about sex and then be encouraged to wait. "What's the rush?" she asks.

11.36. Will, Reni L., & Michael, Jeannine M. (1982). *Mom, I'm pregnant.* Lanham, MD: Madison Books. 239 pp. ISBN: 0-8128-6173-6)

The authors explore the emotional and physical consequences of an unwanted pregnancy and discuss the various options available to young mothers who have an unexpected pregnancy.

Nonfiction References Dealing with Teenage Pregnancy

Journal Articles

Bempechat, J., Stauber, H., & Way, N. (1989). Teenage pregnancy and drug abuse: Sources of problem behaviors. *Clearinghouse on Urban Education Digest, 58* (1), p. 3 ff.

Blum, R. (1987). Contemporary threats to adolescent health in the United States. *Journal of the American Medical Association, 257* (24), p. 3390 ff.

Buie, J. (1987). Teen pregnancy: It's time for the schools to tackle the problem. *Phi Delta Kappan, 68* (10), p. 738 ff.

Cahill, M. (1987, March). Teenage pregnancy and economic self-sufficiency for girls: A sex-equity challenge. *Educational Leadership, 44* (6), p. 86 ff.

Conway, L.J. (1985). GRADS: A program for in-school adolescent pregnant students and young parents. *American Secondary Education, 14* (2), p. 23 ff.

Crosby, E.A. (1993, April). The at-risk decade. *Phi Delta Kappan, 74* (8), p. 598 ff.

Davis, R.A. (1989, spring). Teenage pregnancy: A theoretical analysis of a social problem. *Adolescence, 24* (93), p. 18 ff.

Gibbs, N. (1993, May 24). How should we teach our children about sex? *Time, 140* (21), p. 60 ff.

Hulbert, A. (1984, September 10). Children as parents. *The New Republic, 14* (2), p. 15 ff.

Kennedy, A.M. (1987). Teen pregnancy: An issue for schools. *Phi Delta Kappan, 68* (1), 732 ff.

Krueger, M.M. (1993, March). Everyone is an exception: Assumptions to avoid in the sex education classroom. *Phi Delta Kappan, 74* (7), p. 569 ff.

Levine, A. (1987, March 23). Taking on teen pregnancy. *U.S. News & World Report, 102* (11), p. 67 ff.

Lyons, A. (1985, May). Adolescent pregnancy and parenthood. *The School Guide Worker, 14* (5), p. 24 ff.

Males, M. (1993, March). Schools, society, and 'teen' pregnancy. *Phi Delta Kappan, 74* (7), p. 566 ff.

McClellan, M.C. (1987, June). Teenage pregnancy. *Journal of Home Economics,* p. 789 ff.

Morrison, J. & Jensen, S.   (1982, October).   Teenage pregnancy: Special counseling considerations. *The Clearing House, 56* (2), p. 74 ff.

Polit, D.F.   (1987, January-February).   Routes to self-sufficiency: Teenage mothers and employment. *Children Today, 16* (1), p. 6 ff.

Protinsky, H., Sporakowski, M., & Atkins, P.   (1985, Spring).   Identity formation: Pregnant and non-pregnant adolescents. *Adolescents, 17* (65), p. 73 ff.

Rogers, E. & Hughes Lee, S.   (1992).   A comparison of the perception of the mother-daughter relationship of black pregnant and nonpregnant teenagers. *Adolescence, 27* (107), p. 555 ff.

Schmidt, A.V.   (1985, July-August).   School-based child care puts diploma in reach for teenage mothers. *Children Today, 14* (4), p. 16 ff.

Shostak, A.B.   (1991, July-August).   Abortion in America: Ten cautious forecasts. *The Futurist, 25* (4), p. 20 ff.

Simkins, L.   (1984, Spring).   Consequences of teenage pregnancy and motherhood. *Adolescence, 19* (73), p. 39 ff.

Journal Themes

Teen Pregnancy: An Issue for Schools. (1987, June). *Phi Delta Kappan, 68* (10).

Books

Dash, L. (1990). *When children want children: An inside look at the crisis of teenage parenthood.* New York: Penguin Books. 271 pp. (ISBN: 0-14-011789-X)

Furstenberg, F.F., Jr., Brooks-Gunn, J., & Morgan, S.P. (1990). *Adolescent mothers in later life.* New York: Cambridge University Press. 204 pp. (ISBN: 0-521-37968-7)

Jakobson, C. (1992). *Teenage pregnancy.* New York: Walker. 160 pp. (ISBN: 0-8027-7372-9)

Moore, K. (1989). *Child trends.* Washington, D.C.:   Charles Mott Foundation.

CHAPTER 12

AIDS

Today's adolescents of both sexes face a serious risk of Acquired Immune Deficiency Virus (HIV) infection which causes AIDS and ultimately leads to death. AIDS is often referred to as a gay disease, but, in actuality, it is predominantly found in the heterosexual population. American teenagers are a particularly vulnerable group primarily because of their high-risk patterns of sexual behavior. Many AIDS experts see adolescents as the third wave of individuals affected by HIV--following the concentration found in adult gay men and IV drug users.

STARTLING INFORMATION ABOUT AIDS

- The World Health Organization estimates that 30 million people will be HIV infected by the year 2000.

- The World Health Organization estimates that 60% of HIV transmission worldwide is through heterosexual intercourse, a percentage that will likely rise to 75 to 80% by 2003.

- Most people who have the HIV infection do not know it. (Department of Health and Human Services, 1990)

- Twenty-five percent of the 218,301 reported cases of AIDS in the United States involved persons under the age of 29 which suggests that most of these infections were acquired during adolescence due to the long latency period of the illness. (Tonks, 1993)

- Almost half of sexually active youth said that they were more likely to have sex after drinking, and 17% said they used condoms in sex less often with alcohol than without. (Tonks, 1993)

- There were 3,426 cases of AIDS reported nationwide among children under the age of thirteen. (Centers for Disease Control, 1991)

- More than 140,000 people have died of AIDS-related illnesses, and in 1989, AIDS was the sixth leading cause of death for 15 to 24 year olds. (Tonks, 1993)

- HIV infected women have a one in three chance of passing HIV onto their unborn babies. (Department of Health and Human Services, 1990)

- In 1988, the Presidential Commission on the HIV epidemic recommended that state boards of education should mandate AIDS education.

Risk of AIDS Is Increased By

- Engaging in any kind of unprotected sex.

- Having an increased number of sexual partners.

- Participating in anal intercourse.

- Using drugs or alcohol because sex is more impulsive and use of condoms is less likely.

- Sharing intravenous drug needles; tattoos.

- Receiving blood transfusions but the risk is smaller since the widespread screening and testing of blood began in 1985.

WHAT TO DO AND WHERE TO GO FOR HELP

- Encourage teenagers to learn as much as possible about AIDS.

- AIDS can be prevented. Don't preach to adolescents about sex but do be specific: A more realistic strategy is to encourage the restraint from high risk behaviors with an emphasis on condom use during intercourse. Be adamant about discouraging drug abuse, especially IV drug abuse.

- During prolonged periods of rest or hospitalization, involve the adolescent in a hobby or in the development of a particular talent.

- Try to find ways to establish support groups where teenagers experiencing similar kinds of difficulty can talk to one another.

- Get professional help: Call local AIDS organizations, community health clinics, sexually transmitted disease (STD) clinics, crisis intervention centers, mental health clinics, hospitals, a family physician, a clergy, a guidance counselor, or a teacher. If you or a person you know has AIDS, find a doctor who is experienced with HIV and AIDS-related issues. If you want current updates on AIDS statistics, call the National AIDS Hotline at 1-800-342-AIDS. For more information, write to the American Academy of Child & Adolescent Psychiatry, 3615 Wisconsin Avenue, NW, Washington, D.C., 20016-3007.

Annotated Young Adult Novels Dealing with AIDS

12.01. Arrick, Fran. (1992). *What you don't know can kill you*. New York: Bantam Books. 154 pp. (ISBN: 0-553-97471-7)

Thirteen-year-old Debra Geddes is jealous of all of the attention Ellen is receiving just because of prom and graduation. Debra thinks her older sister's life is perfect, and there isn't much room for her to be any better. Things drastically change, however, when a blood drive reveals that Ellen is HIV positive. Ellen finds out that Jack, her first and only sex partner, had a one-night-stand at a fraternity party while away at college.

12.02. Feinberg, David B. (1990). *Eighty-sixed*. New York: Penguin Books. 336 pp. (ISBN: 0-14-011252-9).

This coming of age novel depicts the history of the AIDS epidemic and the changes it has brought to the Gay Community.

12.03. Hoffman, Alice. (1988). *At risk*. New York: G.P. Putnam's Sons. 219 pp. (ISBN: 0-399-13367-4)

The blood transfusion Amanda received when she was six years old was contaminated, and now she has AIDS. Besides having to deal with her impending death, 11-year-old Amanda faces inordinate rejection from the parents who organize a protest to ban her from school, from her younger brother's best friend's parents who forbid him to visit, and from neighbors who shun the family. Amanda and her family stick by each other and prove, once again, that "blood is thicker than water."

12.04. Kerr, M.E. (1986). *Night kites*. New York: Harper & Row. 216 pp. (ISBN: 0-06-023253-6)

When Erick was five and his older brother, Pete, was 15, Pete made a kite with lights so he could fly it at night. Pete explained its significance to Erick: ". . . most kites fly in the daytime, but some go up in the dark. They go up alone, on their own. . .and they're not afraid to be different. Some people are different too." Erick's life used to be simple and predictable until his senior year in high school when he falls for Nicki, his best friend's girlfriend, and finds out that his brother has AIDS. (an American Library Association Best of the Best Books for Young Adults)

12.05.   Levy, Marilyn. (1990). *Rumors and whispers*. 160 pp.

See Homosexuality

12.06.   Miklowitz, Gloria D. (1990). *Good-bye tomorrow*. New York: Dell. 160 pp. (ISBN: 0-440-20081-4)

Alex Weiss, his family, his friends, and his girlfriend must face their feelings and fears when they learn that Alex has contracted ARC, an AIDS-related complex from a tainted blood transfusion; each responds differently. This novel has been thoroughly researched and deals realistically with the emotional effects of AIDS. (an NCSS-CBC Notable Children's Book in the Field of Social Studies)

12.07.   Uyemoto, Holly. (1989). *Rebel without a clue*. New York: Crown Publishers. 194 pp. (ISBN: 0-517-57170-6)

At 18 years, good-looking Thomas Bainbridge apparently has it all: He is a movie star and the highest paid male model in the country. He and his best friend, Christian, spend a challenging summer together when Thomas acquires one more thing--AIDS. (Note: the author wrote this at 19 years of age.)

12.08.   Young, Alida E. (1988). *I never got to say goodbye*. Worthington, OH: Willowisp Press. 128 pp. (ISBN: 0-87406-359-0)

Traci's Uncle Mark becomes HIV positive after receiving a contaminated blood transfusion because of an automobile accident that killed Mark's parents. At first, Traci's parents try to hide it from her since she had been through so much already. They tell her and Traci witnesses her uncle's "friends" leaving, his inability to get an apartment, and his eventual hospital stay. While visiting him at the hospital, she meets her uncle's roommate, Danny, who got AIDS from a contaminated needle. When Danny dies, Traci and her Uncle Mark attend help groups where they make new friends. They decide to make Danny a panel for the AIDS Memorial Quilt.

Annotated Young Adult Nonfiction Dealing with AIDS

12.09.   Bell, Ruth et.al. (1988). *Changing bodies, changing lives: Revised and updated.* 272 pp.

See Homosexuality

12.10.   Blake, Jeanne. (1990). *Risky times: How to be AIDS-smart and stay healthy: A guide for teenagers.* New York: Workman. 158 pp. (ISBN: 0-89480-656-4)

This book, written specifically for teenagers, addresses their concerns about sex. AIDS is not just a disease that homosexuals and drug users get but is one that affects us all in some way or another. Besides information about safe sex practices and how the disease is transmitted, Blake includes personal testimonials from six teenagers with AIDS.

12.11.   Cohen, Daniel & Cohen, Susan. (1992). *When someone you know is gay.* 162 pp.

See Homosexuality

12.12.   Colman, Warren. (1988). *Understanding and preventing AIDS.* Chicago, IL: Children's Press. 123 pp. (ISBN: 0-516-40592-6)

As the title suggests, the author provides an easy-to-understand overview of AIDS. Addresses, hotline numbers, and other sources for help and information are provided.

12.13.   Hawkes, Nigel. (1987). *AIDS.* New York: Gloucester Press. 32 pp. (ISBN: 0-531-17054-3)

Acquired Immune Deficiency Syndrome was first discovered in 1981 and has spread rapidly since then; over 32,000 cases had been reported in the U.S. when this book was written. There are several ways to get this disease: contaminated needles shared by drug users, homosexual and heterosexual intercourse, contaminated blood transfusions, and intrauterine contact between an infected woman and her unborn fetus. Besides presenting general information about AIDS, the author also describes how to prevent it and current treatment programs.

12.14.   Hyde, Margaret O. & Forsyth, Elizabeth H. (1992). *AIDS: What does it mean to you?* (4th Ed.). New York: Walker & Company. 128 pp. (ISBN: 0-8027-8203-5)

Written specifically for young readers, these authors provide the latest information about AIDS.

12.15.   Kittredge, Mary. (1991). *Teens with AIDS speak out*. New York: Julian Messner. 119 pp. (ISBN: 0-671-74542-5)

Several teenagers share their experiences, both emotional and financial, in dealing with AIDS. Through their stories, readers gain insight into the "it can't happen to me" attitude. Readers also learn ways to prevent AIDS and that it is okay to refrain from sex until they are older. There is also a chapter on the history of AIDS as well as a glossary and a list of resources for further information about AIDS.

12.16.   Landau, Elaine. (1990). *We have AIDS*. Danbury, CT: Franklin Watts. 126 pp. (ISBN: 0-531-10898-8)

Nine adolescents share their moving, personal stories on what it is like to be teenagers with AIDS. The author also provides factual information about the disease throughout.

12.17.   Madaras, Lynda. (1988). *Lynda Madaras talks to teens about AIDS: An essential guide for parents, teachers, and young people*. New York: Newmarket Press. 106 pp. (ISBN: 1-55704-009-5)

This is an informal guide that explains, in simple language, how a person can get AIDS and where a person can go for help.

12.18.   Monette, Paul. (1990). *Borrowed time*. New York: Avon Books. 342 pp. (ISBN: 0-380-70779-9)

Paul and Roger were lovers for 12 years until AIDS put an end to their relationship. *Borrowed Time* is Paul's intensely personal, deeply moving account of their lives together, including their daily struggle for dignity amidst a barrage of physical and emotional attacks. This book "teaches us how to live, how to fight for life, and finally, how to die with courage and grace."

12.19.   Ruskin, Cindy. (1988). *The quilt: Stories from the NAMES Project*. New York: Pocket Books. 160 pp. (includes color photographs by Matt Herron) (ISBN: 0-671-66597-9)

In 1987, a gigantic quilt bearing the names of the victims of AIDS was displayed in front of the United States Capitol. Color photographs of various panels along with the personal stories about the corresponding victims are presented in this book.

12.20.   White, Ryan & Cunningham, Anne Marie.   (1991).   *Ryan White: My own story.* New York: Dial. 277 pp. (ISBN: 0-8037-0977-3)

Ryan White had to face death at the age of thirteen. Rather than sit down and wait for death, Ryan makes a conscientious decision to take great strides with his life. Ryan shares his heroic efforts to maintain his right to attend school with his friends and continue in a healthy relationship with his girlfriend. The reader is privy to the various relationships he has with his family and friends, and the impact his having AIDS has on them.

Nonfiction References Dealing with AIDS

Journal Articles

Allensworth, D.D. & Kerr, D.L.   (1990, June-July).   Every seventh student: How to fight the epidemic of sexually transmitted diseases. *Teacher Magazine*, p. 70 ff.

Bentrup, K.L., Rienzo, B.A., Dorman, S.M., & Lee, D.D.   (1990, November-December).   Cooperative learning: An alternative for adolescent AIDS education, *Clearing House, 64* (2), p. 107 ff.

Fauci, A.S.   (1988, July-August).   How far will AIDS spread in the United States? *The Futurist, 22* (4), p. 41 ff.

Kutzer, M.D.   (1992).   A ghostly chorus: AIDS in the English classroom.   In Mark Hurlbert & Samuel Totten's *Social Issues in the English Classroom.* Urbana, IL: National Council of Teachers of English, p. 206 ff.

Popham, W.J.   (1993, March).   Wanted: AIDS education that works. *Phi Delta Kappan, 74* (7), p. 559 ff.

Scheckler, P.   (1992-1993, December-January).   When a student is HIV positive. *Educational Leadership, 50* (4), p. 55 ff.

Seidel, J.F.   (1992, September).   Children with HIV-related developmental difficulties. *Phi Delta Kappan, 74* (1), p. 38 ff.

Teasley, A.B.   (1993, Spring).   YA literature about AIDS: Encountering the unimaginable. *The ALAN Review, 20* (3), p. 18 ff.

Tonks, D.   (1992-1993, December-January).   Can you save your students' lives? Educating to prevent AIDS. *Educational Leadership, 50* (4), p. 48 ff.

Tonks, D. (1992-1993, December-January). How teenagers are at risk for HIV infection. *Educational Leadership, 50* (4), p. 52 ff.

White, H.L. (1991, May-June). What teachers should know about AIDS. *Clearing House, 64* (5), p. 343 ff.

Books

Harding, P. & Pinsky, L. (Eds.). (1992). *The essential AIDS fact book, No. 3.* New York: Pocket Books. 128 pp. (ISBN: 0-671-73184-X)

Hausherr, R. (1989). *Children and the AIDS virus.* New York: Clarion Books. 48 pp. (ISBN: 0-395-51167-4)

Kubler-Ross, E. (1989). *AIDS: The ultimate challenge.* New York: Collier Books. 329 pp. (ISBN: 0-020-59001-6)

Lerner, E.A. (1987). *Understanding AIDS.* Minneapolis, MN: Lerner Publications. 64 pp. (ISBN: 0-8225-0024-8)

Yarber, W.L. (1989). *AIDS: What young adults should know.* Reston, VA: The American Alliance for Health, Physical Education, Recreation, and Dance. 38 pp. (ISBN: 0-88314-4069)

CHAPTER 13

Death and Dying

There are two major types of involvement a teenager may have with death: having a terminal illness or dealing with the death or long-term illness of a loved one. The adolescent with a serious medical illness usually refuses to believe that it is true and later experiences guilt then anger over the situation. Dying teenagers often feel pulled in opposite directions. On the one hand, they are highly dependent on parents and doctors for their treatments; on the other hand, they are wanting to be independent and social with their friends--a behavior typically associated with normal adolescent development. According to Dr. Kubler Ross, an individual who experiences the death of a loved one must experience five stages in order to fully come to terms with a death. The stages of denial, anger, bargaining, depression, and acceptance do not specifically occur in this order, and each stage period differs from person to person.

STARTLING INFORMATION ABOUT DEATH AND DYING

- Cancer is the 2nd major killer of children. (Schneiderman, 1989)

- More than half of the deaths of children ages 14 or younger can be attributed to accidental causes. (Schneiderman, 1989)

- It is normal for some children to feel immediate grief or persist in the belief that a loved one is still alive for several weeks after the death, but long-term denial or avoidance of grief is unhealthy and can later develop into major problems. (American Academy of Child & Adolescent Psychiatry, *Facts for Families*, 1992)

- A child should not be forced to go to a funeral but should participate in some formal acknowledgment of the death such as lighting a candle, saying a special prayer, or visiting the grave site. (American Academy of Child & Adolescent Psychiatry, *Facts for Families*, 1992)

Dr. Kubler-Ross's Five Stages for Coping with Death

- Denial is the refusal to accept death or dying.

- Anger is directed at self or to others; feelings of rage, betrayal, and envy characterize this stage.

- Bargaining involves the making of deals with God, family, hospital personnel, and others in the hopes of prolonging life.

- Depression refers to the ultimate sadness or feelings of self-pity associated with those facing death.

- Acceptance is where the healing process begins and occurs when the reality of death has been accepted.

WARNING SIGNS OF A PERSON WHO IS HAVING DIFFICULTY ADJUSTING TO DEATH

- An extended period of depression in which the child loses interest in daily activities or events.

- Inability to sleep, loss of appetite, prolonged fear of being alone.

- Acting much younger for an extended period of time.

- Excessively imitating the dead person, making repeated statements about wanting to join the dead person.

- Withdrawal from friends.

WHAT TO DO AND WHERE TO GO FOR HELP

- Respond not only to the teenager's illness but also to his or her strengths.

- Encourage the teenager to learn as much as possible about the illness.

- During prolonged periods of rest or hospitalization, involve the adolescent in a hobby or in the development of a particular talent.

- Try to find ways to establish support groups where teenagers with similar illnesses or problems can talk to one another.

- Get professional help: Call local community health clinics, crisis intervention centers, mental health clinics, hospitals, a family physician, a clergy, a guidance counselor, or a teacher. If you or a person you know needs immediate help, call the National Crisis Alert at 1-800-231-1295. For more information, write to the American Academy of Child & Adolescent Psychiatry, 3615 Wisconsin Avenue, NW, Washington, D.C., 20016-3007.

Annotated Young Adult Novels Dealing with Death and Dying

13.01.   Adler, C.S. (1992). *Ghost brother*. New York: Avon-Camelot. 128 pp. (ISBN: 0-380-71386-1)

Everyone is in a state of disbelief when Jon-o dies, especially his brother Wally who has always felt less important than his older brother. Jon-o was the one who was exciting, athletic, and Mom's favorite. Eventually, Jon-o's ghost starts appearing to Wally and offers him advice on how to handle his grieving mother and his overbearing aunt. Unfortunately, what might have worked for Jon-o often backfires for Wally. Wally has to learn how to value his own personality and trust his own instincts while remembering his brother.

13.02.   Allen, Richard E. (1989). *Ozzy on the outside*. New York: Delacorte Press. 196 pp. (ISBN: 0-385-29741-6)

Ozzy has always had a special relationship with his mother who's encouraged him to be his own person. He's never minded being on the outside at school, especially since he dreams of a solitary profession as a novelist. Things go awry for Ozzy when his mother suddenly dies, and the reactions of his family prompt him to run away. Fortunately, he meets a young woman on a bus who helps him through his guilt and sorrow.

13.03.   Ames, Mildred. (1984). *The silver link, the silken tie*. New York: Charles Scribner's Sons. 215 pp. (ISBN: 0-684-18065-0)

Tim and Felice have something in common: They are both sophomores trying to deal with the deaths of loved ones. Tim is trying to get over the accidental death of his sister, the accident being his fault. Felice, on the other hand, is haunted by her parents' death while on a cruise. Tim and

Felice initially dislike each other, but as they get to know one another, they develop an understanding and empathy unlike the rest of the students.

13.04.   Asher, Sandy. (1986). *Missing pieces*. New York: Dell Laurel-Leaf. 144 pp. (ISBN: 0-440-95716-8)

After Heather's father dies unexpectedly, she gets comfort from Nicky. He helps her to understand her own as well as her mother's feelings about their loss.

13.05.   Bacon, Katherine Jay. (1987). *Shadow and light*. New York: Margaret K. McElderry. 197 pp. (ISBN: 0-689-50431-4)

Emma's delighted to find out that she can spend another carefree summer with her grandmother on the horse ranch she loves. She can't think of a better person to share her 16th birthday with than her Grandma Gee. Unfortunately after Emma arrives on the ranch, she learns that her grandmother is dying. Although Grandma Gee makes Emma promise not to tell anyone, Emma is confronted with a major decision after she notices a drastic decline in Gee's health.

13.06.   Bauer, Marion Dane. (1987). *On my honor*. New York: Dell. 90 pp. (ISBN: 0-440-46633-4)

Tony's life changes the day he and his friend Joel ride their bikes to Starved Rock State Park to climb the bluffs. Tony dares Joel to jump in and swim across the Vermilion River forgetting that Joel doesn't know how to swim. When Joel drowns, Tony is overcome with guilt and is left having to confess what happened to both his parents and Joel's parents. (1987 Newbery Honor Book)

13.07.   Benjamin, Caro Lea. (1991). *Nobody's baby now*. New York: Bantam Books. 176 pp. (ISBN: 0-553-28896-2)

Fifteen-year-old Olivia Singer has to learn how to cope with her grandmother's Alzheimer's disease, especially when she moves in.

13.08.   Bennet, Jay. (1982). *The executioner*. New York: Avon Flare. 176 pp. (ISBN: 0-380-79160-9)

Bruce wishes that Raymond never offered to take him, Elaine, and Ed home one night. While rough-housing in the car, Bruce inadvertently causes Raymond to lose control of the car. As a result of the accident, Raymond dies and Bruce is severely injured. Everyone is in denial, and Bruce feels he must hide the truth about the accident. A person, who goes by the name "the

Executioner" feels that all of the survivors of the crash must pay. The novel incorporates many problems that teenagers might face: drinking and driving, dealing with the death of a close friend, and the emotional problems resulting from denial and lies.

13.09. Bennet, Jay. (1987). *The haunted one*. New York: Franklin Watts. 176 pp. (ISBN: 0-531-15059-3)

Paul Barrett has everything going for him: He's a champion swimmer, he's got a great job as a lifeguard at a beach resort, and he's just fallen in love with a beautiful dancer named Jody Miller. In one tragic afternoon, Paul's life changes forever. While swimming, Jody gets a cramp and cries for Paul's help. Because Paul has been smoking marijuana, he doesn't hear her and she drowns. Not only does he have to deal with the loss of his girlfriend's life, but he also must come to terms with his own guilt and irresponsibility which led to her death.

13.10. Blume, Judy. (1982). *Tiger eyes*. New York: Dell. 221 pp. (ISBN: 0-440-98469-6)

Davey Wexler's father was violently killed one night at his 7-Eleven store beneath his family's home. Davey, a fun-loving high school student, is now acutely afraid and constantly haunted by everything and everyone. Davey, her mother, and younger brother move from Atlantic City to New Mexico to be with relatives who help them try to adjust to the tragedy. Her childless aunt and uncle take away many of her privileges and her grieving mother is too helpless to intervene. Besides finding it difficult to understand the night of her father's death, Davey has also got to cope with a new school and making new friends. Fortunately, Davey meets Wolf who senses her despair, especially since his own father is dying of cancer in the hospital. Wolf helps her to resolve her fears, accept her life as it is, and see the world once again as a place where good can happen. She learns to forget about that night and to remember the wonderful times she shared with her father. (an American Library Association Best Book for Young Adults and a California Young Readers Medal)

13.11. Bottner, Barbara. (1988). *Nothing in common*. New York: Bantam Books. 179 pp. (ISBN: 0-553-27060-5)

Sara's mother, Mrs. Gregori, is the live-in family maid for Melissa's family; both girls are 16. Like Sara, however, Melissa regards Mrs. Gregori like a mother. When Mrs. Gregori dies, both girls suffer the same kinds of feelings but don't realize it. Sara feels that Melissa's family worked her mother to death and that they now "owe" her for her loss. Melissa, on the other hand, writes letters to the dead woman in the hopes that she will find some answers.

Eventually both girls develop an understanding for each other and for death as well.

13.12.   Bridgers, Sue Ellen. (1988). *Home before dark*. 150 pp.

See Poverty

13.13.   Bunting, Eve. (1990). *A sudden silence*. 105 pp.

See Alcohol and Drugs

13.14.   Byars, Betsy. (1980). *The night swimmers*. New York: Delacorte Press. 131 pp. (ISBN: 0-440-06261-6)

Since her mother's death two year's ago, Retta has had to take care of her two younger brothers.   Their father is a country-western singer who performs at night. When he isn't singing, he's busy writing songs in his head that he hopes will top the charts; his children rarely penetrate his imaginary world. He has no idea that his kids go swimming at night in an unsuspecting neighbor's pool until a near-tragedy occurs. He makes a tacit acknowledgment that he must resume his responsibilities as their father and allow Retta to drop the pseudo-mother role she has assumed.

13.15.   Carillo, Charles. (1986). *Shepherd avenue*. Boston: Atlantic Monthly Press. 299 pp. (ISBN: 0-871-13043-2)

After his mother's death, a shy 10-year-old boy is sent to live with his grandparents. His grandparents are Italian, lively, and loud, and he struggles to find his place in this new family situation.

13.16.   Carter, Alden R. (1989). *Sheila's dying*. New York: Scholastic. 207 pp. (ISBN: 0-590-42045-3)

This is the story of three teenagers who are confronted with death for the first time. Jerry Kinkaid has been casually dating Sheila, but Sheila wants to go steady. Because they don't have enough in common and he wants a more sexually satisfying relationship, Jerry decides to break up with her. Before he has a chance to break things off, Sheila is diagnosed with cancer and his involvement with her changes dramatically. He becomes heavily involved in her everyday care, sharing the responsibilities of her care with Sheila's only other close friend, Bonnie Harper. (an American Library Association Best Book for Young Adults & an ALA Recommended Book for the Reluctant YA Reader)

13.17.   Carter, Alden R. (1990). *RoboDad*. New York: G.P. Putnam's Sons. 144 pp. (ISBN: 0-399-22191-3)

When Shar is in the 9th grade, not only does she have the typical problems facing most teenagers--looks and boys--but she has to deal with her father's illness as well. Shar's father had a major artery burst in his brain which debilitated his ability to express higher emotions. Although he alternates between placid stares and violence, Shar is determined to help her father act like a loving dad again.

13.18.   Cleaver, Vera & Cleaver, Bill. (1969). *Where the lilies bloom*. Philadelphia: J.B. Lippincott Company. 174 pp. (ISBN: 0-397-31111-7)

Four children become orphans and each grieves when their father dies. Knowing they'll be separated if its found that they are orphans, Mary, a 14-year-old girl, makes an extraordinary attempt to hold the family together. In the Great Smoky Mountain region, life is extremely difficult for these children who try to manage without the help from any adult.

13.19.   Clymer, Eleanor. (1989). *My brother, Stevie*. New York: Holt, Rinehart, & Winston. 73 pp. (ISBN: 0-440-40125-9)

Young Mary Stover and her brother live with their grandmother in New York City after their father dies and their mother disappears. Stevie starts running around with a bad crowd, but a teacher befriends the two of them and has a positive influence on Stevie.

13.20.   Colman, Hila. (1989) *Suddenly*. New York: Fawcett. 128 pp. (ISBN: 0-449-70321-5)

Sixteen-year-old Emily likes to party, and this Halloween she's planning a wonderful bash. Things are going just fine until Emily's involved in a tragic car accident that kills Joey, a little boy she babysits and loves. She and her boyfriend, Russ, were on Halcyon when the child was struck and killed. Emily learns that life isn't always fun, especially when you have to deal with the death of someone you care about. Various other topics are covered: acceptance of others, facing friends and family after a scandal, and dealing with mental illness.

13.21.   Cooney, Caroline. (1992). *Flight #116 is down*. New York: Scholastic. 201 pp. (ISBN: 0-590-44465-4)

Heidi Landseth wakes up as an ordinary teenager but will be a 16-year-old going on 50 by the time she recovers from the ordeal of her life. As

fate would have it, a 747 crashes on her family's property leaving her to do what she can for the survivors of the burning aircraft. Vignettes from the lives of some of the survivors are intermixed in the story giving the reader a genuine sense of concern for their well being.

13.22.   Cormier, Robert. (1983). *The bumblebee flies anyway*. New York: Pantheon Books. 241 pp. (ISBN: 0-394-86120-5)

Sixteen-year-old Barney Snow is a guest at The Complex, an experimental hospital. He meets some boys who are regarded as human guinea pigs by their doctor, known as "the Handyman." In spite of their terminal illnesses, these boys all become close friends. Barney discovers that he isn't as different from the other boys as he thought. The plot intensifies, however, as he uncovers truths and memories that threaten his life. (an American Library Association Best Book for Young Adults)

13.23.   Cormier, Robert. (1986). *The chocolate war*. New York: Dell. 192 pp. (ISBN: 0-440-94459-7)

See Dropouts and Delinquency

13.24.   Cormier, Robert. (1991). *Now and at the hour*. New York: Dell Laurel-Leaf. 165 pp. (ISBN: 0-440-20882-3)

Alph is dying of cancer and he is angry about it. As his family begins to crumble with the stress, Alph becomes sensitive and compassionate and helps keep everyone together.

13.25.   Cormier, Robert. (1992). *Tunes for bears to dance to*. New York: Delacorte Press. 101 pp. (ISBN: 0-385-30818-3)

Henry Cassavant's family moves from Frenchtown to Wicksburg to escape the horrible memories of the death of his older brother, a victim of a hit-and-run accident. Henry's father is severely affected, having lost all motivation and his willingness to work to support his family. His mother works extra hours to help, and Henry, even though he is only 11 years old, takes a job at the Corner Market to contribute what he can. While working at the Corner Market, however, Henry suspects that his boss is abusing his wife and daughter. In a climactic scene, Henry is forced to choose between his family's financial well being or his new friendship with an elderly survivor of the Jewish Holocaust.

13.26.   Craven, Margaret. (1991). *I heard the owl call my name*. Cutchogue, NY: Buccaneer Books. 250 pp. (ISBN: 0-89966854-2)

This is the touching story of a young, mortally ill priest who spends the last days of his life working among the Kwakiutl Indians of British Columbia. The ultimate truths of life are found in many places, and Mark Brian finds his in Kingcome, an Indian village in the cold, unforgiving climate of the Northwest. Mark is adopted by the Indians he ministers to. When Mark hears the owl call his name, he knows his death is imminent. He learns to face his death with the spirit and courage of a great Indian chief.

13.27. Crutcher, Chris. (1983). *Running loose.* New York: Greenwillow Books. 190 pp. (ISBN: 0-688-02002-X).

Louie Banks's senior year is one that he'll never forget: He refuses to play dirty and challenges his football coach, falls in love, and loses his girlfriend in a fatal accident. Louie is caught in a world that appears to value winning and appearances over honesty, love, and fairness. (an American Library Association Best of the Best Books for Young Adults)

13.28. Davis, Jenny. (1987). *Goodbye and keep cold.* New York: Orchard. 210 pp. (ISBN: 0-531-05715-1)

After Edda Comb's father is killed in a strip mining accident, her mother's best friend, Annie, helps them through their hard times. Edda is extremely confused by the romantic relationship that her mother has developed with Henry John, the man responsible for his death. Additionally, Edda finds herself taking care of her younger brother. While coping with her own emotions, she is puzzled by the behavior of the adults in her life. When Annie suddenly leaves without saying good-bye, Edda is left wondering why. (an American Library Association Best Book for Young Adults, a *School Library Journal* Best Book of the Year, an NCSS-CBC Notable Children's Book in the Field of Social Studies)

13.29. Davis, Jenny. (1988). *Sex education.* 150 pp.

See Abuse

13.30. Deaver, Julie Reece. (1989). *Say goodnight, Gracie.* New York: Harper & Row. 224 pp. (ISBN: 0-06-447007-5)

Jimmy Woolf and Morgan Hackett have grown up together, developing a strong friendship based on their common interests in theatre and dance. When Jimmy is tragically killed by a drunk driver, Morgan suffers her own crash by staying in bed for weeks with his jacket on. Morgan must come to terms with her grief and let their hopes and dreams become her own.

13.31.   DeClements, Barthe. (1986). *I never asked you to understand me.*
New York: Viking/Kestrel. 138 pp. (ISBN: 0-670-80768-0)

Didi's life falls apart while her mother is dying from cancer. Because
she has trouble concentrating in school, her grades begin to drop and she finds
herself in Cooperation High better known as "The Coop," an alternative school.
She makes two new friends, Stacy and T.J., but neither of them are much help
to her because Stacy is preoccupied with her abusive father and T.J. is a heavy
drug user. As Didi becomes more involved with the lives of her two new
friends, they help each other to overcome the problems each faces.

13.32.   Ehrich, Amy. (1991). *The dark card.* New York: Viking Press. 197
pp. (ISBN: 0-670-83733-4)

After the sudden death of her mother, 17-year-old Laura has a
particularly difficult time trying to cope. Unable to communicate her feelings
to her father or older sister, Laura becomes increasingly more apathetic and
listless. They leave Laura to spend a lot of the summer alone in their house on
the Jersey Shore, but Laura finds the nearby casinos in Atlantic City just the
distraction she needs. Unfortunately, her escapist attitude only brings her more
trouble and heartache as she begins to dabble in a lifestyle uncharacteristic of
her former, teenage self. It is Laura's boyfriend who finally gets Laura's family
to respond to her needs and problems.

13.33.   Ellis, Sarah. (1988). *A family project.* New York: Margaret K.
McElderry. 137 pp. (ISBN: 0-689-50444-6)

Eleven-year-old Jessica is ecstatic to learn that her mother is pregnant
and is even more thrilled when her baby sister, Lucie, arrives. They bond
together immediately, and Jessica is caught up in her big sister role. Joy
suddenly turns to unbelievable grief when Lucie dies unexpectedly of sudden
infant death syndrome. Jessica is devastated and has difficulty accepting the
senselessness of the tragedy.

13.34.   Ethridge, Kenneth E. (1985). *Toothpick.* New York: Holiday House.
118 pp. (ISBN: 0-8234-0585-0)

Jamie Almont, better known as "Needle Legs", is a skinny, shy,
insecure 11th grader whose personality improves when he befriends Janice
Brooks. Not understanding why, he is immediately drawn to the new, skinny
girl who has been saddled with the nickname, "Toothpick." While his friends
tease her unmercifully, he takes the time to get to know her. While helping
him with some homework, Janice confides in him that she is dying of cystic
fibrosis. Through Janice's courage and friendship, Jamie begins to rethink his

old values; reevaluates his own sensitivity and convictions; and becomes self-confident, compassionate, and loyal.

13.35. Evernden, Margery. (1984). *The kite song*. New York: Lothrop, Lee & Shepard. 186 pp. (ISBN: 0-688-01200-0)

After the death of his mother, 11-year-old Jamie stops talking to everyone except his older cousin, Clem. Pretty soon, people mistake his silence for stupidity and he's treated accordingly. A savvy teacher, a poem about a kite, and Clem help him to face the past and deal with the terrors of his mind.

13.36. Ferris, Jean. (1989). *Invincible summer*. New York: Avon Books. 176 pp. (ISBN: 0-374-33642-3)

During the fall of her senior year of high school, Robin finds herself battling leukemia. While in the hospital for tests, she meets Rick who is receiving chemotherapy for his cancer. Eventually the two of them fall in love, and life takes on a new meaning. More good news is in store for Robin as her leukemia goes into remission during the spring. Just when everything is looking so hopeful, things take a turn for the worse and tragedy must be faced.

13.37. Florey, Kitty Burns. (1987). *Real life*. New York: New American Library. 320 pp. (ISBN: 0-451-40029-1) (Out of Print)

Fourteen-year-old Hugo has had a lot to deal with. First, both of his parents were killed and then his grandfather, with whom he had been living, dies. Now he has to deal with a 38-year-old aunt whose single lifestyle doesn't lend itself to child rearing. At a time when he is in need of emotional support, Aunt Dorrie is not doing anything right. Through the help of Alex, a friend of Aunt Dorrie, and Nina, a 16-year-old neighbor, Hugo manages to resolve some of his problems about death and his new living arrangement.

13.38. Forman, James. (1981). *The pumpkin shell*. New York: Farrar, Straus & Giroux. 156 pp. (ISBN: 0-374-36159-2)

Seventeen-year-old Robin Flynn constantly relives the guilt he feels about his mother's sudden death. He's also had to adjust to his father's remarriage and his new beautiful but angry stepsister. During a hurricane, he is trapped with his new stepsister for awhile. During this experience, Robin begins to regain control over his life.

13.39. Forman, James D. (1989). *The big bang*. New York: Charles Scribner's Sons. 160 pp. (ISBN: 0-684-19004-4)

Kids will be kids, but sometimes kid-things can turn out to be their worst nightmares. Such is the case for Chris Walker on the night that he, his older brother, and seven friends decide to outrace a train. The train won, leaving 14-year-old Chris having to sort out his feelings about the tragedy and answering to a father who cannot understand.

13.40.   Forshay-Lunsford, Cin. (1986). *Walk through cold fire*. 205 pp.

See Dropouts and Delinquency

13.41.   Fosburgh, Liza. (1990). *The wrong way home*. New York: Bantam Starfire. 192 pp. (ISBN: 0-553-05883-5)

Bent Roland's mother has Huntington's Chorea, and her health has increasingly deteriorated since the divorce. After she is hospitalized, Bent's father asks Bent to move in with his new family which she does with reluctance. Not only does 14-year-old Bent have to accept the impending death of her mother, but she also has to accept a new family including the problems that come with it. Confused, Bent makes matters worse by resorting to the temporary escape of marijuana. Bent realizes that she is responsible for her own happiness and eventually comes to terms with her own life.

13.42.   Fox, Paula. (1980). *A place apart*. New York: Farrar, Straus & Giroux. 183 pp. (ISBN: 0-374-35985-7)

When Victoria is only 13 years old, her father suddenly dies leaving her to deal with many problems: reduced family income, a move from Boston to New Oxford, and her mother's plans to remarry.

13.43.   Freeman, Gaail. (1982). *Out from under*. New York: Bradbury Press. 186 pp. (ISBN: 0-878-88188-3)

Teenagers often have difficulties with their parents, but things get really bad for the protagonist when her father dies and she finds herself arguing with her mother, being manipulated by a friend, and developing a relationship with a guy.

13.44.   Gabhart, Ann. (1991). *For Sheila*. New York: Avon Books. 160 pp. (ISBN: 0-380-75920-9)

A family grieves and has to come to terms with the death of a young family member.

13.45.   Gibbons, Faye. (1985). *Mighty close to heaven*. New York: William Morrow. 183 pp. (ISBN: 0-688-04147-7)

After the death of Dave Lawson's mother, his father decides that Dave would be better off in the care of his maternal grandparents. At 12 years of age, Dave wants to be with his father and doesn't understand. To make matters worse, he is angered when his dead mother's furniture is missing from the storage shed and accuses his grandfather of selling it. Dave takes it upon himself to find his father, and when he does, he is very disappointed. When he returns to his grandparents, Dave is more receptive to the love that they offer him.

13.46.   Graber, Richard. (1986). *Doc.* New York: Harper & Row. 160 pp. (ISBN: 0-06-022064-3) (Out of Print)

Doc is Brad Bloodworth's grandfather, a man who's deserved much admiration. When Doc develops Alzheimer's disease to such a degree that he must stop practicing medicine, Brad thinks that taking him to Cape Cod for a traditional family summer will be the miracle cure. When Doc continues to worsen in spite of Brad's well-intentioned vacation, Brad must come to terms with the harsh reality of his grandfather's condition.

13.47.   Grant, Cynthia D. (1989). *Phoenix rising or how to survive your life.* New York: Atheneum. 148 pp. (ISBN: 0-689-31458-2)

After 18-year-old Helen dies of cancer, her family nearly falls apart. Her 17-year-old sister, Jessie, becomes very depressed and withdraws. Jessie finds Helen's diary which helps her understand her sister and her death a little better. Eventually, Jessie finds the strength to get on with her life. The novel effectively alternates between Jessie's thoughts and Helen's words.

13.48.   Greenberg, Jan. (1983). *No dragons to slay.* New York: Farrar, Straus & Giroux. 119 pp. (ISBN: 0-374-35528-2)

Thomas Newman has always been a very capable young man who's good in sports and popular among the girls. Things change rapidly when Thomas learns that he has a malignant tumor and has to undergo painful tests, treatments, and medication. Through all of this, Thomas learns that you don't have to necessarily have cancer to have to face a life-threatening situation.

13.49.   Greene, Constance C. (1988). *Beat the turtle drum.* New York: Dell Laurel-Leaf. 128 pp. (ISBN: 0-440-40875-X)

Kate and her family try to hold it together when Kate's younger sister, Joss, dies suddenly.

13.50.   Guest, Elissa Haden. (1987). *Over the moon.* New York: Bantam Books. 208 pp. (ISBN: 0-553-26565-2)

Kate Baker's parents were killed in an accident when she was eight years old. For the most part, Kate, Jay, and Mattie have been raised by their Aunt Georgia. Mattie moved out four years ago, and Kate, now 16, is confronting the death of her parents and related family issues. She and Jay go to New York and visit their old house. There, they reminisce about old times-- times when their parents were alive. Prompted by a birthday gift from Mattie, Kate sets out to visit her sister in order to make things right again. Since Mattie's husband deserted her, Mattie's been raising her baby with money she earns by sewing. Kate convinces Mattie to visit Aunt Georgia in an attempt to get the family together again.

13.51. Halvorson, Marilyn. (1986). *Cowboys don't cry*. New York: Dell Laurel-Leaf. 176 pp. (ISBN: 0-440-91303-9)

Shane Morgan still suffers from his mother's death four years ago, and he still can't help but hold his father responsible for the accident that killed her. To make matters worse, his father has resorted to drinking which has Shane concerned. He's hoping that things will improve after he and his father, an estranged rodeo clown, move to a ranch in Alberta, Canada. As he gets more involved with a girl and school affairs, things do start to improve but not without work.

13.52. Hamilton, Virginia. (1990). *Cousins*. New York: Philomel. 125 pp. (ISBN: 0-399-22164-6)

Cammy lives with her mother and 16-year-old brother in a modest household. Cammy finds it easier getting along with her 94-year-old grandmother, who lives in a nursing home, than she does getting along with her cousins. Patty Ann is about her age of 12 but is too perfect for Cammy. Elodie is not only adopted, but her mother is nothing but a poor, migrant worker. One day during a camping trip, Patty Ann loses her life while saving Elodie from drowning. Everyone concerned must learn to accept this tragic loss.

13.53. Harlan, Elizabeth. (1982). *Footfalls*. New York: Margaret K. McElderry Books. 144 pp. (ISBN: 0-689-50255-9)

Stephanie is the most promising member of her track team and is a 13-year-old in every sense of the word. She is involved in her school, enjoys her friends, and is beginning to have romantic feelings. There is a lot going on in her life, and now her father is dying of cancer and her parents won't discuss it with her or her brother.

13.54. Hassler, Jon. (1980). *Jemmy*. 180 pp.

See Poverty

13.55. Haven, Susan. (1990). *Is it them or is it me?* New York: G.P. Putnam's Sons. 176 pp. (ISBN: 0-399-21916-1)

Molly Snyder has an unbelievable freshman year. Not only does she have all of the problems associated with going to a new school, but Molly's mother has just been diagnosed with cancer. All of this is compounded by the fact that her best friend is attending a private school instead.

13.56. Hinton, S.E. (1989). *The outsiders*. 156 pp.

See Dropouts and Delinquency

13.57. Holland, Isabelle. (1977). *Of love and death and other journeys*. New York: Dell Laurel-Leaf. 140 pp. (ISBN: 0-440-96547-0)

As the title indicates, the main character, Meg, moves through several phases in her life: She begins to understand how open love is, she sees how easy it is to hurt others, and she realizes the value of life. Meg's mother dies, and Meg works through the grief process and develops an understanding of how to live.

13.58. Howe, James. (1985). *A night without stars*. New York: Avon Books. 192 pp. (ISBN: 0-380-69877-3)

At 11 years of age, Maria has to face what most people will never have to face--open heart surgery. It is no wonder that she is very frightened and has questions that her parents and doctors can't answer totally. Maria finds some relief when she goes to the hospital and meets Donald, a boy called "Monster Man" because of disfigurement caused from burns several years ago. The two of them meet when each needed a friend, and they help each other through some rough times.

13.59. Howe, Norma. (1986). *God, the universe, and hot fudge sundaes*. New York: Avon Books. 160 pp. (ISBN: 0-380-70074-3)

Sixteen-year-old Alfie Newton has just experienced the death of her younger sister who died of a congenital muscle disease which affected her all of her life. Following her sister's death and parents' divorce, Alfie is forced to come to terms with her own attitudes about death, religion, and love. She turns to Kurt, an older college student, who helps her get her life back together.

13.60.   Howker, Janni. (1986). *Isaac Campion*. New York: Greenwillow Books. 83 pp. (ISBN: 0-688-06658-5)

Isaac Campion is a young boy growing up in rural England in the late 19th century. Isaac has struggles and hardships because of the poor relationship he has with his father. Their relationship gets worse when his older brother, his father's favorite, is killed in an accident. Isaac's father reacts to the death by becoming more detached and less patient with him and his mother. Things eventually improve for Isaac as events draw him closer to his father. Isaac learns from his mother about the difficult and sometimes terrible upbringing his father had because of a tyrannical father. Isaac's understanding and compassion helps him draw his father out of his depression.

13.61.   Hughes, Monica. (1983). *Hunter in the dark*. New York: Atheneum. 131 pp. (ISBN: 0-689-30959-7)

Sixteen-year-old Mike has acute lymphocytic leukemia, but his parents tell him that he is just anemic. Knowing that something is awry, Mike runs away to the Canadian bush to sort things out and hunt for his dream--the head of a whitetail deer. (an American Library Association Best Book for Young Adults, a Notable Children's Trade Book in the Field of Social Studies, and a Children's Book of the Year)

13.62.   Hunt, Irene. (1987). *Up a road slowly*. New York: Berkeley. 100 pp. (ISBN: 0-425-10003-0)

After her mother's death, 7-year-old Julie Trelling chooses to live with her Aunt Cordelia instead of her father and his new wife. This novel traces Julie's development through her 18th birthday. While growing up in the country, Julie learns many things about life, death, school, relationships, her family, and herself. (Newbery Medal Winner)

13.63.   Irwin, Hadley. (1982). *What about Grandma?* New York: Atheneum. 165 pp. (ISBN: 0-689-50224-9)

Rhys, a 16-year-old girl, finds herself in a situation that forces her to grow up a little faster than anticipated. Rhys and her mother go to help Grandmother Wyn auction off her property one summer, but this focused purpose turns into quite another when Grandma tells them that she is dying. The generation gaps become closer as they learn to listen and love each other, in some ways, for the first time. During this summer, Rhys also meets Lew, a handsome, 26-year-old golf pro who is there for her while she learns about death as well as life and loving. (an American Library Association Best Book for Young Adults and a Notable Children's Trade Book in the Field of Social Studies)

13.64.   King, Buzz. (1990). *Silicon songs*. New York: Doubleday. 160 pp.
         (ISBN: 0-385-30087-5)

Although Max is only 17 years old, he lives on the street and wanders
Venice Beach by day and works as a part-time computer programmer by night.
His Uncle Pete is in the hospital dying of cancer, and Max is trying to earn the
money to help. As his uncle's prognosis deteriorates and his agony becomes
increasing more noticeable, Max's own life falls more and more apart.

13.65.   Klaveness, Jan O'Donnell. (1990). *Ghost island*. 224 pp.

See Divorced and Single Parents

13.66.   Klein, Norma. (1986). *Going backwards*. New York: Scholastic.
         182 pp. (ISBN: 0-590-40328-1)

When Charles is about to embark on his most terrific year of school,
his senior year, Grandmother Gustel moves into his house and almost ruins
everything. Charles's grandmother has Alzheimer's disease and can no longer
take care of herself. Charles's father makes matters worse because he won't
acknowledge that there is a problem, and Charles is left to sort through his
feelings by himself.

13.67.   Klein, Norma. (1987). *Sunshine*. New York: Avon Books. 224 pp.
         (ISBN: 0-380-00049-0)

Kate, Jill's mother, is informed that the lump on her leg is not bursitis
but is cancer. As Kate goes through the various stages of dying, Jill is there to
receive her mother's undying love for her.

13.68.   Klein, Norma. (1988). *Confessions of an only child*. New York:
         Bullseye Books. 93 pp. (ISBN: 0-394-80569-0)

Antonio has been accustomed to being an only child for the last nine
years, and now she has to get used to the idea that her parents are having a
baby. She and her best friend, Libby, think that babies are a real pain, and
Antonio is not happy about having a little brother or sister. When Antonio's
baby brother is born prematurely and dies, she learns to cope with her guilt and
is much more receptive to the idea the next time.

13.69.   Koertge, Ron. (1990). *Where the kissing never stops*. 224 pp.

See Divorced and Single Parents

13.70.   Lasky, Kathryn.   (1988).   *Home free*.   New York: Dell.   244 pp.
         (ISBN: 0-440-20038-5)

Sam Brooks has two major adjustments to make--his father's death and his new move with his mother to Massachusetts. Sam's personal concerns take a back seat to the problems faced by his two new friends. Gus, a wildlife photographer, is dying but he feverishly takes pictures of a local reservoir in an effort to keep it a wildlife preserve. His 13-year-old friend, Lucy, is a mute autistic orphan. Sam's friends help him sort out what's important in life.

13.71.   L'Engle, Madeleine.   (1990).   *A ring of endless light*. New York: Dell
         Laurel-Leaf. 336 pp. (ISBN: 0-440-97232-9)

Sixteen-year-old Vicki Austin spends the summer on Seven Bay Island where her grandfather, a retired minister, is dying of leukemia. Her older brother and a boy named Adam work with dolphins at a marine research center. Vicki befriends a boy named Leo whose father, a member of the Coast Guard, has just died after rescuing Zachary, a suicidal, wealthy boy. Zachary and Leo compete for Vicki's affections, but Vicki is more interested in Adam and the special gift she has for communicating with dolphins. Vicki is weighed down by all of the suffering around her, but she survives and grows through the advice of her wise grandfather. She develops a maturing sense of love and meaning in life as she confronts the problems of first love and the slow death of her grandfather.   (a Newbery Honor Book and an American Library Association Notable Children's Book)

13.72.   Little, Jean.   (1986).   *Mama's going to buy you a mockingbird*. New
         York: Puffin Books. 213 pp. (ISBN: 0-14-031737-6)

In the summer before entering the 6th grade, Jeremy has to come to grips with the fact that his father, who has always been so strong and healthy, is now very sick with cancer. Jeremy and his sister, Sarah, have to spend the summer with their aunt while their parents deal with frequent visits to the hospital. After their father's death, they have to sell their house and move to an apartment which was once owned by the grandfather of a girl named Tess. Tess and Jeremy become friends because they know what it feels like to lose a parent--Tess through abandonment and Jeremy through death. (Literary Merit)

13.73.   Lowry, Lois.   (1977).   *A summer to die*. Boston: Houghton Mifflin.
         154 pp. (ISBN: 0-395-25338-1)

Molly Chalmers is attractive, vibrant, popular with the boys, and is excited about life. Her younger sister, Meg, the novel's 13-year-old narrator, is just the opposite: She wears glasses, hates boys, and loves to be alone in her photography darkroom. Meg has always been envious of Molly's beauty and easy going manner until the family learns that Molly is terminally ill. Meg must sort out her feelings for her sister and come to grips with her sadness about Molly's eventual death from leukemia. During their final summer together in the country, the girls meet and befriend Will Banks, the 70-year-old owner and caretaker of the farmhouse their parents are renting. The girls also make friends with their new neighbors, Ben and Maria, a young couple about to have their first child. As the girls face their fears about Molly's eventual death, their new friends help them see that life goes on. Through her love of photography, Meg deals with her grief over her sister's death, experiences joy at the birth of Ben and Maria's baby, and finds comfort in her special friendship with Will Banks. (an American Library Association Notable Children's Book, International Reading Association Children's Book Award, an NCSS-CBC Notable Children's Book in the Field of Social Studies, and a California Young Readers Medal)

13.74.   Mahy, Margaret. (1989). *Memory*. New York: Dell Laurel-Leaf. 288 pp. (ISBN: 0-440-20433-X)

Five years ago, Jonny Dart used to be a television tap dancer with his twin sister, Janine. Now, at 19, Jonny decides that he must confront the issues surrounding his twin sister's death. He seeks out Bonny Benedicta, his sister's best friend, but finds Sophie West instead. Sophie, an eccentric woman suffering from Alzheimer's disease, lives alone with a houseful of cats. Jonny is drawn to her and their relationship helps him deal with the painful memories of his sister's accidental death. By helping Sophie, who has only bits of memory, and becoming caught up in the present, he begins to let go of some of his tormenting memories. (a Carnegie Medal winner in England in 1982 and 1984, an American Library Association Best Book for Young Adults, a *School Library Journal* Best Book of the Year, and a *Boston Globe/Horn Book* Honor Book)

13.75.   Major, Kevin. (1980). *Hold fast*. New York: Delacorte Press. 170 pp. (ISBN: 0-440-03506-6)

Michael and his younger brother are split up after their parents' death. Michael is sent to live with an uncle and aunt, but his uncle is mean. Not tolerating his bullying any longer, Michael and his cousin run away to Michael's old home. (Winner of the Canadian Award for Best Children's Book)

13.76.   Malmgren, Dallin. (1987). *The whole nine yards*. New York: Delacorte Press. 137 pp. (ISBN: 0-385-29452-2)

When Storm Russell's father dies unexpectedly during his sophomore year of high school, he pursues distractions rather than dealing with the reality for the next three years. As each year passes, his adventures become increasingly more dangerous. His older brother, Forrest, tries to help, but Storm constantly makes excuses for his behavior. It isn't until Storm is confronted with death for a second time that he learns what it means to go "the whole nine yards."

13.77.   Martin, Ann M. (1986). *With you and without you*. New York: Holiday House. 179 pp. (ISBN: 0-8234-0601-6)

Liza's father is dying from a heart ailment, so the family makes plans to have the best Christmas ever while he's still alive. After his death, Liza's family must learn to adjust to life with one income. Besides dealing with his death, they suffer many other hardships: They are forced to move from their home into a smaller house, her mother has to take a second job, and her older brother has to get a job to help make ends meet. The story addresses the changes Liza's family goes through, both emotionally and economically, as they learn to accept the death of a loved one.

13.78.   Mazer, Harry. (1981). *The island keeper*. New York: Delacorte Press. 165 pp. (ISBN: 0-440-03976-2)

Cleo Murphy is desolate after the deaths of her mother and sister. She tries to escape her loneliness by running away to a deserted island in the middle of a Canadian lake. Her loneliness is worsened and compounded by fear when her canoe is destroyed, and she must face a brutal Canadian winter by herself.

13.79.   Mazer, Harry. (1985). *When the phone rang*. New York: Scholastic. 181 pp. (ISBN: 0-590-32167-6)

When 16-year-old Billy answers the phone, the tragic message he hears changes the three Keller children's lives forever. Their parents have been killed in a plane crash. Although relatives offer to take care of Billy and his younger sister, his older brother, Kevin, returns home from college in the hopes of keeping the family together. Things are tough as they struggle against the advice of relatives, financial difficulties, and overwhelming personal problems. Kevin, not accustomed to being in charge of the family, resents his new responsibilities; and their sister, Lori, gets involved in shoplifting. It isn't until they suffer through another crisis that the three of them are brought together and start behaving as a family again.

13.80.   Mazer, Harry. (1991). *Someone's mother is missing*. New York: Dell. 166 pp. (ISBN: 0-440-21097-6)

Lisa and Robyn are two sisters trying to cope after their wealthy father's death. To compound matters, their mother leaves after creditors repossess their personal effects. The girls have no other choice but to go and live with their Aunt Renee and her teenage son, Sam. The girls' initial negative opinion of them change, and they learn the true meaning of family love.

13.81.   Mazer, Norma Fox. (1987). *After the rain*. New York: William Morrow. 291 pp. (ISBN: 0-688-06867-7)

Rachel's parents and cantankerous, old grandfather are getting on her nerves. She finds writing in a journal and her older brother, Jeremy, helps for relieving her frustrations periodically. After her grandfather is diagnosed with cancer and is only given a short time to live, Rachel finds herself walking with him every day--and listening. During these walks, she realizes that she really does love him. While her grandfather becomes weaker, he helps this 15-year-old to discover her special abilities as a writer. (a Newbery Honor Book)

13.82.   Mazer, Norma Fox. (1991). *When we first met*. New York: Scholastic. 199 pp. (ISBN: 0-590-43823-9)

This sequel to *A Figure of Speech* finds Jenny Pennayer a senior who's about to fall in love for the first time. Unfortunately, her boyfriend's mother is the drunk driver who killed her sister in an accident two years before. Emotions fly like a hurricane with Jenny at the center, especially when her parents find out.

13.83.   Mazer, Norma Fox & Mazer, Harry. (1989). *Heartbeat*. New York: Bantam Books. 165 pp. (ISBN: 0-533-28779-6)

Tod Ellerbee knows about death: His mother died when he was three, and his best friend, Amos, saved him from drowning when they were kids. At the time, Tod promised Amos that he would do anything for his friend if he asked. Amos waited until their senior year before asking Todd to make good on that promise. He wants Todd to fix him up with Hillary, another senior who works after school as an auto mechanic. Tod had intended to get Hillary for Amos as agreed, but he didn't count on his own feelings getting in the way. Feelings really get out of hand when Amos is hospitalized for a rare disease.

13.84.   McDaniel, Lurlene. (1985). *Six months to live*. Worthington, OH: Willowisp Press. 144 pp. (ISBN: 0-874-06007-9)

Dawn and Sandy form a deep friendship while being hospitalized for leukemia. Both teens go to a special summer camp together after their cancer goes into remission. At this camp for children with cancer, they form friendships and romances with two teenage boys. They have a wonderful, fun-filled summer and all keep in touch through letters afterwards. When Sandy's cancer returns, her father takes her to Mexico for treatment because he is unable to see her go through the agony of chemotherapy again. Dawn's anguish is almost unbearable as she experiences the loss of her friend.

13.85.   McDaniel, Lurlene.   (1987).   *I want to live*.   Worthington, OH: Willowisp Press. 128 pp. (ISBN: 0-874-06237-3)

I Want to Live is a sequel to *Six Months to Live*. Dawn Rochelle, now 14, finds she has to fight once again for her life when her leukemia becomes active again. Losing her hair because of the chemotherapy is only part of Dawn's fight. She wants to be treated like everyone else, not like some fragile doll. Dawn's relationship with her older brother, Rob, brings warmth to the story as he must donate bone marrow to Dawn who barely clings to life on the operating table. Rob's wedding plans are ruined when he realizes his fiancee can't deal with the sickness his family deals with daily, but he finds comfort from a pretty nurse who appreciates the love he has for his little sister.

13.86.   McDaniel, Lurlene.   (1986).   *Why did she have to die?*   Worthington, OH: Willowisp Press. 128 pp. (ISBN: 0-87406-071-0)

At 13 years of age, Elly Rowan learns some hard lessons. She has always felt overshadowed by her older sister, Kathy. The way Elly sees it, Kathy is prettier, more popular, smarter, and even more loved by their parents. The day that 17-year-old, basketball star, Russ Canton offers them a ride home in his flashy, new Firebird changes things forever. In order to avoid hitting a child on a bicycle, Russ rams his car into a pole. Kathy is killed on impact, Elly's leg is severely broken and she is comatose for a week, and Russ escapes serious injury. Elly and her family struggle to cope with their lives without Kathy; resentments abound. After Elly gets into trouble a few times at school, her parents decide they need professional counseling. Through the help of a support group, Elly comes to terms with her feelings. She is able to identify why she wishes it had been her who died, why she is mean to her friends, and why she is still angry at Kathy for dying.

13.87.   McDaniel, Lurlene.   (1989).   *Too young to die*.   New York: Bantam Books. 166 pp. (ISBN: 0-553-28008-2)

Things change drastically when Melissa Austin, a bright high school junior with big plans for scholarships and college, discovers she has leukemia. Through the support of her family and best friend, Jory, she becomes determined to live her life to the fullest and refuses to let go of her dreams. She learns to live for the here and now.

13.88.   McDaniel, Lurlene.   (1989).   *Goodbye doesn't mean forever*.   New York: Bantam Books. 166 pp. (ISBN: 0-553-28007-4)

Melissa's cancer was in remission during their junior year in high school but returns just before their senior year. In this sequel to *Too Young to Die*, Melissa and Jory are determined not to let the cancer interfere with their plans for their last year in high school. Unfortunately, Melissa's condition deteriorates so fast that she must be hospitalized. Melissa opts to have a bone marrow transplant rather than let the disease run its course, and Jory heads up a carnival fund-raiser to help pay for Melissa's operation. Jory is heartbroken when Melissa dies but finds comfort from Melissa's family, and surprisingly, from her own mother. All who loved her find help in rediscovering the sense of hope Melissa left behind.

13.89.   McDaniel, Lurlene. (1991). *A time to let go*. New York: Bantam Starfire. 176 pp. (ISBN: 0-553-28350-2)

Erin's world falls apart after her younger sister's tragic death. She is overcome by constant headaches and family conflicts arising out of uncontrolled emotions. Fortunately, David Devlin, a good friend with an upbeat personality, and a support group help Erin to go through the grief process and start thinking about her future.

13.90.   McDaniel, Lurlene. (1991). *Somewhere between life and death*. New York: Bantam Starfire. 160 pp. (ISBN: 0-553-28349-9)

After a car accident leaves Amy in an irreversible coma and brain dead, her family is forced to make some difficult decisions.

13.91.   McDaniel, Lurlene. (1991). *Now I lay me down to sleep*. New York: Bantam Starfire. 160 pp. (ISBN: 0-553-28897-0)

Carrie and Keith, two teenage friends, both have cancer. Carrie's cancer is in remission, but Keith's is terminal. Keith decides to participate in the hospice program and wants to die at home surrounded by his loving and supportive family. In direct contrast is Carrie's home situation: Her parents are still bitter from their divorce and are unable to accept their daughter's disease. Carrie's parents cannot understand why she wants to spend all of her free time with this dying boy, but it is through Keith's courage that Carrie develops a strong will to live.

13.92.   Miller, Sandy. (1988). *Allegra*. New York: Signet. 208 pp. (ISBN: 0-451-15413-4) (Out of Print)

Allegra Stephenson's life is shattered when her parents are killed in a car accident. Being 11 is hard enough without having to deal with such a loss. Somehow, Allegra must muster all of her courage to face life and continue with her dream of becoming a concert pianist.

13.93. Montgomery, Robert. (1985). *Rabbit ears*. New York: New American Library. 160 pp. (ISBN: 0-451-13631-4) (Out of Print)

The only thing keeping Jason going right now is his being catcher on a winning baseball team. After practice, he goes home and reality sets in--his father is dying. Jason befriends the new pitcher on his team and helps him to overcome his "rabbit-eared" sensitivity to the crowd's jeering. His new friend, in turn, helps Jason with his own "rabbit-eared" knowledge of his father's death.

13.94. Naughton, Jim. (1989). *My brother stealing second*. New York: Harper & Row. 213 pp. (ISBN: 0-06-024374-0)

Billy and Bobby were the kind of brothers parents dream about--they liked each other. Billy was athletically inclined with some real talent in baseball, and Bobby tried to be just like him. When a fatal car accident takes Billy, Bobby's life loses its vitality until Bobby can get past the tragedy.

13.95. Nixon, Joan Lowry. (1982). *The specter*. New York: Delacorte Press. 160 pp. (ISBN: 0-385-28948-0)

Diana is 17 years old and is in the hospital being treated for cancer. Her roommate, 9-year-old Julie, believes that her parents' fatal car accident was no accident. Julie believes that a man, Bill Sikes, killed them and is threatening her life.

13.96. Nixon, Joan Lowry. (1986). *The ghosts of now*. New York: Dell-Laurel Leaf. 192 pp. (ISBN: 0-440-93115-0)

Angie's brother is now in a coma after a hit-and-run accident. It seems as though she is the only one concerned about finding out who did this to her brother. Even her parents don't seem concerned, and she gets little help from the people who witnessed what happened that night.

13.97. Olsen, Violet. (1985). *Never brought to mind*. 176 pp.

See Stress and Suicide

13.98. O'Neal, Zibby. (1982). *A formal feeling*. New York: Viking Press. 162 pp. (ISBN: 0-670-32488-4)

Emily Dickinson said, "After great pain, a formal feeling comes." Ever since her mother's death a year ago, Anne Cameron has experienced a great emptiness, "a formal feeling" that separates her from her family and friends. Her father is able to remarry, and her brother continues his education, but it seems to Anne that she was the only one who really loved her perfect mother. When something happens which makes Anne realize her mother wasn't perfect, her emptiness vanishes and she lets the "formal feeling" go. The admission of imperfection doesn't diminish the love they once shared, and Anne is able to once again secure her place in the world and care again.

13.99.   Paterson, Katherine. (1987). *Bridge to Terabithia*. 144 pp.

See Growing Up: Alienation and Identity

13.100. Peck, Richard. (1981). *Close enough to touch*. New York: Delacorte Press. 133 pp. (ISBN: 0-440-01362-3)

Seventeen-year-old Matt Moran deeply loves his first girlfriend, Dory, so when she dies suddenly from an aneurysm he doesn't think he will ever get over it. While struggling to accept her loss, he meets Margaret Chasen, a senior who encourages him to take a second chance at love and get back to living his own life. (an American Library Association Best Book for Young Adults)

13.101. Peck, Robert Newton. (1982). *A day no pigs would die*. New York: Alfred A. Knopf. 150 pp. (ISBN: 0-394-48235-2)

The main character, Robert Peck (the novel's based on the author's childhood), is a 12-year-old boy growing up in a Shaker family on a farm in Vermont during the Depression. Robert is a happy boy who is well acquainted with work and family responsibilities. His prized possession is a pet pig, given to him as a reward for saving a neighbor's cow. His first touch of manhood occurs when he must help his father slaughter his pig when they realize the pig is infertile; it's a harsh, cruel reality that a man must face. Rob is able to put the harshness of life into perspective, which aids him in his transition into manhood, when he accepts his own father's death and becomes the man of the house. (an American Library Association Best Book and Notable Children's Book)

13.102. Pershall, Mary K. (1990). *You take the high road*. New York: Dial Books. 245 pp. (ISBN: 0-8037-0700-2)

Samantha, a teenager, is delighted when her mother announces that she is pregnant. Samantha shares in the planning and naming of her baby sister and is in the delivery room when she gets a baby brother instead. Nicholas turns out to be the joy of the family until he dies in an accident when he is one-and-a-half years old. The family is shattered, and Sam has to learn to help herself and her grieving mother. (an American Library Association Best Book for Young Adults)

13.103. Pfeffer, Susan Beth. (1987). *The year without Michael*. New York: Bantam Books. 176 pp. (ISBN: 0-553-05430-9)

One day, Jody's 13-year-old brother, Michael, disappears somewhere between the ballfield and home. The family doesn't know what's worse--the loss or not knowing. For Jody and her younger sister, Kay, the months that follow are horrible. Not only do they have to deal with their own feelings of loss, but they have to deal with their mother's irrational behavior and their father's withdrawal. (an American Library Association Best Book for Young Adults, a *School Library Journal* Best Book of the Year, *Booklist* YA Editors' Choice, an NCSS-CBC Notable Children's Book in the Field of Social Studies, a YASD Recommended Book for Reluctant Readers, a *Publisher's Weekly* Best Book of the Year, an *American Bookseller* Pick of the Lists, an International Reading Association Young Adults' Choice)

13.104. Phelan, Terry Wolfe. (1985). *Making half whole*. New York: New American Library/Signet Vista Books. 160 pp. (ISBN: 0-451-13630-6) (Out of Print)

Because Allison is a "Navy brat" and is constantly on the move with her family, she has learned to adjust to making new friends knowing that they will only be temporary. A new reality for the word "temporary" strikes when her family moves from the beaches of California to the suburbs of New Jersey. There she befriends twin sisters, Jane and Marnia, and finds herself caught up in Marnia's struggle with a life-threatening kidney disease.

13.105. Phipson, Joan. (1981). *A tide flowing*. New York: Atheneum. 156 pp. (ISBN: 0-689-50196-X)

A young boy wonders if he is responsible for his mother's death and his father's rejection.

13.106. Radley, Gail. (1984). *CF in his corner*. New York: Four Winds Press. 134 pp. (ISBN: 0-590-07901-8)

Fourteen-year-old Jeff thinks it is unusual that he has to take care of his 7-year-old brother, Scotty, over the summer while his mother works. Scotty has always been a sickly child. Although he eats a lot, he remains very small. He's constantly having to take vitamins, and he has to sleep with a vaporizer in his room. His mother says it is just asthma, but Jeff finds out that Scotty has cystic fibrosis and is shocked that Scotty doesn't even know about it. Jeff thinks Scotty should be told, but his mother disagrees.

13.107. Rawls, Wilson. (1992). *Where the red fern grows*. New York: Bantam Starfire. 256 pp. (ISBN: 0-553-08900-5)

Billy, a country boy from rural Iowa, wanted two hunting hounds so badly that he saved his money for two years so he could buy them. After Billy buys his dogs, they roam the hills and valleys of the Ozarks where they hunt and think as one. Billy's love for his dogs gave him a deep sense of fulfillment and a start into manhood. The novel is Billy's recollection of these childhood hunting days, the days before Old Dan died to save Billy and Little Ann died of a broken heart. (the Great Stone Face Award)

13.108. Russell, Stephanie. (1986). *A quiet ember*. New York: Ballantine/Fawcett Juniper. 212 pp. (ISBN: 0-449-70112-3)

Miranda Greene is about to return to New York after she spent the last year in England trying to get over her father's death. She discovers that many of her old friends have changed, but there's hope in her new friendship with Vivi. Miranda faces the final challenge of accepting her father's death when her mother develops a relationship with Vivi's widowed father.

13.109. Schwandt, Stephen. (1988). *Holding steady*. New York: Henry Holt. 161 pp. (ISBN: 0-8050-0575-7)

When Brendon and his father nickname their Volkswagen "D.C." for "Death Car," neither of them had any idea that the nickname would come true. Brendon's father is killed, leaving 17-year-old Brendon to adjust to his father's death and become a man.

13.110. Schwemm, Diane. (1990). *Always*. New York: Fawcett. 160 pp. (ISBN: 0-449-14607-3).

Shelly Carlson thinks she has her priorities in order during her senior year of high school: She's working hard in her classes, trying to be a good softball team captain, leading student government projects, and applying to good colleges. Her priorities change dramatically when her boyfriend, Jay, is diagnosed with Hodgkin's disease. Shelly practically drops everything to spend all of her time with him. Through encouragement from family, friends, and Jay, Shelly learns how to preserve her own life while adjusting to the impending loss of a loved one.

13.111. Sebestyen, Ouida. (1980). *Far from home*. Boston: Little, Brown, & Company. 191 pp. (ISBN: 0-316-77932-6)

Thirteen-year-old Salty Yeager's mute, unmarried mother dies leaving him in charge of his grandmother. Before she died, his mother left him a note telling him to love Tom Buckley who owns the boarding house where she used to work. Salty goes to work in the Buckley Arms Hotel and finds out that Tom is his father. Salty must learn to cope with the fact that his father will never claim him.

13.112. Snyder, Anne. (1986). *My name is Davy, I'm an alcoholic.* 144 pp.

See Alcohol and Drugs

13.113. Stolz, Mary. (1974). *The edge of next year.* New York: Harper & Row. 195 pp. (ISBN: 0-060-25857-8)

The Woodwards are very happy on their little farm until Mom is accidentally killed. Fourteen-year-old Orin has to run the house and care for his brother, Victor, when their father tries to drink away their mother's death. Bitter and resentful of their father's abandonment, Orin and Victor make a desperate bid for attention. After their father regains control, Orin is able to get on with his own life.

13.114. Strasser, Todd. (1982). *Friends till the end.* New York: Dell Laurel-Leaf. 224 pp. (ISBN: 0-440-92625-4)

David Gilbert is a teenage soccer star who befriends Howie Jamison. Their relationship intensifies when Howie develops leukemia, and David learns that there is more to life than sports and parties. David and his friends acquire a new and deeper appreciation for life after this experience. (an American Library Association Best of the Best Books for Young Adults)

13.115. Strasser, Todd. (1990). *The accident.* New York: Dell Laurel-Leaf. 192 pp. (ISBN: 0-440-20635-9)

After a group of friends are killed in a car wreck pegged as a drunk driving accident, Matt learns that high-powered individuals sometimes reinvent the truth in order to protect themselves. Although this teenager finds himself alone in his quest for the truth, he doggedly sets his mind in its pursuit.

13.116. Sweeney, Joyce. (1992). *Piano man.* 227 pp.

See Abuse

13.117. Talbert, Marc. (1985). *Dead birds singing.* Boston: Little, Brown, & Company. 170 pp. (ISBN: 0-316-83125-5)

Matt's jubilance over his first place win at his junior high school's track meet is brought to a screeching halt when his family is hit by a drunk driver on the way home. Although Matt survives, the car accident kills his mother and puts his sister in a coma. Matt suddenly finds himself being taken care of by his best friend's family and having to deal with all kinds of feelings of grief, sadness, and anger toward the drunk who hit them. (an American Library Association Best Book for Young Adults)

13.118. Thesman, Jean. (1990). *Erin*. New York: Avon Books. 139 pp. (ISBN: 0-380-75875-X)

Erin Whitney's life has been miserable ever since her parents' death when she was 10 years old. Now, at 15, she is given an ultimatum: Either she is to get along with Uncle Jock and his family or she will get placed in a foster home.

13.119. Thomas, Karen. (1986). *Changing of the guard*. New York: Harper & Row. 186 pp. (ISBN: 0-060-26163-3)

Caroline's beloved grandfather dies when she is 16 years old. She chooses to be a loner or to spend time with her grandmother rather than socialize with her friends. Finally, a very outgoing, new girl starts attending Caroline's school, befriends her, and helps her get over her despondency.

13.120. Ure, Jean. (1989). *One green leaf*. New York: Delacorte Press. 192 pp. (ISBN: 0-385-29751-3)

Four teenagers, who are the best of friends, learn what friendship is all about when one of them suddenly has to go to the hospital for a cancer operation.

13.121. Voigt, Cynthia. (1982). *Tell me if the lovers are losers*. New York: Atheneum. 241 pp. (ISBN: 0-689-30911-2)

Three unlikely girls, Ann, Niki, and Hildy, become friends during their freshman year at college due to their being on the same intramural volleyball team. Ann, a product of a girls' prep school, has fine manners and a sensible, responsible nature. Niki, on the other hand, is often rude. Her extroverted personality coupled with her competitive nature often interferes with her "win at all costs" mentality. Finally, Hildy is a North Dakota farm girl with an unusual accent, strong religious convictions, and a mysterious background. When Hildy is suddenly killed by an automobile, Ann and Niki are left to reexamine their own lives and deal with their memories of Hildy.

13.122. Voigt, Cynthia. (1984). *Dicey's song*. 211 pp.

See Divorced and Single Parents

13.123. Wersba, Barbara. (1976). *Run softly, go fast*. New York: Atheneum. 205 pp. (ISBN: 0-689-20611-9)

Dave Marks and his father have a love-hate relationship. Not until his father dies does Dave examine his own life, values, and beliefs.

13.124. White, Ellen Emerson. (1987). *Life without friends*. New York: Scholastic. 250 pp. (ISBN: 0-590-33781-5)

Beverly Johnson has a lot on her plate for her senior year. She has not adjusted well to living with her father, her stepmother, and new brother, and she is definitely not yet over her mother's death or possible suicide. She befriends a guy named Tim Connors who is the worst possible choice for a friend. Not only is he abusive towards her, but she fears he is guilty of much worse. Her suspicions are confirmed when Tim is found guilty in the death of two teenagers, but now nobody at school will associate with her because of their friendship. Beverly gradually regains control of her life through the help of a psychiatrist and her friendship with Derek, a groundskeeper of a local park.

13.125. Winthrop, Elizabeth. (1978). *Knock, knock, who's there?* New York: Holiday House. 192 pp. (ISBN: 0-823-40337-8)

Two boys mourn the death of their father. To complicate matters, their mother seems to be slipping out of touch with reality which causes them even more worry. The boys learn about her longtime problem with alcoholism which gets much worse after the father's death. The sons seek help for her, but she refuses the help which threatens to break up the family. The boys realize that their father had a lot to do with keeping them together now that they are faced with similar issues without the knowledge of how to deal with them.

13.126. Wood, Phyllis Anderson. (1986). *Then I'll be home free*. New York: Dodd-Mead. 238 pp. (ISBN: 0-396-08766-3)

Sixteen-year-old Rosemary Magnuson has always taken the security of living with her doting grandparents for granted. When Gram suddenly dies, Gramps becomes a lonely, dependent old man right before her eyes. He used to be so happy and cheerful, but Gram's death is about to kill him too. Not only must Rosemary deal with her own grief for Gram, but she also must worry about what will happen to her if Gramps dies too.

13.127. Zindel, Paul. (1984). *Confessions of a teenage baboon*. New York: Bantam Books. 176 pp. (ISBN: 0-553-27190-3)

Chris Boyd moves with his mother, a practical nurse, from one live-in job to the next. Chris tells his shocking story of spending his 15th year with a dying lady and Lloyd Dipardi, her 30-year-old misfit son. Lloyd helps Chris learn that he must take responsibility for his own life if he is ever to become a man. (an American Library Association Best Book for Young Adults)

13.128. Zindel, Paul. (1990). *A begonia for Miss Applebaum*. New York: Bantam Books. 180 pp. (ISBN: 0-553-28765-6)

Miss Applebaum, Henry and Zelda's favorite high school teacher, is going on an early retirement. The teens decide to bring her a pink begonia as a gift and learn that she is really dying of cancer. Henry and Zelda make it a point to visit her often, and Miss Applebaum continues to teach them new things about the world, New York City, and themselves. Henry and Zelda become increasingly concerned about their teacher, especially since it appears that Miss Applebaum's niece is more concerned about her will than about her health. Henry and Zelda arrange for her to receive a specialist's care, and Miss Applebaum entrusts her strongbox of important documents in their care. Before she dies, Miss Applebaum teaches them one final lesson that they will never forget. (an American Library Association Best Book for Young Adults)

13.129. Zindel, Bonnie and Paul. (1980). *A star for the latecomer*. New York: Harper & Row. 185 pp. (ISBN: 0-060-26847-6)

Brooke Hillary, a 16-year-old girl, wants to be an ordinary teenager but her mother wants her to be a star. Faced with the tragedy of her mother's terminal illness, Brooke desperately tries to become famous before her mother dies of bone cancer. Brooke struggles with her own life goals in an effort to satisfy her mother's dying wish.

Annotated Young Adult Nonfiction Dealing with Death and Dying

13.130. Blinn, William. (1983). *Brian's song*. New York: Bantam Books. 128 pp. (ISBN: 0-553-26618-7)

This is the story of Brian Piccolo's courageous battle with cancer.

13.131. Bombeck, Erma. (1989). *I want to grow hair, I want to grow up, I want to go to Boise: Children surviving cancer*. New York: Harper & Row. 174 pp. (ISBN: 0-06-016170-1)

In a collection of anecdotes and interviews, Bombeck shares what it is like for families that have children with cancer. These remarkable families somehow manage to keep a sense of humor, a characteristic with medicinal properties.

13.132. de Beauvoir, Simone. (1985). *A very easy death.* New York: Pantheon. (ISBN: 0-394-72899-8)

De Beauvoir writes about her mother's slow death from terminal cancer. She realistically portrays the prolonged agony and slow deterioration of her mother's condition and what it felt like for her staying by her mother's side throughout the ordeal. The author tells about her own childhood, her mother's happiness and unhappiness, and explores her thoughts about the mystery of human existence.

13.133. Donnelly, Katherine F. (1982). *Recovering from the loss of a child.* New York: Macmillan. 224 pp. (ISBN: 0-02-532150-1) (Out of Stock)

Over 400,000 thousand children under the age of 25 die each year in this country. The author shares the stories of parents and siblings who have been in this awful situation and captures how they have dealt with their anger, guilt, and grief. Addresses and descriptions of agencies that are designed to assist the bereaved are also included.

13.134. Fine, Judylaine. (1986). *Afraid to ask: A book for families to share about cancer.* New York: Lothrop, Lee, & Shepard. 178 pp. (ISBN: 0-688-06196-6)

Using actual case histories, the author describes cancers in 19 different parts of the body. Information is also included that explains what cancer is, who gets it, how to prevent it, the different types of treatment, typical symptoms, and survival rates.

13.135. Gaffney, Donna A. (1989). *The seasons of grief: Helping your children grow through loss.* New York: New American Library. 176 pp. (ISBN: 0-452-26243-7)

Parents and teachers are given helpful information on how to help young people deal with the loss of a loved one.

13.136. Gordon, Jacquie. (1988). *Give me one wish.* New York: Norton. 350 pp. (ISBN: 0-393-02518-7)

Little did Christine know, but the journal requirement given to her by an English teacher when she was 14 years old would later become the basis for this book published by her mother. Chris kept the journal far after the assignment was over. In fact, she persistently recorded her thoughts and feelings about living with cystic fibrosis until her death at 21 years of age.

13.137. Gunther, John. (1971). *Death be not proud*. New York: Harper & Row. 264 pp. (ISBN: 0-060-11634-X)

This is Gunther's moving story about his son's courageous battle against a cancerous brain tumor. Throughout the battle, Johnny never lost his spirit or his sense of humor.

13.138. Hyde, Margaret O. & Hyde, Lawrence E. (1989). *Meeting death*. New York: Walker. 132 pp. (ISBN: 0-8027-6873-3)

The authors promote the hospice attitude of accepting death as a part of life. They use the stages identified by Dr. Kubler-Ross to describe the process of dying. Using case studies, the feelings of the terminally ill and remaining loved ones are examined. A chapter is included that deals with issues concerning suicide.

13.139. Kosof, Anna. (1986). *Why me? Coping with family illness*. New York: Franklin Watts. 95 pp. (ISBN: 0-531-10254-8)

When a life threatening illness strikes within a family, the tendency for its members is to ask a rhetorical, "Why me?" This book is a compilation of case studies and interviews in which the author presents the stories of families besieged with tragedy and how they learn to deal with and accept their various situations. The book focuses on young people who have to deal with a chronic or fatal disease or illness that they have or a relative has. The reader will meet a family whose baby is born with a birth defect, a teenager and a mother with cancer, a father who's had a heart attack, and an 8-year-old who's the victim of an accident. In some cases, the lack of knowledge is more frightening than the illness itself.

13.140. Krementz, Jill. (1989). *How it feels to fight for your life*. Boston: Little, Brown, & Company. 132 pp. (ISBN: 0-316-50364-9)

Fourteen young people, ages 7 to 16, share what it is like for them having to cope with serious illnesses. With touching honesty, these adolescents share their concerns about life and death, religion, and relationships. For many, it is highly frustrating being so dependent on parents at a time when most teenagers are wanting their independence.

13.141. Landau, Elaine. (1987). *Alzheimer's disease*. New York: Franklin Watts/First Books. 67 pp. (ISBN: 0-531-10376-5)

Alzheimer's Disease, a degenerative, progressive disease of the central nervous system, is becoming increasingly more common in the United States. When this book was written, there were over two million reported cases in the

U.S. alone.   Several topics are covered in this book: how the disease affects families, how one copes with the disease, and what treatment programs are available.

13.142. L'Engle, Madeleine. (1974). *The summer of the great-grandmother.* New York: Harper. 245 pp. (ISBN: 0-816-42259-1)

This is actually the autobiographical account of L'Engle's dealing with her mother's death, the woman who was "the great-grandmother of the extended family." L'Engle writes about her mother's life and how she helped her mother die with dignity.

13.143. LeShan, Eda. (1986). *When a parent is very sick.* Boston: Atlantic Monthly Press. 112 pp. (ISBN: 0-316-52162-0)

This book explores the many typical feelings a child experiences when a parent is very ill. The author explains where to get helpful information, what to ask the medical professionals, the pressures on the family, and what to expect if the parent dies or gets well.

13.144. Lightner, Candy & Hathaway, Nancy. (1990). *Giving sorrow words: How to cope with grief and get on with your life.* New York: Warner. 243 pp. (ISBN: 0-446-51509-4)

Candy Lightner, the founder of Mothers Against Drunk Driving, shares first hand experiences, as well as those of others, who have faced the death of loved ones.

13.145. Lund, Doris. (1990). *Eric.* New York: Dell Laurel-Leaf. 272 pp. (ISBN: 0-440-94586)

Seventeen-year-old Eric is dying of leukemia, but he lives his last four years with courage and exuberance. This true story is told by Eric's mother and includes some of Eric's drawings.

13.146. Miller, Robyn. (1986). *Robyn's book: A true diary.* New York: Scholastic. 179 pp. (ISBN: 0-590-41331-7)

Although Robyn was diagnosed with cystic fibrosis at 13 months, she lived a relatively normal life until her 16th birthday. Robyn kept a journal, *Robyn's Book*, and recorded what it was like for her coming to terms with the knowledge of having a terminal disease. From 16 to 21, Robyn was in and out of hospitals and lived through the deaths of close friends who had the same disease.   Somehow, she managed to keep a positive attitude about life, appreciating the little things--especially her writing. She died in the summer of 1985 at the age of 21 before this book was published.

13.147. Morris, Jeannie. (1990). *Brian Piccolo: A short season*. New York: Dell. 192 pp. (includes photo inserts) (ISBN: 0-440-10889-6)

Jeannie Morris tells the story of Brian Piccolo, a courageous football player who died of cancer at 26 years of age.

13.148. Peck, Richard. (1990). *Something for Joey*. New York: Bantam Books. 192 pp. (ISBN: 0-553-27199-7)

This true story is about two brothers who really love each other. The older is a Heisman Trophy athlete and the other, Joey, is dying of leukemia. This novel poignantly describes their relationship and their struggle to cope with the inevitable.

13.149. Richter, Elizabeth. (1986). *Losing someone you love: When a brother or sister dies*. New York: G.P. Putnam's Sons. 80 pp. (ISBN: 399-21243-4) (Out of Print)

Fifteen young people, ranging in age from 10 to 24, describe the feelings and emotions they experienced after the death of a brother or sister. This nonfiction collection of vignettes vividly expresses each individual's sorrow, fear, loneliness, anger, and the difficulties experienced both at home and at school. Their desire to be heard and understood stems from two concerns: They hope that what they have suffered will help kids in similar situations and will also help those who haven't shared this experience to understand what they are going through. Richter manages to draw out the words from these adolescents and effectively recaptures their stories using their language.

Nonfiction References Dealing with Death and Dying

Journal Articles

Auten, A. (1982, March). Why teach death education? *Journal of Reading, 25* (6), p. 602 ff.

Gooden, K.W. (1989). Surviving a death in the family. In *Coping with family stress*. New York: Rosen. p. 23 ff.

Justin, R.G. (1988). Adult and adolescent attitudes toward death. *Adolescence, 23* (90), p. 429 ff.

Spruce, M. (1991, February). When a student grieves: Helping children cope with the loss of a parent or friend. *Teacher Magazine, 2* (5), p. 30 ff.

Wilson, L.W. (1984, November). Helping adolescents understand death and dying through literature. *English Journal, 73* (7), p. 78 ff.

Books

Corr, C. & McNeil, J.N. (1986). *Adolescence and death.* New York: Springer Publishing. 290 pp. (ISBN: 0-826-14930-8)

Kubler-Ross, E. (1983). *On children and death.* New York: Macmillan. 279 pp. (ISBN: 0-025-67110-3)

Miller, J.H. (1986). *Death education and the educator.* Illinois: Charles C. Thomas. 100 pp. (ISBN: 0-398-05266-2)

Raab, R.A. (1989). *Coping with death.* New York: Rosen. 135 pp. (ISBN: 0-823-90960-3)

Schneiderman, G. (1989). *Coping with death in the family.* Toronto: NC Press Limited. 154 pp. (ISBN: 1-550-21055-6)

CHAPTER 14

Stress and Suicide

Despite the adult view that youth is a carefree time, many adolescents are obviously not coping very well with the stresses in their lives. It is painfully evident that adolescent stress and suicide are major problems confronting our society. For many adolescents, an accumulation of many stresses ultimately overwhelms them to the extent that they start believing that suicide is their only alternative. Suicide victims often cry for help, but, unfortunately, their cries often fall on deaf, unknowing ears. If you do hear someone say that he or she doesn't want to live anymore, take that person seriously and don't try to handle the situation alone.

STARTLING INFORMATION ABOUT TEENAGE STRESS AND SUICIDE

- Most adolescents communicate their intent to commit suicide before they attempt to do so because most really do not want to die; suicide is preventable. (American Association of Suicidology)

- Suicide is the 2nd leading cause of teenage deaths; "accidents" rated first. (National Center for Health Statistics, 1988)

- The National Adolescent Student Health Survey given to 11,000 8th and 10th grade students revealed that 34% (25% of the boys and 42% of the girls) reported that they had thought seriously about committing suicide; adolescent suicide has quadrupled in the last 30 years. (Centers for Disease Control, 1987)

- Between 1986 and 1990, the suicide rate for teenagers doubled. (National Association of State Boards of Education and the American Medical Association, 1990)

- An adolescent commits suicide every one hour and 47 minutes. (National Center for Health Statistics, 1987)

- The suicide rate for alcoholics is 58 times higher than non-alcoholics. (National Council on Alcoholism)

- In a youth suicide study, victims who used firearms were five times more likely to have been drinking than those who used other means. (American Academy of Child & Adolescent Psychiatry, *Facts for Families*, 1992)

- It is well documented that four times as many boys than girls succeed in their suicide attempts but three times as many girls than boys attempt it; boys tend to use violent means, while girls tend to use pills.

- Guns were nearly twice as likely to be found in homes of suicide victims: Of the 2,059 adolescents between 15 and 19 years of age who committed suicide in 1988, 1,261 used a gun. (Centers for Disease Control)

- Catholic and Jewish young people commit suicide less often than do those youth belonging to other religious groups with fewer traditions and rituals. (The Division of Child and Adolescent Psychiatry at the University of Minnesota Hospital and Clinic, 1988)

WARNING SIGNS OF A PERSON CONTEMPLATING SUICIDE

- Low self esteem caused by repeated failure and unhappiness.

- Preoccupation with themes of death or expressing suicidal thoughts.

- Giving away prized possessions and getting personal affairs in order.

- Dramatic changes in behavior: sleeping too much or too little, eating too much or too little, suddenly losing interest in school, dropping out of activities, taking dangerous risks, withdrawing from family and friends.

- Becoming suddenly cheerful after a period of depression.

- Dramatic changes in personality: having sudden outbursts of anger, being apathetic about appearance and health, becoming fidgety and restless, crying frequently, feeling hopeless and helpless.

- Losing a steady boyfriend or girlfriend, moving to a new town, unemployment.

- Using drugs or alcohol.

- Talking about committing suicide and saying things like, "I wish I were dead," "It's no use," or "You'll miss me when I'm gone."

- Seeing depressed parents or experiencing family problems.

- Having previous suicide attempts or knowing someone who has committed suicide.

WHAT TO DO AND WHERE TO GO FOR HELP

- It is better to engage in discussions and strategies that develop assertiveness and coping techniques than it is to discuss suicide as a topic.

- If someone you know is suicidal, discuss the problem openly and frankly while showing genuine concern.

- Take all suicidal threats seriously.

- Get professional help: Call suicide prevention centers, crisis intervention centers, mental health clinics, hospitals, a family physician, a clergy, a guidance counselor, or a teacher. For immediate help, call the National Suicide Hotline at 1-800-621-4000 or the National Crisis Alert at 1-800-231-1295. For more information, write to the American Association of Suicidology, 5459 South Ash Street, Denver, Colorado, 80222.

Annotated Young Adult Novels Dealing with Stress and Suicide

14.01. Arrick, Fran. (1988). *Tunnel vision*. New York: Dell Laurel-Leaf. 160 pp. (ISBN: 0-440-98579-X)

An apparently happy 15-year-old boy commits suicide, and his family and friends try to find out why. The novel sensitively exposes the feelings of those left behind. (an American Library Association Best of the Best Books for Young Adults)

14.02. Bennett, James. (1990). *I can hear the mourning dove*. Boston: Houghton Mifflin. 197 pp. (ISBN: 0-395-53623-5)

After the sudden death of her father, Grace Braun fails at a suicide attempt and winds up spending most of her junior year in a mental institution. With the help of a psychologist, teacher, and friend, Gracie starts rebuilding her life only to fall apart again after another tragedy. Luke, a delinquent who's been passed around several foster homes, helps her come to terms with her own troubles. (an American Library Association Best Book for Young Adults)

14.03. Bridgers, Sue Ellen. (1989). *Notes for another life*. 208 pp.

See Divorced and Single Parents

14.04. Bunting, Eve. (1985). *Face at the edge of the world*. New York: Clarion Books. 158 pp. (ISBN: 0-899-19399-4)

Jed's best friend, Charlie, commits suicide and Jed doesn't find out about it until he reads about it in the newspaper! Everything had been normal and plans had been made between the two of them to be roommates when they went away to college together next year. Charlie was moody at times but isn't everybody? Puzzled and determined to find out why Charlie resorted to such an end, Jed and Charlie's girlfriend, Annie, search Charlie's past and discover his secret life. (1987 Young Adults' Choice)

14.05. Byars, Betsy. (1988). *The burning question of Bingo Brown*. Bergenfield, NJ: Viking Penguin. 160 pp. (ISBN: 0-670-81932-8)

Bingo Brown wonders if Mr. Markham, his favorite 6th grade teacher, was asking for help when he asked the class to write a letter trying to convince someone not to commit suicide. When Mr. Markham has a mysterious motorcycle accident, Bingo wonders what he should do.

14.06. Christian, Mary Blount. (1990). *Singin' somebody else's song*. New York: Macmillan. 192 pp. (ISBN: 0-02-718500-1) (Out of Print)

After Gideon's friend, Jeremy, commits suicide, Gideon decides to publish two of their country songs in his memory. Gideon realizes that their lifelong dream of becoming country music stars is not the same without his friend.

14.07. Crutcher, Chris. (1991). *Chinese handcuffs*. New York: Dell. 220 pp. (ISBN: 0-440-20837-8)

Dillon Hemingway likes two girls: Stacy is his brother's ex-girlfriend and mother of Preston's child, and Jennifer is an all-star basketball player for their high school team. Although the novel focuses on Dillon and his attempts at dealing with his brother's suicide, it also deals with Dillon's attempted relationships with these two girls. Stacy's issues are obvious, but Jennifer seems to have everything going for her. Dillon eventually learns that Jennifer's problems with intimacy are due to her stepfather's sexual abuse and threats. Dillon **will not** witness another suicide and is determined to help Jennifer find a way to rebuild her life. (an American Library Association Best Book for Young Adults)

14.08. Engebrecht, Pat. (1983). *The promises of moonstone.* 182 pp.

See Handicapped Youth

14.09. Faucher, Elizabeth. (1985). *Surviving.* New York: Scholastic. 168 pp. (ISBN: 0-590-41068-7)

Rick's father constantly pushes him to study so he can become a doctor "just like his father." Up until recently, Rick has been the model 16-year-old son. Rick's life is shattered after he discovers that his father is having an affair with another woman. Because he can't handle the pressure, he confides everything to his girlfriend Lonnie, a "problem teen." Lonnie, who had previously tried to commit suicide because she felt like an unwanted child, has parents who also think that they are providing the perfect home life for their daughter. The two teens take action when Lonnie's parents decide to send her to a boarding school which she does not want to attend. The two of them decide that life just isn't worth the hassle. (Based on the television movie by Joyce Eliason).

14.10. Ferris, Jean. (1985). *Amen, Moses Gardenia.* New York: Farrar, Straus, & Giroux. 200 pp. (ISBN: 0-374-30252-9)

At 15, Farrell has everything that money can buy, but she is desperately unhappy. Money can't buy love, and Farrell wants to feel loved by her family and friends. She gets into a deep depression that takes her to the brink of suicide. Her friends and counselor are there to help her, but Farrell has to be able to see and feel the help.

14.11. Fleagles, Anita Macrae. (1976). *The year the dreams came back.* New York: Atheneum. 146 pp. (ISBN: 0-689-30438-9)

After her mother's suicide, Nell has emotional problems for over a year. When Nell meets Amy, a lady who runs a local bookstore, she begins to let go of her grief, guilt, and worry. Things get even better when Amy meets and marries Nell's father.

14.12.   Guest, Judith. (1976). *Ordinary people*. New York: Ballantine Books. 245 pp. (ISBN: 0-345-30734-8)

Conrad Jarrett is a sensitive, teenage boy who is recovering, both physically and emotionally, from his attempted suicide. While staying in a mental hospital for eight months, Conrad learns that the road to recovery is full of rough spots and he must overcome some major obstacles: his strained relationship with his cold, seemingly uncaring mother and his guilt over the death of his 17-year-old brother whom he idolized. A psychiatrist helps Conrad to get in touch with his feelings and deal with his problems. Fortunately, Conrad and one of his parents learn from their trying experiences and eventually realize the secret to survival. (an American Library Association Best of the Best Books for Young Adults)

14.13.   Hale, Janet Campbell. (1991). *The owl's song*. New York: Bantam Books. 144 pp. (ISBN: 0-553-28829-6)

Billy White Hawk, a 14-year-old Indian, confronts loneliness and prejudice as he searches for his heritage and future as a man. Billy's mother died when he was young, and his father has a difficult time communicating with his son and resorts to alcohol too often. After witnessing his best friend's suicide, Billy decides he must leave the Indian Reservation and goes to a high school in a large city where the other students taunt him. After his experiences, Billy returns to the Benewah Reservation determined to talk with his father.

14.14.   Hughes, Dean. (1982). *Switching tracks*. New York: Atheneum. 180 pp. (ISBN: 0-689-30923-6) (Out of Print)

Mark blames himself for his father's suicide and tries to escape the pain by absorbing himself in video games at a local arcade. An elderly neighbor dying of cancer helps Mark to confront the truth about his father's death. (a Notable Children's Trade Book in the Field of Social Studies)

14.15.   Irwin, Hadley. (1988). *So long at the fair*. New York: Margaret K. McElderry. 202 pp. (ISBN: 0-689-50454-3)

Joel Wendell Logan III and Ashley come from extremely affluent families and neither has a need for anything, at least not material things. The novel begins with Joel spending a week at the State Fair trying to figure out why Ashley, his best friend, committed suicide. As Joel reminisces about the times he spent with Ashley, he realizes that she had been crying out for help from the very beginning. Ashley's survivors are left with the chore of trying to figure out why a pretty, intelligent, young, rich girl who seemed to have everything would resort to such a thing, and Joel is left with the task of living his life without his best friend.

14.16. Knudson, R.R. (1984). *Just another love story.* New York: Avon Flare. 208 pp. (ISBN: 0-380-65532-2)

Dusty Blaisdale intentionally drives off a Long Island pier after he and his girlfriend break up. He is saved by a body builder who encourages him to make something of himself.

14.17. L'Engle, Madeleine. (1990). *A ring of endless light.* 336 pp.

See Death and Dying

14.18. Madison, Winifred. (1979). *A portrait of myself.* 239 pp.

See Eating Disorders

14.19. Mango, Karin N. (1990). *Just for the summer.* New York: Harper Collins/Zolotow. 204 pp. (ISBN: 0-06-024038-5)

Jenny Smith is a lifeguard at a New Hampshire Beach for the summer where she meets Rollo, an introverted musician who lives in the next cottage. At first, Rollo doesn't want to have anything to do with her, but her persistence gets him to eventually open up to her. Rollo suffers from guilt in not being able to prevent his father's suicide. With Jenny's help, he is able to get a better perspective on things through interviewing his father's past associates. Jenny finds that she can draw on what she has learned from Rollo to help her with relationship problems she's been having with Alec, a deaf teen back home.

14.20. McCuaig, Sandra. (1990). *Blindfold.* New York: Holiday House. 176 pp. (ISBN: 0-8234-0811-6)

Sally O'Leary, a 15-year-old, is left behind to deal with the suicides of two of her best friends, Joel and Benji. The newspaper headline reads "Young Brothers Jump to Death: Loved the Same Girl" which makes Sally feel guilty about their deaths. Through the help of Dr. Jago, a psychiatrist, and a friend she calls "Lifesaver," Sally becomes aware of the responsibility she had in their deaths and is able to cope with their suicides.

14.21. Meyer, Carolyn. (1990). *Because of Lissa.* New York: Bantam Books. 192 pp. (ISBN: 0-553-28802-4)

Four teenagers decide to make some good come out of Lissa's suicide. They establish a school hotline for troubled students. Actual training techniques in handling hotline calls are detailed.

14.22. Morris, Winifred. (1987). *Dancer in the mirror*. New York: Atheneum. 158 pp. (ISBN: 0-689-31322-5)

Carole Palermo and Marty Land become friends shortly after Carole's parents' divorce. Marty is wild and reckless and temporarily serves as a good distraction for the ailing Carole. Carole, unaware that Marty has problems with her own family, is jolted into reality when Marty proposes that the girls swear to a suicide pact to get back at their parents.

14.23. Nixon, Joan Lowery. (1990). *Secret, silent screams*. New York: Dell Laurel-Leaf. 192 pp. (ISBN: 0-440-20539-5)

Marti knows that her friend, Barry, didn't kill himself but no one will listen to her. It is assumed that Barry's death is a copycat suicide, just another tragedy in a string of recent high school suicides. Marti searches for the truth in spite of the generally accepted evidence and adult authority; she believes he was murdered. The novel's message is clear: Parents and friends need to listen to a depressed teenager's cry for help. (a YASD Recommended Book for Reluctant Readers)

14.24. Olsen, Violet. (1985). *Never brought to mind*. New York: Atheneum. 180 pp. (ISBN: 0-689-31110-9)

Joe Conway's life is shattered when his best friend and former girlfriend are killed over New Year's. Hollis and Mary Beth die in a car accident when Hollis smashes his car into a tree right after Joe's fight with her. As school starts again, Joe is not ready emotionally to continue with his senior year. He skips school and avoids his friends and family. He feels dead inside and thinks that he would be better off physically dead as well. It isn't until he's standing on a bridge ready to plunge to his own death that he finally faces his grief and guilt regarding the tragedy. He realizes that forgetting is impossible, and he finally accepts the understanding and love from the people in his life who have wanted to help all along. His adjustment and return to life is an education for all who read this book.

14.25. O'Neal, Zibby. (1980). *The language of the goldfish*. New York: Viking Press. 179 pp. (ISBN: 0-670-41785-8)

Carrie Stokes, a 13-year-old teenager, attends a private school with her older sister, Moira, who seems to have forgotten what it's like to be Carrie's age. When they were younger, the two girls used to talk to the goldfish. They had a magic vocabulary and the goldfish pond became their special, enchanted escape-world. As they grew older, Moira became more interested in boys, and Carrie's parents typically ignored her too. Carrie takes an overdose of pills, in a suicide attempt, and her mother, who is unable to face the truth, tells everyone that Carrie's been hospitalized for bronchitis. Through the help and encouragement of a teacher and a psychiatrist, Carrie reconstructs the past and builds a better future. Carrie finds she can no longer hear the vocabulary of the goldfish but passes the magic vocabulary to her young friend, Sara, who promises to pass it on when she outgrows it.

14.26.   Peck, Richard. (1986). *Remembering the good times.* New York: Dell Laurel-Leaf. 181 pp. (ISBN: 0-440-97339-2)

Three teenagers, two boys and a girl, strike up a friendship that ends in tragedy. Buck befriends Kate the summer before seventh grade, and the two of them become friends with Trav, a wealthy student, in the beginning of the eighth grade. Soon, they feel that as long as they have each other, they don't need anyone else. No one could figure them out, or, at least, that's what they thought. When one of them decides at 16 years of age that the future is just too great of a risk, it leaves the other two wondering just how well they knew their friend. (a *School Library Journal* Best Book of the Year, 1990 ALAN Award, an American Library Association Notable Children's Book and YASD Author Achievement Award, and Best Book for Young Adults)

14.27.   Peck, Richard. (1988). *Father figure.* 182 pp.

See Divorced and Single Parents

14.28.   Pevsner, Stella. (1989). *How could you do it, Diane?* New York: Clarion Books. 183 pp. (ISBN: 0-395-51041-4)

Fourteen-year-old Bethany discovers her well-loved, older stepsister's body after she commits suicide. Beth doesn't understand why Diane, who was outgoing and seemingly happy, would do such a thing; no note was left. With time, Beth takes it upon herself to try to force her family to accept Diane's death, while not realizing that she hasn't yet accepted it herself.   When problems develop with Beth's younger brother and sister, the entire family goes in for counseling. The first session is almost the last session, but they all continue until the family is able to remember "but not dwell on" Diane.

14.29.   Pfeffer, Susan Beth. (1990). *About David.* New York: Dell Laurel-Leaf. 176 pp. (ISBN: 0-440-90022-0)

After David kills his parents and himself, his close friend Lynn is left to figure out why he could do such a thing. Lynn struggles to understand his murders and suicide and their implications for her. In diary form, she tries to piece the parts together to figure out why it happened. Eventually she comes to terms with her own feelings about life and about David. (an American Library Association Best Book for Young Adults)

14.30. Roos, Stephen. (1989). *You'll miss me when I'm gone*. 208 pp.

See Alcohol and Drugs

14.31. Sachs, Marilyn. (1988). *The fat girl*. New York: Dell Laurel-Leaf. 176 pp. (ISBN: 0-440-92468-5)

Jeff Lyons has no idea what effect his insults to Ellen, a fat classmate, is having on her until he learns she is contemplating suicide. Jeff apologizes and befriends her in an attempt to help her with her self-esteem problems. Both teens learn a lot from each other. (an American Library Association Best Book for Young Adults)

14.32. Sparks, Dr. Beatrice. (Ed.). (1979). *Jay's journal*. New York: Times Books. 179 pp. (ISBN: 0-812-90801-5)

This novel is a collection of a young boy's daily journal entries. It chronicles Jay's downward spiral into drug abuse, crime, and Satanism. Jay's farewell note points to the despair and isolation which eventually lead up to his taking his own life. Although this book makes a powerful statement about the dangers inherent in losing control of oneself to outside forces, its strong language, upsetting religious theme, and depiction of violence against people and animals make this novel a tough one to recommend to teenagers. The book could be valuable for adults in that it depicts many of the warning signs of impending suicide and could teach adults the signs to look for in a troubled youth.

14.33. Sweeney, Joyce. (1991). *Right behind the rain*. New York: Delacorte Press. 160 pp. (ISBN: 0-440-20678-2))

Carla Bryce's brother has everything going for him, or so everyone thinks. Kevin can sing and dance and can just about do anything well. While rehearsing for a summer stock production, Carla notices that he looks pale and thin. His parents, on the other hand, think its just the demands of the theatre. Fortunately, his pending suicide is prevented, and the reader is left with a sense of hope as well as gaining insight to some worthwhile advice.

14.34. Tapp, Kathy Kennedy. (1989). *The sacred circle of the hula hoop.* 208 pp.

See Abuse

14.35. White, Ellen Emerson. (1987). *Life without friends.* 250 pp.

See Death and Dying

Annotated Young Adult Nonfiction Dealing with Stress and Suicide

14.36. Cohen, Daniel. & Cohen, Susan. (1992). *Teenage stress.* New York: Dell. 175 pp. (ISBN: 0-440-21391-6)

The Cohens examine several stressful areas involving teenagers such as sex issues, parental concerns, school matters, peer pressure, etc.

14.37. Gardner, Sandra & Rosenberg, Gary B. (1990). *Teenage suicide.* New York: Julian Messner. 128 pp. (ISBN: 0-671-70200-9)

This is a collection of stories from teenagers who attempted suicide and lived to tell about it. Information is included about the warning signs and what to do if you suspect a friend is suicidal.

14.38. Hermes, Patricia. (1987). *A time to listen: Preventing youth suicide.* San Diego: Harcourt, Brace, & Jovanovich. 132 pp. (ISBN: 0-15-288196-4)

Hermes, through a series of interviews, presents the lives of teenagers who have attempted suicide, psychologists who have counseled teenagers with suicidal tendencies, and the parents and friends who were left behind when a suicide occurs. Hermes documents what the interviewees say with research data and provides an interpretation of what it all means.

14.39. Hyde, Margaret O. & Hyde, Lawrence E. (1989). *Meeting death.* 132 pp.

See Death and Dying

14.40. Kolehmainen, Janet & Handwerk, Sandra. (1986). *Teen suicide: A book for friends, family, and classmates.* Minneapolis: Lerner Publications. 70 pp. (ISBN: 0-8225-9514-1)

Suicide is one of the leading causes of teenage deaths in this country. Through case studies, the authors present the stories of six teenagers in order to present to the reader various options to suicide, typical causes of suicide, and the warning signs of suicide. The authors also include information about where and when to go for help and advises how to cope with grief and guilt if someone you know commits suicide.

14.41.   Langone, John. (1986). *Dead end: A book about suicide*. Boston: Little, Brown, & Company. 176 pp. (ISBN: 0-316-51432-2)

This book presents several aspects of suicide: physical and psychological causes, society's view, warning signs, prevention, and its history.

14.42.   Leder, Jane Mersky. (1989). *Dead serious: A book for teenagers about teenage suicide*. New York: Avon Books. 141 pp. (ISBN: 0-380-70661-X)

It is possible to prevent suicide but a person has to be knowledgeable about how to act. This book presents accounts of actual suicides, discusses the reasons why people choose to end their lives, discloses the warning signs, and gives helpful advice for what to do if a person you know is thinking about suicide.

14.43.   Newman, Susan. (1992). *Don't be S.A.D.: A teenage guide to handling stress, anxiety, and depression*. New York: Julian Messner. 122 pp. (ISBN: 0-671-72610-2)

Teenagers who have experienced stress, anxiety, or depression share their stories. The author analyzes each scenario and offers plausible suggestions in each instance. The bottom line is that no situation is so tough that it cannot be broken down into manageable elements that can be dealt with. Information is given regarding the following problem areas: alcohol and drug abuse, alienation and identity, death and dying, divorce, eating disorders, physical and sexual abuse, school problems, etc.

14.44.   Wilson, Miriam J. Williams. (1992). *Stress stoppers for children and adolescents*. Cameron, West Virginia: William Gladden Foundation. 111 pp.

In a simple to read format, this book alerts the reader to indicators of stress and how to alter stress producing behaviors. Self esteem issues and methods to enhance it are also addressed.

Nonfiction References Dealing with Stress and Suicide

Journal Articles

Brophy, B. (1986, October 27). Children under stress. *U.S. News & World Report, 101* (17), p. 58 ff.

Cannold, S. (1985, September). Teenage suicide: What can be done about it? *Thrust, 15* (1), p. 38 ff.

Crowder, W.W. (1983, September). Teaching about stress. *The Clearing House, 57* (1), p. 36 ff.

Edwards, T.K. (1988, December). Providing reasons for wanting to live. *Phi Delta Kappan, 70* (4), p. 296 ff.

Elias, M.J. & Clabby, J.F. (1988, March). Teaching social decision making. *Educational Leadership, 45* (6), p. 52 ff.

Feinour, P. (1989, February). A high school play helps suicidal teenagers. *America School Board Journal.* p. 29 ff.

Frymier, J. (1988, December). Understanding and preventing teen suicide: An interview with Barry Garfinkel. *Phi Delta Kappan, 70* (4), p. 290 ff.

Garbowsky, M. (1984, September-October). Teaching teens to cope with stress. *Curriculum Review, 24* (1), p. 21 ff.

Gooden, K.W. (1989). Suicide. In *Coping with family stress.* New York: Rosen. p. 80 ff.

Manning, A. (1984, April 18). Teen-age suicide: We should all be on the alert for cries of help. *U.S.A. Today,* p. 4D.

Reese, F.L. & Roosa, M.W. (1991, August). Early adolescents report on major life stressors and mental health risk status. *Journal of Early Adolescence,* p. 363 ff.

Seibel, M. & Murray, J.N. (1988, March). Early prevention of adolescent suicide. *Educational Leadership, 45* (6), p. 48 ff.

Steinberg, L. (1987, September). Bound to bicker. *Psychology Today, 21* (9), p. 36 ff.

Strother, D.B. (1986, June). PAR, Suicide among the young. *Phi Delta Kappan, 67* (10), p. 756 ff.

Stupple, D.M. (1987, January). Rx for the suicide epidemic. *English Journal, 76* (1), p. 64 ff.

Wolfle, J. (1988, December). Adolescent suicide: An open letter to counselors. *Phi Delta Kappan, 70* (4), p. 294 ff.

Young, T.J. (1985, October-November). Adolescent suicide: The clinical manifestation of alienation. *The High School Journal, 69* p. 55 ff.

Journal Themes

Teen Suicide. (1985, February). *People, 23* (7).

Recycling Anxiety. (1985, Winter). *Voices: The Art of Science of Psychotherapy, 20* (4).

Youth Suicide. (1984, Summer). *Educational Horizons, 62* (4).

Suicide. (1984). *Death Education, 8.*

Books

Davis, P. (1983). *Suicidal adolescents.* Springfield, IL: Charles C. Thomas, Publisher. 89 pp. (ISBN: 0-3980-4866-5)

Klagsburn, Francine. (1976). *Too young to die: Suicide and youth.* Boston: Houghton Mifflin. 201 pp. (ISBN: 0-3952-4752-7)

Maloney, M. & Kranz, R. (1993). *Straight talk about anxiety and depression.* New York: Dell.

Pardeck, J.A. & Pardeck, J.T. (1984). *Young people with problems: A guide to bibliotherapy.* Westport, CT: Greenwood. 176 pp. (ISBN: 0-3132-3836-7)

Patross, P. & Shamoo, T. (1989). *Depression and suicide in children and adolescents: Prevention, intervention, and postvention.* Boston: Allyn & Bacon. 214 pp. (ISBN: 0-205-11670-1)

Author Index

Title Index

About the Author

JOAN F. KAYWELL is Assistant Professor of English Education at the University of South Florida, where she specializes in literature for young adults and middle and secondary teaching methods in English education. She is the author of the book *Adolescent Literature as a Complement to the Classics* (1993), and many articles on teaching language arts and using young adult literature in the classroom.